CREATED TO WALK WITH GOD

How to Walk with God

written by
Rev. Carlton P. Gleason, Sr.
January 1996

All rights reserved by the author.
Published by Mocking Bird Hill Publications,
211 North Saratoga Drive, Lynchburg, VA 24502.

Library of Congress Catalog Card Number: TXu 739-857

Gleason, Sr., Carlton P.
How to Walk with God / Carlton P. Gleason, Sr.
ISBN 0-9653588-0-1

CREATED TO WALK WITH GOD

Acknowledgments

To our daughter, Jyl Dawn VanDusen and my wife Joyce Brooks Gleason for many hours of valuable assistance in the editing of this book. To Dr. Maurice Stone, then professor at Liberty University, for his strong encouragement that this book be written: even though he would not, necessarily, endorse all my personal beliefs and convictions.

How to Walk with God

Dedication

To our children, grandchildren, great grandchildren and our children In The Faith that they clearly see the pathways along which the Lord has lead us; and one day join with us and those who have gone before us for a wonderful reunion at Our Heavenly Father's Eternal Home. May each of them, like Enoch of old, learn to "Walk With God," in such fellowship, He may be able to walk them all the way home! *Genesis 5:24*

Chapter Contents

1 Created to Walk with God *11*
    Physical Creation
    The Fall of Man
    Spiritual Creation and Recreation
    Witness of Creation

2 Learning to Walk *20*
    Our Spiritual Destiny
    Reciprocating God's Love
    Our Hearts His Temples
    Soul-Winner's Destiny

3 Systems of Guidance *26*
    Call to the Heights
    Launched in Time and Space
    The Mind of God
    The Son of God
    The Spirit of God
    Sustaining Energy from the Heart and Hand of God

4 Walking in the Spirit *31*
    Our Father's Children
    Beginning to Walk
    Working the Works of God
    Unity of The Trinity
    Fruits of the Spirit

5 Walking in Love *46*
    Secret of Praying in Jesus' Name
    Learning to Listen
    Water from the Rock
    Relay Beacons
    Call in the Wilderness

6 Walking in Holiness *66*
    Fullness of the Spirit
    God Cares
    Conflicting Concepts
    Hung Up on Perfection

7 God's Love is Sufficient *89*
    Learning to Love
    Levels of Love
    Cross Bearing
    Language of Love
    Bearing Spiritual Burdens

8 Walking in Peace *113*
    Peace with God
    Peace Among Men
    Conformed or Transformed
    Peace in the Family

9 Playground or Battlefield *129*
    The Church a Conservatory
    Miracles
    Gifts or the Giver
    Spiritual Gifts
    God's Call to Service

10 Secrets of the Lord *154*
    No Scientific Atheists
    Descendants of Witch Doctors
    Interim at Trenton
    God's Call to Jury Duty
    Wilderness Wandering?

11 In the Presence of the Enemy *167*
    Understanding the Opposition
    Spiritual Fifth Column
    Playing the Fool or Keeping the Faith
    God Developing Character
    Humility and Self-Image
    Living by Faith
    God's Internet
    Seeing the Invisible
    Mastery Through the Spirit

12 When God Steps In *202*
    Will God Step and Speak Peace?
    National Survival
    Historical Witness
    Biblical Witness
    Current History

13 Mysteries of Godliness *214*
    By Revelation Only
    Owner's Manual
    Three Days and Three Nights
    Viewing Calvary and the Resurrection

14 Going Home *219*
    Special Home Goings
    Memory Cassettes
    Best Yet to Come
    Your Inheritance
    Homeward Bound!

Preface

God's Word teaches us that He created mankind for fellowship with Himself! When God said, "Let us make man in our own image," among other things, it was His purpose to give man intelligence to access His own mind; conscience, or moral and spiritual sensitivity, to access His heart and the capacity to receive, experience, reciprocate and communicate His love. Thus God established the basis for our warm, personal, living relationship with Himself in a fellowship of love! He did not choose to create us as robots, clones, nor even as angels but as His created children. I personally believe God created mankind to have children with whom to share His great love. He longed to have children to reciprocate His love freely and completely. Neither morality nor love is a command performance! **Without freedom of choice** both lose their meaning! Love and morality are **inspired** responses.

God did walk with Adam and Eve, in loving fellowship, through the Garden of Eden in the cool of the evenings! One tragic evening God came for fellowship and man was not there to meet Him! Adam and Eve, through disobedience, had given Satan access to their hearts and minds! A great barrier of sin had risen between God and mankind. Fellowship with God was broken! Brokenhearted, our Heavenly Father walked the garden that night crying, "Adam, Adam where art thou?" **That cry for reconciliation has come echoing down the corridors of time ever since!** God has sought reconciliation through His own direct efforts; through angels, patriarchs, His prophets and finally through the sacrifice of His only begotten Son. We read in His Word, "**God was in Christ, reconciling the world to Himself!**"

CREATED TO WALK WITH GOD

Prologue

This book is not a biography! Even though it has many biographical sketches. It is not meant to be a theological treatise on doctrine, nor is there any attempt to discredit the belief of another. It does confront many of my own doctrinal dilemmas. It is not a book of philosophy: although it does seek to present truth, as I understand it, under the criterion of coherence. I am not qualified to write a book on human psychology and the malfunctions of the mind. Yet I share, what are considered to be **self-evident truths** relating to mental health, and emotional and spiritual stability. These psychological factors are seen as keys to vital elements in God's systems of communication with His created children.

I wish to share wonderful memories of fellowship established and victories through His grace. The Psalmist, David, in the twenty-fifth Psalm, verse fourteen, states "The secret of the Lord is with them that fear Him." When I speak of shared secrets, this is **not** in reference to extra-Biblical revelations, but refers to clearer insight into the Word as the Author of the Book explains it to me! The Holy Spirit has spoken so clearly, so many times during my lifetime of seeking a loving relationship with the living God! He has helped me to walk with Him in personal and intimate fellowship! No apologies are offered for references to personal experiences. These thoughts are **not the compilations of an eclectic**; but are the **personal witness** of one who has "tasted and seen" that my God is good!

There is sincere apology for the frequent use of personal pronouns. This book is largely a transcript from memory cassettes programmed through the years. It is very subjective in point of view. Every literary devise known to me, has been used to avoid personal reference, without clouding the issue; or lessening the impact of an eye witness. This is a sincere attempt to share what God has given me, under tutelage of the Holy Spirit, in the classroom of life. The privilege of "Walking with God" is not that of a favorite few. It is the birthright of every one of His children! It is His legacy to all of them, for this was a central purpose of creation!

To attempt writing a book on "How to Walk with God," may on the surface, seem highly presumptuous. Ask a little boy, who has a loving, wise dad and he will tell you anything and everything about his dad! But what does he actually know about his father?

How to Walk with God

What does he know of his father's work, dreams, plans, problems, frustration and heartbreak? That small boy knows so little about his dad: how can he be so confident and secure? Simply because there is so much that **he does know** for certain! He knows that his daddy loves him! If he is in danger his daddy will protect him! If he is hungry, daddy will feed him! If a long way from home and in the darkness of night he can reach up and feel his daddy's hand: he is secure for his father knows the way home! **My Heavenly Father is a wonderful Dad!** Throughout life's experiences he has demonstrated His love, care and omnipresence! I'll not try to tell you what I don't know about Him, but let me share my confidence in His love and some of the secrets I have learned concerning how to **walk with Him in a fellowship of love**! I "do hold these truths to be self-evident!"

This book could be more accurately characterized as a **travelogue**. Hopefully, it contains supplemental information to help travelers as they "Walk with God" in their journey through time and space. May the Lord give you a wonderful passage! **I hope to see you in the morning!**

1 Created to Walk with God

Why did God create mankind? Many have questioned why a holy, loving God would create man in His own spiritual image and give him the power of self-determination while knowing what man would do with those privileges. It would appear that God, Himself, had second thoughts concerning the matter. In Genesis 6:6 we read, "And it repented the Lord that He had made man on the earth, and it grieved Him in His heart." Knowing what man would do, why did God go ahead and make him anyway? God, the Father, had His only begotten Son, the angels and the hosts of Heaven: why then create a physical, material world and physical mankind, giving him dominion over His own creation? It seems obvious to me that God, the very essence of love, wanted created children with whom He could share that love!

God's Word plainly teaches us that He created mankind for fellowship with Himself! When God said, "Let us make man in our own image," among other things, it was His purpose to give man intelligence to access God's own mind; conscience, or moral, sensitivity, to access His heart; and the capacity to receive, experience, reciprocate and communicate His love! Thus God established the bases for our warm, personal, living relationship with Himself in a fellowship of love. He did not choose to create us as robots, clones, nor even as angels; but as His created children. I believe He longed for children capable of reciprocating His love freely and completely. Neither love nor morality is a command performance! Without freedom of choice both lose their meaning. Love and morality are inspired performances. God wanted children who would respond with all their heart, soul and mind. He placed His created children in a **temporary setting** to prove and develop them for an **eternal relationship** as His adopted children, joint heirs with His only begotten Son. "Behold, what manner of love the Father hath bestowed upon us; that we should be called the sons of God!" *I John 3:1* God did walk with Adam and Eve, in loving fellowship, through the garden of Eden in the cool of the evenings. How beautifully soul-satisfying that must have been! What wonderful joy and comfort to stroll with God knowing they were created for just such moments as the objects of His love!

Satan Given Access Through Disobedience

One tragic evening, God came seeking their companionship; and they were not there to meet Him! According to Genesis 3:8, "They heard the voice of the Lord God walking in the garden in the cool of the day: and Adam and his wife hid themselves from the presence of the Lord God." Through disobedience, Adam and Eve had given Satan access to their hearts and minds and fellowship with God was broken! God, with an aching, broken heart walked throughout the garden crying, "Adam! Adam! Where art thou?" **That cry for reconciliation** with His estranged, guilt-ridden children **has come echoing down the corridors of time ever since**!

Men That Walked Faithfully

Enoch, father of Methuselah the oldest man that ever lived, responded to God's call for reconciliation; and exercised his privilege of walking with God! In Genesis 5:24 we are informed, "Enoch walked with God and was not; for God took him." Enoch walked the earth with God for more than three hundred years. It seems that one day as they were walking in precious fellowship, God must have said something like, "Enoch, let me walk you all the way home to My house where we can continue our fellowship without interruption." He was one of only two men who went to Heaven without going through the grave! God knew he was ready for Heaven and would be perfectly at home there. So many are so in love with this world, and so estranged from God they wouldn't be happy in Heaven even if they got there! (Which will not happen!) Heaven is a place prepared for a people who walk with God while on this earth!

God was so disillusioned and disappointed with mankind that He decided to destroy the human race with a flood; but there was Noah! Noah feared God and loved Him; and we are told Noah found grace in the eyes of the Lord. "Noah was a just man and perfect in his generation, and **Noah walked with God**!" *Genesis 6:9*

The Law, as given to Moses, was another effort by God to effect reconciliation. In Leviticus 26:12, God promised Israel: "And **I will walk among you**, and will be your God, and ye shall be My people." Through the Law and the Prophets God sought to prepare a people through which He could reach mankind. However, as Paul realized, the law of sin in his members prevented him from truly living according to the Levitical Law. Romans chapter seven gives a detailed description of his struggle with sin under the Law. Romans chapter eight tells of victory as a born-again child of God.

Thank God! The Scripture records the lives of extraordinary men, filled with His Spirit, who did indeed, **walk with God**! Joseph and Daniel have been inspirations to me since early childhood. Joseph, betrayed by his own brothers and sold into slavery, was victimized again because he would not be sexually immoral or betray his trusts. Through it all he kept his faith and maintained a right spirit. Joseph gave living proof that you can live a clean, holy life in a filthy, immoral world. He was faithful to God and God was faithful in honoring him. Daniel, the young prince of Israel, taken into slavery, physically mutilated, "Purposed in his heart that he would not defile himself!" God did not fail him! He preserved him from his enemies, delivered him from the den of lions and revealed His own plans for the future to him. God even sent a special messenger from Heaven to tell Daniel He loved him, very much! Except

CREATED TO WALK WITH GOD

for a few such heroes of faith, mankind has compiled a very dismal record of defeat and degradation.

Satan Takes Dominion

Adam received dominion over the earth along with his opportunities as a child of God. He surrendered that dominion to Satan through disobedience to God, betraying himself and the human race into spiritual bondage. Satan has held dominion over the world ever since. What Satan could not accomplish through direct confrontation with God, he realized through the disobedience of man. **Man failing to walk with God**: now found himself **ruled by Satan**. Satan has no power over God at all. Fallen man gives Satan preeminence and the opportunity to strike at the heart of God through His estranged children.

Adam and Eve were told they would die if they ate of the forbidden tree. Satan argued they would not surely die but rather be very wise like God Himself. These are the basic tenets of The New Age Movement. There is nothing new about such beliefs. They had their genesis with that first rebellion in Heaven when Satan said, "I will be as God!" Adam and Eve **disobeyed**, did eat the forbidden fruit and **they did die**! In fact, death came upon them and succeeding generations in three ways. They experienced immediate spiritual death in that they were separated from God by a barrier of sin. Physical death became the appointment for all mankind. Eternal death became the inheritance of everyone who is not spiritually reborn before physical death takes place. The unredeemed are lost forever.

Spiritual death is not annihilation of the soul for our spirit is eternal. It will live forever, somewhere. We will never just cease to be. Death is essentially a matter of separation. When two friends separate and become enemies, a **friendship dies**. When a husband and wife divorce because of adultery, a **marriage dies**. When the soul leaves the body, the **body dies**. When man is separated from God by the sin-barrier, that person is **spiritually dead** in trespasses and sin! Every human being is spiritually **stillborn**: dead in trespasses and sin. We are born into satanic bondage: in a world where Satan is the prince of the power of the air because Adam surrendered dominion to him by sinful disobedience. When David in his penitential Psalm said, "Behold, I was shapen in iniquity; and in sin did my mother conceive me," he was not declaring sexual relations as sinful. He was simply stating that he inherited a sinful nature from his human parents. We are born with our backs toward God and heading in the wrong direction! If we ever meet God and walk with Him in fellowship **we must turn around**! This underlies the meaning of the term, converted! There is an often repeated truism: there are **two births** and **two deaths**! If we are **born once** we **die twice**; if **born twice** we **die once**!

How to Walk with God

When Adam sinned and separated himself from God, God immediately sought reconciliation and redemption for His estranged children. The entire Bible is a record of His efforts to rescue lost mankind. He attempted the rescue Himself through direct dealings with mankind. At the time of the flood, only one man was listening. God started all over again with that one man and his family. He called out Abraham to establish a dynasty of faithful men. He worked through the patriarchs; and then through Moses and The Law. God sought reconciliation through special men, and then through the prophets.

When all other efforts had failed God made the ultimate sacrifice. He ordained that His only begotten Son should take upon Himself the limitations of human flesh; become incarnate and effectively redeem mankind. John 3:16 records, "God so loved the world that He gave His only begotten Son, that whosoever believeth in Him should not perish, but have everlasting life." We are informed in II Corinthians 5:19, "God was in Christ reconciling the world to Himself."

Jesus suffered and died to serve our death sentence: providing atonement for our redemption. **Jesus broke the sin-barrier!** When we believe in Him, repent, confess and forsake our sins: God has promised to forgive our sin and to cleanse from all unrighteousness. With the sin-barrier removed, that which separated us from God is gone and we are reconciled. No longer separated from God, we become spiritually alive. We have been "born-again"! Reunited with our Heavenly Father we now **begin our walk with God**! He who walked with Adam and Eve in the garden, not only walks with us: **He walks in us**! We have become living, walking temples of His Holy Spirit and have established a living relationship with The Living God!

Reconciled to God

We are clearly informed that those who would reconcile with God "Must believe that He is and that He will reward all who diligently seek Him." *Hebrews 11:6* We are also instructed in I Corinthians 2:14 that, "The **natural man** cannot receive or know the things of the Spirit, because they are spiritually discerned." When man sinned, **the lights went out!** Adam learned the truth of what was written later in Matthew six, "If therefore the light that is in thee be darkness, how great is that darkness!" The sin-barrier that arose between God and man brought such horrible spiritual darkness that man, not only lost his way in that darkness; but through the ages has come to question the very existence of God himself.

Witness of Creation

God has sought, from the beginning, **to speak to man through His created things**. In Isaiah 45, verses 6, 12, 22: "That they may know from the rising of the sun, and from the West, there is none beside Me. I Am the Lord, and there is none else. I have made the earth, and created man upon it: I, even my hands, have stretched forth the heavens, and all their host have I commanded. Look unto Me, and be ye saved, all the ends of the earth: for I am God, and there is none else."

"In the beginning God created the Heaven and the earth. And the earth was without form, and void; and darkness was upon the face of the deep. And the Spirit of God moved upon the face of the waters." *Genesis 1:1-2*

"And God saw everything that **He had made**, and, behold it was **very good**. And the evening and the morning were the sixth day." *Genesis 1:31*

"The heavens declare the glory of God; and the firmament sheweth His handiwork. "...Day unto day uttereth speech, and night unto night sheweth knowledge. ...There is no speech nor language, where their voice is not heard. "...Their line is gone out through all the earth, and their words to the end of the world." *Psalms 19:1-4*

If there ever was truth that is **self evident** it is the **truth concerning creation**. We look through the **telescope** viewing the world of the **Macrocosm** and see a seeming infinity of space, galaxy after galaxy, innumerable stars, planets and other heavenly bodies all being governed by the same forces and laws. These heavenly bodies maintain precise orbits and time frames. We have sent out man-made **space probes**, controlling them with precision, for the laws and principles of physics on earth, apply in space. When we look through the **microscope** into the world of the **Microcosm** we discover the same laws and physical principles apply there also with precision. Could man ever develop microscopes or telescopes capable of probing the extremes? In one **light year**, light travels over 5.8 trillion miles. Scientists now talk of millions or billions of **light years** to distant stars and galaxies. It is small wonder that men without faith, or the guidance of the Holy Spirit, consider God to be **unknowable** and beyond human comprehension. Truly, the heavens do declare the glory of God and their words magnify God to the **ends** of His universe! How big is God? We must conclude **He is big enough**!

Nothing Just Happens

How can any thinking person recognize the common design apparent in the study of physics today, and evident also in the worlds of the microcosm and macrocosm; and not realize there must also have been a **common designer**? Most of us recognize what is known as the law of adequate, or efficient, causation. Simply stated, the lesser cannot produce the greater. The cause has to be equal to or greater than the effect produced! When we realize the **Designer/**

Creator of the universe is, of necessity greater than all of His creation: it is easy for me to say, "**My Lord and my God!**" Only God exists without causation. Many philosophers refer to God as "**The Unmoved Mover**". The Bible simply states, "In the beginning, God created..." *Genesis 1:1*

Truth Absolute, Comprehension Is Not

When studying at Brown University, the skeptics accused me of "filling the gaps of my understanding with God to escape the impact of my own ignorance!" I did not **fill the gaps with God ... I committed them to God**! I am confident He knows everything for **He is Truth**! The frontiers of my knowledge kept advancing as I learned new facts of truth and discovered new reasons for the hope that dwelt in me! The better I understood truth as **it was**: the better I understood **God as He is**! We finite beings know so little of the truth inherent in our Infinite God! We will always "know in part" and the frontiers of our knowledge will always be so limited. **Only faith** can bridge the gap that stretches beyond the limits of our human understanding. **Truth is absolute and never changes**. What God has established as truth is, and always will be, the truth! Our **concepts of truth vary** with our information and experience. However, we can live in harmony with absolute truth if we are but led by God's Holy Spirit. What a wonderful gift to be able, through His Spirit, to access the heart and mind of God! In Daniel twelve, four: we are informed that in these last days there will be an explosion of knowledge! Well educated people today experience reaches of the mind not experienced by the Greek philosophers. We have access to data bases not known until this very present generation. How wonderful it would be if our advancing frontiers of knowledge would bring us into a more warmly, personal relationship with the God of Creation!

God has spoken to me, personally, so many times through His Creation. Much of my childhood and youth were spent in His fields and forests. I could see His handiwork and feel His presence everywhere. Deep within, my heart has exalted, "This is my Father's world!" **Scientific facts** have never been a **challenge to my faith**. They have always come as a deeper revelation of God's creativity. All that is scientifically factual, truly does "Declare the glory of God and show His handiwork!" He created it all! "Without Him was nothing made that was made!" One can learn a lot about someone by studying the workings of his hands. In God's wilderness one can see the beauty of harmony in the color combinations. (Who else could present so many shades of green and make them harmonize?) We see the beauty of symmetry where everything is in proper proportion. I feel that I am a part of the wilderness scene when alone in it; not merely a spectator but a participant. The sight of the flora and fauna; the scent of the flowers, the pine and the balsam; the sounds of a running brook; the wind sighing in the pines, the rustle of the leaves, the songs of the birds and the calls of living things effect me much the same as when listening to light symphony. I feel that I am part of the whole, especially, when assured, God is the great Conductor of this symphony. Much of the peace we feel when alone in the forest or meadow is experienced because nature is functioning in harmony with, and according to, the purpose of its Creator.

Have you ever stood on the rim of The Grand Canyon, watching as the setting sun changed the color of patterns on the canyon walls: with their seemingly endless rock formations and colorations, creating shadows on the canyon floor? Have you been privileged to view the majestic British Columbia Mountains and studied their snow-capped peaks, glaciers and the small trees that trace the beginnings of the tree lines? Trees that increase in size and density to that of the majestic fir and spruce as they extend down the slopes to line the shores of lakes and rivers at the bottom of the canyons? One memorable October day, I flew, in a light plane, just above the Muskoka Lakes in Ontario, Canada. There was not a cloud in the sky. The blue of the sky reflected upon the waters of the lakes, causing the fall foliage of the trees to stand out against the sparkling blue of the slightly rippled waters. The sugar maples were at the peak of their splendor: the deep red, the scarlet and various shades of yellow stood out among the green of the pines, spruce and fir. The large islands in the lakes looked like huge floral displays on a table cloth of deep blue; and entire forests, in their indescribable beauty, traced the rocky shores of lakes and streams. Who but God could even conceive such beauty: let alone create it?

My Father's World

One day, I stood on the fan tail of the USS Rochambeau, a troop ship, just off the coast of California headed for a very uncertain future in the South Pacific. The Japanese invasions of many lands were raging unchecked. They had not been defeated anywhere. We were not thinking of a limited tour of duty. It could be years before we returned home, if ever! We were part of a U.S. Naval amphibious force sent to confront the enemy and turn back their tide of conquests. I watched that day as the Golden Gate Bridge of San Francisco disappeared behind the fog banks blanketing the coast. Back there was everything I had known and loved: home, family, friends, churches and familiar scenes. Looking out to sea, there was nothing but gray fog and the white-capped ground swells slowly lifting and lowering our ship. What lay beyond that ominous fog? Looking back toward the coast, the Golden Gate Bridge was visible for a few moments then lost again to the fog. Suddenly, I felt overwhelmed with loneliness, uncertainty and foreboding. It was at that moment my Heavenly Father spoke to me through the twenty-fourth Psalm: "The earth is the Lord's and the fullness thereof; the world and they that dwell therein. For He hath founded it upon the seas, and established it upon the floods." Instantly, I was reminded, **"This is My Father's world!** All of it! **No matter where I go in it I cannot get out of my Father's backyard**! I shall be at home everywhere and anywhere I go!" At that very moment, my uncertainty and foreboding disappeared and I faced the future with full confidence in my Father's loving care. I was a **child of destiny**, assured by my Heavenly Father, that no one or nothing could harm me unless He permitted it! Once again God had spoken of His presence throughout His creations.

God permitted a great moment of ecstasy one unforgettable morning. So vivid is that memory, were I an artist, I could paint that scene today. It occurred just after daybreak on a February morning. I was snowshoeing out to meet a relief convoy bringing food and supplies to our snowbound logging camp at the East Branch dam, on Medunkeunk Stream, in the wilderness of Maine. With the temperature at 55 degrees below zero, Fahrenheit, my dark mackinaw jacket was snow white from hoarfrost. Hoarfrost icicles hung from my eyebrows, into the line of vision, as I approached an open ridge in the trail. By chance, looking back across thirty miles of snow-laden wilderness, I saw the rising sun as it caught the tip of snow-capped Mt. Katahdin, the first place in North America to catch the light of sunrise. I stood transfixed as the deep purple shadows at the base of the mountain gave way to the blazing light of the rising sun. That descending line of golden fire displaced the various shades of purple as it crept down the mountain until the whole mountain shimmered like blazing gold. Many of us have seen dust particles revealed by the sunlight, streaming through a window, but I had not realized that in still, sub zero air, golden frost particles fill the air like dust particles in an old house. By the time the rising sun had turned Katahdin into golden fire, the sunlight also touched the tops of the birches and white pine trees of Pea Ridge, the high "horseback" along which I was traveling. Those golden flecks of frost sparkled in the entire air about me and added their golden sheen to the snow-laden trees on the ridge and across the glens below. No queen in all her jewels had shimmered with greater beauty than the entire wilderness setting in which I found myself. Everything there proclaimed the glory of God, showing forth His creative handiwork! When I view the indescribable wonders of God's creation, here on earth, sensing his own love for beauty: I think, "If God can do all this down here, in time; what must Heaven be like where He has had eternity to make it up and nobody to trash or pollute His creation!"

Earth for Time Mankind for Eternity

During World War II, it was my privilege to visit the Grand

Sequoia Forest at Santa Cruz, California. I felt so small and insignificant in the presence of such forest giants. One huge tree had a cavity in it's base the size of a small room. It has been said that the Mexican General, Santayana, used that cavity as a headquarters during his California campaign. Those trees were living organisms when Moses led the children of Israel out of bondage. It is quite possible they took root as seedlings just after The Flood. They were huge trees when our Lord hung on the cross at Calvary. Countless generations of men have lived and died since those trees were seedlings. Why, then, would God assign so brief a life span to His crowning creation made in His own image? It suddenly dawned on me that He did not create me for time, but for eternity! Long after those sequoia have crumpled to dust or become petrified, I shall be alive in His presence, if I truly conform to my Father's will and purpose!

Why Me, Lord?

It is not difficult to believe God big enough and wise enough to create the heavens and the earth. However, I do find it difficult to believe His love for me was great enough, and His interest in me compelling enough to identify me among His creatures and know me intimately and completely, actually being concerned about me! I am reminded that King David expressed the same thoughts in Psalm eight: "When I consider thy heavens, the work of Thy fingers, the moon and the stars, which Thou hast ordained; What is man, that Thou art mindful of him? And the son of man, that Thou visitest him?" God knew the truly sensitive among mankind would find difficulty believing He cared for them, individually, personally. That is why He had Jesus tell of His care for lilies and sparrows; and that He even knew the number of hairs on our heads. All this to assure us He cared and would hear us when we called upon Him! How wonderful the assurance of John three, sixteen, "God so loved the world that He gave His only begotten Son that **whosoever** believed on Him should not perish but have everlasting life." **He made a new creation out of me!** I was born the **physical son** of Ralph Emerson Gleason and Christine Marple Gleason. Spiritually stillborn, dead in trespasses and sin. I was **born-again** because Christ had broken the sin-barrier and made possible my reconciliation with God. Spiritually reborn, I became a **spiritual son** of God! Do we not read, "If any man be in Christ, he is a new creation, old things pass away and all things become new." ❖

2 Learning to Walk

As the Spirit of God once brooded over the waters of an earth without form and void: that same Holy Spirit moves in our hearts and lives to bring holy order to the sinful chaos within us! In the words of a precious hymn, "What a wonderful change in my life has been wrought since Jesus came into my heart!" God created a physical, temporal **world for us to live in**. When we are spiritually reborn: created new creatures in Jesus Christ, it is that **He might live in us**! Jesus did not have to die to create the world or work miracles! He did all that before He died. He died that we might become new creations: spiritually reborn to eternal life! "What? Know ye not that your body is the temple of the Holy Ghost which is in you, which ye have of God, and ye are not your own? For ye are bought with a price: **therefore glorify God in your body, and in your spirit, which are God's**." *I Corinthians 6:19-20*

Our Hearts His Temple

God took Isaiah to Solomon's Temple to reveal Himself, His holiness, and His will. Since Pentecost, God has sought to reveal His presence, His holiness and His will through the ministry of His Holy Spirit operating within the temples of His created children who have been born of the Spirit, filled with the Spirit, and are led by the Spirit. Our Lord said that it was the wicked who sought physical and material signs and wonders that God might prove Himself! God is providing spiritual proof of His presence, His power, His holiness, His will and His love **through spirituality reborn** mankind, shining as His lights in the world. **We are His witnesses!** "Let your light so shine before men, that they may see your good works and glorify your Father which is in Heaven!" *Matthew 5:16* We need to remember, in the strict sense of the words, it is not truly **our good works**: but according to Ephesians 2:10, "We are **His workmanship** created in Christ Jesus unto good works, which God hath ordained that we should walk in them." May we all respond, "**Let the beauty of Jesus be seen in me!**" "How beautiful upon the mountains are the feet of him that bringeth good tidings, that publisheth peace: that bringeth good tidings of good that publisheth salvation; that say unto Zion, thy God reigneth!" *Isaiah 52:7* In Philippians we are admonished to be, "Blameless and harmless, the sons of God, without rebuke, in the midst of a crooked and perverse generation, among whom **ye shine as lights** in the world." *Chapter 2:15*

Lying Signs and Wonders

There is grave danger for those who need to see miracles to believe. In the last days Satan will perform many miracles, even to the raising of the dead. Many will be misled simply because a miracle has been performed. In Luke chapter sixteen, Jesus quotes Abraham, telling the rich man in Hell, "They have Moses and the prophets ... If they hear not Moses and the prophets neither will they be persuaded though one rose from the dead." Today, we have far more light than Moses and the prophets! We have also the ministry of His only begotten Son, the presence of His Holy Spirit, the New Testament and nearly two thousand years of church history as bases for our faith and hope. Signs and wonders appeal to the carnal, natural man. He wants material proof to establish his beliefs. Such a man says in effect, "**Show me** and **I will believe**!" God says, "**Believe** and **I will show you**!" First Corinthians, chapter two, speaks directly to the true bases of our faith. "The **natural man** receiveth not the things of the Spirit: for they are foolishness unto Him: neither can he know them for they are **spiritually discerned**." *verse 14* "But **God hath revealed** them unto us **by His Spirit**: for the Spirit searcheth all things, yea the deep things of God." *verse 10* "Now we have received, not the spirit of the world, but the Spirit which is of God; that we might know the things that are freely given of God. Which things also we speak, not in words which man's wisdom teacheth, but which the Holy Ghost teacheth; comparing spiritual things with spiritual." verses *12-13* It was said of Moses, "He endured, as **seeing** Him who is **invisible**." *Hebrews 11:27* People **do not believe because they see miracles! They see miracles because they believe!** It cost God far more to redeem mankind than it did to create the universe! Many believe God created the universe in six days. It took His Son almost thirty-three years ... **and His life** to provide for our redemption.

What Time Was It?

The one great question for many firm believers in creationism involves the time element. The chronology of events listed in the Biblical account of creation and the chronological sequence of events theorized by the evolutionists are very similar. The big differences are in the causative factors and the time element. For fundamental believers in God's Word, the causative factors are unquestioned. It is the time element that raises questions for many of them. Just what constitutes a day? We think of a day as the twenty-four hour period between sunrise and sunrise, or sunset to sunset: the time it takes the earth to make one complete turn in the face of the sun. This presents difficulty, for, according to God's own account of creation, He did not create the sun **until the fourth day**. Genesis one, tells us exactly what God did on that fourth day. In verse fourteen God said, of the sun and the moon He created on the fourth day, "Let them be for signs, and for seasons, and for days, and years."

Paleontologists, geologists and other research scientists, who study earth's history; have concluded that the physical world to be millions, if not billions of years old. They use fossils and petrified rock formations and trees to sustain their beliefs. When God said, one of His days was as a thousand years, I do not believe He was giving the precise value of a unit of time. My confidence is, He was simply saying, in fact, "So what! I do not deal in years; but eternities!"

God forbid that my open mind on the matter should undermine the faith of one believing the earth to have been created within a time frame of one hundred and forty-four hours. Please do not brand me a heretic either. I do know that millions of believers who love God and believe the Bible, have found it difficult, even impossible to accept the six day period as now measured, in the light of archaeological digs and rock formations.

What God could have done and what He did do are two entirely different matters. I suppose He could have created the universe in six hours, had He chosen to do so. Whatever the time frame, it was His timing for He scheduled it all. This matter poses no challenge whatsoever to my faith, nor confidence in His Word. If God had thought this question vital, He would have explained it precisely as He has so many other things.

Millions of years of history seem relatively unimportant, in the face of untold trillions of years of eternities yet to come. The Bible flatly states, "In the beginning, God created the heavens and the earth." He did it on His own schedule of sequence and time frame. That is all I need to know. Of course, I would like to broaden my data base on the subject! He assures us all, "We will understand it better by and by, when we no longer see through a glass darkly." One day we will know as we are known. When those ancient fossils are reduced to dust, I hope to be praising their Creator in Heaven.

I fear that we do not fully understand Philippians two, six: quote, "Who, being in the form of God, thought it not robbery to be equal with God." Some have translated this, "Thought it not to be grasped at, or clung to." I firmly believe this described Jesus' attitude about surrendering His role as co-regent with His Father in Heaven, to submit to being born as a human infant and know the restrictions of being as one of His own creations, and to suffer physical death that He might redeem and reconcile mankind with the Father. Verse seven of that chapter states, "He made Himself of no reputation, and took upon Him the form of a servant, and was made in the likeness of sinful men." As eternal Spirit He could not die! He released His authority; and surrendered His glory to become flesh that He could die. He was born to die, that I might live! He expects me to die out to myself, that He might live in me! One Jewish maiden in all history was honored by God to provide a body for His Son that **He might die**! However, each of us is honored with the privilege of **providing our Lord a body through which He can live**! He wants to walk the earth in our shoes, lift burdens with our hands, look with compassion through our eyes, love through our hearts and win other lost souls, for whom, He also died! If we could but realize the price He paid to redeem us, none of us could ever complain about what it costs us to provide a body for Him who gave life for us! He surrendered His glory to come and share our burdens of sin, providing reconciliation. We will have to **surrender the world**, and all it means to us **to share His glory**!

Soul Winner's Eternal Destiny

The heavens shall pass away with a great noise, and the elements shall melt with fervent heat, the earth also and the works that are therein shall be burned up." *II Peter 3:10*   The earth that God created in the beginning will pass away. "**Then shall the righteous shine forth as the sun in the Kingdom of their Father.**" *Matthew 13:43* "And they that be wise shall shine as the brightness of the firmament and **they that turn many to righteousness as the stars for ever and ever**." *Daniel 12:3*   "And this is the promise that He hath promised us, even eternal life." *I John 2:25*

God's Executive Agent

How can anyone so insignificant as man find reconciliation and fellowship with the God of Creation? First of all God sent His Son. The Son, in turn, promised the Father would send the Holy Spirit to teach us everything He would have us know that was vital to our eternal salvation. *John 14:26*   The Greeks, by reason, knew not God! "No man can say, Jesus is the Lord, but by the Holy Ghost." *I Corinthians 12:3* "As many as are led by the Spirit of God, they are the sons of God." *Romans 8:14*   The Holy Spirit is absolutely vital to our total relationship with God! That is why the sin against the Holy Spirit is the sin unto death! **He is God's Administrative Agent in the total process of man's redemption, and his preparation for eternity**. Through the Holy Spirit God reveals His truth, His holiness, His will and man's own standing before God. Hence the warnings: "Quench not the Spirit." *I Thessalonians 5:19* ; and "Grieve not the Spirit whereby ye are sealed unto the day of redemption." *Ephesians 4:30*   We have this wonderful assurance too: "**As many as are led by the Spirit of God, they are the sons of God!**" *Romans 8* When the Holy Spirit is rejected, our contact with God is broken!

Truly Reciprocating God's Love

It was so important to God that we love Him too! That is why He made us free to choose, for we know love cannot be commanded or coerced! We repeat, Love is not a command performance: it is inspired! Our love is the one thing He cannot command. How tragic then that so many of us should love the world He created more than we love the Creator Himself! God created the earth as a temporal proving ground; and a place to prepare His created children to feel at home in Heaven. How horrible then when we "Set our affections on things on the earth" and fail to qualify for admission to our heavenly and eternal home! Let us learn to walk with Him here that He may be able to walk us all the way home! What a place that must be! The heavens do declare the glory of God and the firmament does show His handiwork! But what about us? Are we glorifying God in our bodies which are His? Does His Spirit abide in us? Are our feet beautiful upon the mountains of earth as we declare "our God reigneth"? Are we, the creations of His love, permitting Him to love others through us? Will we shine forever, when the earth of His creation has passed away; because we have "turned many to righteousness"? Let us truly reciprocate His love; enjoy our walk with Him through time and have a wonderful journey!

Our daughter, Lynne, was a very sensitive, gentle child. She would cringe if there was strife or contention about her. One day she was corrected for some misdemeanor; and she was shattered. Perhaps I had come across more harshly than I felt or intended. She was so shaken up, we both grieved. Hesitant, lest I weaken the point of discipline, I sat trying to read the evening newspaper. It seems the paper could have been upside down, for my thoughts were centered in that grieving four year old. The newspaper rustled in my hands, looking down I saw a tear-stained pixy face looking up at me from beneath the paper. Her lips were quivering as she said, "Daddy, I wuv ya!" How precious those moments when we found relief hugging one another!

What must it be like for our Heavenly Father, as He looks down upon our upturned, tear-stained faces; and hears us say, "Father, I don't understand all this! I only know I love you!" How wonderful when He sees our hearts responding, reciprocating His love; because nothing else really matters! I believe our Heavenly Father is far more compassionate and understanding than we could ever be. This assurance is such a comfort to me.

> Praise ye the Lord, Praise ye the Lord from the
>   heavens: praise Him in the heights.
> Praise ye Him, all His angels: praise ye Him, all
>   His hosts.
> Praise ye Him, sun and moon: praise Him, all ye
>   stars of light.
> Praise Him, ye heavens of heavens, and ye waters
>   that be above the heavens.
> Let them praise the name of the Lord: for He
>   commanded and they were created.

He hath made a decree which shall not pass.
Praise ye the Lord from the earth, ye dragons and all deeps.
Fire, and hail; snow and vapour; stormy wind fulfilling His word.
Mountains, and all hills; fruitful trees, and all cedars:
Beasts, and all cattle; creeping things, and flying fowl:
Kings of the earth, and all people; princes, and all judges of the earth:
Both young men, and maidens; old men and children:
Let them praise the name of the Lord: for His name alone is excellent; His glory is above the earth and Heaven.
He also exalteth the horn of His people, **the praise of all His saints; even of the children of Israel, a people near unto Him, praise ye the Lord!** *Psalm 148* ✢

3 Systems of Guidance

A farmer, we know, found the nest of a Canada goose. Taking the eggs home, he placed them under a setting hen that hatched the young goslings. When those young goslings, happily, took to the water in the barnyard pond, that hen was frantic! She would run up and down the water's edge, trying to call them out of the water. My mother often said she knew just how such a hen would feel, having raised six very adventurous boys! The farmer clipped the wings of the goslings as they matured. That fall the calls of wild geese, flying southward in a ragged V formation, reached the hearing of the young geese in the barnyard. They ran about the yard flapping their wings, trying to take flight. Though, raised by a hen, there was an instinctive call to the heights within them. The farmer failed to clip the wings of a young gander before the wild geese again flew overhead in their northward migration. This time as the haunting honking stirred the geese in the barnyard, that young gander had found his wings and took flight, joining the V formation overhead. With that compelling **call to the heights** he could no longer be content in a barnyard!

We too, are **called to the heights**, simply because we were created in the **image of God**! As His created children, we cannot be content and truly fulfilled in the "barnyards" of an earthbound existence. We will find true fulfillment only through our fellowship with God as we learn to walk with Him. In Psalm forty-two, David cried, "As the hart panteth after the water brooks, so panteth my soul after Thee, O God. My soul thirsteth for God, for the living God: when shall I come and appear before God?" When Satan told me as a youth that I did not have what it took to escape my spiritual barnyard: God spoke to me through the beatitude, "Blessed are they that **hunger** and **thirst** for righteousness, for **they shall be filled**." That hunger and thirst was not only my assurance that I would be filled, but the evidence that there was a God out there who had instilled that hunger. Certainly, Satan did not inspire that hunger for purity, righteousness and holiness: nor could it have arisen from within my own sensuous nature. Just as our natural body craves food and water to sustain life and body functions; our spirit hungers and thirsts for a right relationship with our God! We do well to remember God created us in His own likeness, a **spiritual being destined** for eternity! Please remember our physical bodies are but temporary accommodations for our existence in time. We are prone to indulge the sensual demands of the body while neglecting the care for our soul. We will consider this conflict of values, later in the book.

CREATED TO WALK WITH GOD

Launched In Space

We are all familiar with many details of our National Space Program. Not many years ago, few thinking persons would believe we could launch men into space, have them walk on the moon, and return them safely home. We marvel at the scientific inventions assembled to provide transportation, life support systems, control and communication systems to achieve such an objective. Our space agencies provided mechanisms that the astronauts might control their own space craft. Space program scientists also provided back up systems and controls that would permit control by NASA ground units. Success of the missions; and the safety of those in space depended upon close cooperation by all personnel involved.

Radio, television, computer systems and system controls played tremendous roles in success after success. Can you imagine astronauts in space deliberately destroying, or turning off life supports and communication systems? Can you visualize them rejecting ground control, sabotaging their own spacecraft just because they felt someone was interfering with their life styles, or being too demanding? Men who rejected assistance from the ground or who destroyed their means of communication would be forever lost in space, and nothing Ground Control could do would save them! How preposterous!

When God made man and established him on earth, He too had plans to provide everything necessary to sustain him, enabling him to survive in a hostile environment, keep in communication with him until He could bring him safely home. Tragically, man is so self-willed and rebellious that he often interferes with his Creator and rejects the controls and communication systems God has provided for his successful journey through time and a safe trip home. So many of God's created children will be **lost in time, making it impossible for Him to bring them home**!

God has carefully designed us for a safe and successful journey through time! Through intelligence and conscience He brought us in touch with His own heart and mind. He placed within us an instinctive homesickness of the soul! He seeks to keep in constant communication with us through His Holy Spirit.

God's Guidance Systems

How do birds know how, when and where to migrate? What impels and guides salmon back, from vast oceans, to the very streams and rivers where they were spawned, hatched and left as fingerlings? **I do not know!** We call it instinct; but it is clearly evident that some thing, inherent within them, guides them unerringly. **Most all nature responds to, and is controlled by, the will of it's Creator.** God looked upon all that He had made and said, "**That is good**"! How horrible that **Man**, God's crowning creation, **abusing his freedom of choice**, would be **the exception**!

God provided for guidance systems in the physical universe of His creation. I know so little about electricity and electronics! In fact, many say that nobody knows just what electricity really is. This has been scientifically established as factual: **the universe is electrical in its very composition**! All matter is composed of building blocks we call atoms. Each of them is an electrical sphere in itself that can be reduced to pure energy. **Scientists have created none of this!** They have merely discovered principals and laws of physics that God established at the time of creation! Unlocking these secrets has permitted man, in a very brief span of time, to develop these latent powers and harness them to provide vast systems of physical communication, and proliferate the world with electrically powered devices. **Every physical thing created by God, or invented by man is a composition of atoms.** To create: all God has to do is **call up, yet another, configuration of atoms**.

Men discovered the magnetism of the earth's poles, early in their scientific quests. They put this knowledge of magnetism to work in the development of the compass. The needle point of the compass, unerringly pointing to the magnetic pole, provided sure guidance systems for travelers on land and sea. Later knowledge of electricity, and associated electronics, enabled the scientific community to invent all the systems that have enabled man, with reasonable safety, to conquer space.

Energy from Hand of God

Speaking, strictly **personally**, I believe it a **self-evident fact** that **electricity is creative energy from the very hand of God operative in the world of matter**! I believe He **spoke** the world into existence "**And sustains it by the power of His presence!**" This belief concerning the source and nature of electricity is held with the force of **conviction**. I do hold this truth to be self-evident! Electricity energizes, purifies, enlightens, provides cohesion and communication, among other powers and potentials.

Energy from Heart of God

God's love is the central force of His guidance systems! Love is probably the most talked about word in the English language; and the least understood. When speaking of love, we most often speak about what love does rather than what it is. We speak of symptoms and results. **Love is not emotion nor feeling.** It is a **spiritual force that** causes, or creates, emotion or feeling. Like the wind, you see what love does, not what it is! It is my firm conviction that true love is a **positive flow of spiritual energy!** Just as electricity is a positive flow of **physical** energy, from the **hand** of God operative in the world of matter: **God's love is a positive flow of creative energy, from the heart of God, operative in the realm of spiritual reality**! God wants to channel His love, as a positive flow of creative, spiritual energy through the hearts, minds and lives of His created children. Born of the Spirit and filled with the Spirit, as new creatures in Jesus Christ, we do become channels for His love and power.

Everything, and more, that electricity does in the world of matter, love does in the realm of the spiritual. Love bonds, bringing cohesion: it purifies, enlightens, enables communication and energizes. We also speak of **grace** in terms of its expressions rather than its identity. **Grace is God's love in motion!** We do not see what grace is: we see what it does. Saving grace, healing grace, enabling grace, forgiving grace and all other expressions of grace are evidences of **God's love in motion** and power in and through human personality and lives. Our Lord said, "If I be lifted up, I **will draw** men unto me." Just as forces of gravity, and other electrically related powers keep heavenly, physical bodies in their fixed orbits: so God's love maintains order, preventing chaos in the realm of spiritual things.

Love inspires responsive, reciprocal love. We love to cuddle baby animals, primarily, because they are so loving. When we realize how much God loved lost mankind, and how much that love cost Him, we should not find it difficult to keep the first great commandment to love God with all our hearts, soul, mind and strength. If we do truly reciprocate the love of God; we will have little difficulty communicating that love to others. We are informed in His word, "He that loveth not, knoweth not God, for God is love." *I John 4:* We will discuss, more completely, our fulfillment of the two great commandments, later in this book. Failure to respond to God's love **aborts the key element in God's program for our safe return home**!

Guidance from the Mind of God

When God gave us intelligence, He gave us the power to access His own mind. Yet reason alone in insufficient. "The Greeks by wisdom knew not God." The reach of the mind falls far short because of our minuscule data base and finite limitations. How can the finite mind fully fathom the infinite mind of God? We do not understand but a fraction of what was and now is. What about the future? What does God have in mind for us? Through faith, love and the guidance of His Holy Spirit **we are given the access code to the mind of God** who does know the past, present and future!

Guidance from the Son of God

God launched His only begotten Son into our time and space warp that He might provide, instruct and inspire us for a safe journey home. He told the disciples, during His last evening with them, "I am the way, the truth, and the life: no man cometh to the Father but by Me." He knows the way home! If we follow Him, we too, will return to the Father!

In World War II, I believe, during the Battle of Savo Sound, a cruiser received a direct hit on the bridge, knocking out all systems of navigation and communication. The captain, of the crippled ship, signaled the admiral on his flagship up ahead, by a portable short-wave radio. Reporting his distress, He asked for instructions. The admiral radioed back, "Follow my wake!" Those who have sailed the South Pacific are familiar with the phosphorescent trails of light in the turbulent waters behind a passing ship. I am told that phosphorescence is the result of dying marine life. That crippled cruiser did follow the wake of the flagship, out of the battle zone to safety. Our Lord, having lived and died as one of us, rose again to leave a path of light, guiding us to safety. Jesus said to His disciples, in their crucial times of decision, "Follow thou Me!"

Guidance by the Spirit of God

When Jesus was about to leave His disciples, He knew they could not make it on their own. In the fourteenth, fifteenth and sixteenth chapters of John's Gospel, He assured them, "Let not your hearts be troubled. I will not leave you comfortless. I will pray the Father and He will send another Comforter and He will abide with you forever. He is the very Spirit of Truth who will teach you all things, whatsoever I have commanded." In Romans eight, we have this assurance, "As many as are led by the Spirit of God, they are the sons of God." God promised, through Ezekiel, "I will put My Spirit within you, and cause you to walk in My statutes, and ye shall keep My judgments, and do them." *Chapter 36:27* God has done everything possible to ensure our successful journey throughout our allotted time, and of a safe recovery when our mission is completed. Let us walk carefully and be alert and cooperative with our mission controls lest we be lost in time! ✤

4 Walking in the Spirit

One of the key secrets of Walking with God is found in Acts 17:28, "In Him we live, move and have our being." Wonderful facets of truth are revealed through the prism of this text. **God's truth** is like a **many-faceted diamond**! Each time you approach it and turn it over in your heart and mind, new light flashes from the exposed prisms and new brilliance and beauty flows from unfathomable depths.

"**In Him we live!**" In Christ we are brought back to spiritual life, resurrected from our death in trespasses and sin, spiritually reborn to live in His presence forever! I repeat the quote, "There are two births and two deaths. If we are born but once we die twice. If we are born twice, we die just once!" I love that song, "Nothing between my soul and the Savior, so that His blessed face may clearly be seen, nothing preventing the least of His favor, keep the way clear. Let nothing between." *John Peterson* **In Him we Live!**

"In Him we **move**!" Colossians two, six admonishes us, "As ye have received Christ, so walk ye in Him." Christianity is not just a belief, a system of theology. It is a way of life! It is a life shared with God! Through His indwelling Spirit He presents His own value system, principles and patterns for living. He calls upon us to so live that He need not be embarrassed to be in our presence, or have us identified as His children. "In all thy ways acknowledge Him, and He shall direct thy path." *Proverbs 3:6*

During the seventies, when counseling members of that estranged subculture known as hippies, I often assured them that many of them were looking for the right things, but in the wrong ways and wrong places. Many were seeking love, peace, direction and purpose for living. They were advised, "You will not find true love in erotica. You will find no peace storming up and down the streets shouting, 'Hell no! I won't go!' Nor will you find a meaningful purpose in life trying to destroy what others build." They were instructed that if they accepted Jesus Christ as Savior and Lord, they would find the fullness of love, a peace that was beyond all understanding, and God's own will would provide direction for a creative life filled with joy; and the world could be a better place just because they had lived in it.

There are ministers, missionaries, pastors, educators, teachers, layworkers in churches and their wives, from that subculture, who did discover their true fulfillment in Christ! **In losing their self-indulgent and futile life styles, they found their true identity as His created children.** How wonderful to have the privilege of telling them they were not just trash or flotsam on a heaving, restless sea! And have God confirm my witness as He spoke to them with the assurance they were indeed created by Himself for a mutually shared love, victorious living here, and a destiny that is eternal! "**In Him we Have our Being!**"

This realization that in Him I lived, moved and had my being came early in my life as God witnessed to His presence. However, I had missed a most precious and beautiful facet of that diamond of truth! God shed light on that precious passage and I realized the **converse** was also true! We not only **live** and **move** and **have our being in Him**! **He lives** and **moves** and **has His being in us**! Even as God had found it necessary to provide a human, fleshly body for His only begotten Son that He might die: He also needed to provide human bodies **through which His Son should live**! He does indeed **live within us**! Jesus said in John 14:23, "If a man love Me, he will keep My words: and My Father will love him, and we will come unto him and make our abode with him." "Now ye are the body of Christ, and members in particular." *I Corinthians 12:27* **In us He lives!**

Jesus, in His High Priestly prayer recorded in John seventeen explains the **very essence of reconciliation**. He prayed, "**I in them, and Thou in Me, that they may be made perfect in one; and that the world may know that Thou hast sent Me, and hast loved them, as Thou hast loved Me.**" Many have stumbled throughout the ages over the **mystery of the Trinity**! The Bible assures us, "**Great is the mystery of Godliness.**" The Jews found in him a "stumbling block" as teaching polytheism to a people taught by the Law, "Behold, O Israel, the Lord thy God is **one** God." How could three be one? Jesus taught there were indeed: three entities, three individual personalities. This is illustrated at His baptism when He, standing in the Jordan River, was confirmed as God's Son by God's own voice from Heaven; and The Holy Spirit descending as a Dove! There have been many other references to three distinct personalities in the Word.

Many are still troubled today by the mystery of the Trinity. Some believe that they will see only **God the Father** in Heaven. Others believe that they will see but **God the Son**. To many, **God the Holy Spirit** is but a phantom-like Spirit. Surely these mysteries are beyond the reach of human reasoning alone. We simply lack the data base. What we know concerning them must come as **revelations** from God. I too, as a young Christian, was troubled by aspects of the problem. Should I pray to God the Father, the Son, or confide in the Spirit? To whom should I say, "Thank you!"? These questions were laid to rest one day by the truth revealed in the high priestly prayer that all believers should **be one; even as We are One**! How can the millions of believers, of all times, all nations, each with their own personalities **be one**? How can we be "**One Body**" ... **The Church, the bride of Christ**? How can a man and a woman, two distinct personalities **be one**? God said that when He joined man and woman in holy wedlock, they **became one flesh**!

CREATED TO WALK WITH GOD

How can this be? **In the same way God the Father, God the Son and God the Holy Spirit are one! In spiritual unity!**

Our Lord prayed that **the unity of the Trinity** should bind us, not only to the God-head; but to each other! The **power**, or **force** that bonds us in this unity **is His love**! Do I think such unity in love is possible? Of course! **Jesus, Himself prayed that it should be!** Would not the Father answer His prayer?

In presenting the roles of Father, Son and Holy Spirit, as related to our Walking with God: I seek to carefully avoid the appearance of dividing the Trinity. Where One is present, all are present. Where One is honored, all are honored. Where One is involved, all are operative. The **unity of the Trinity cannot be broken**.

We are able to **Walk with God** when **the Son is revealed** by **the Spirit** and we, walking in the light, are **born of** the Spirit, **filled with** the Spirit and are **led by** the Spirit. We may now truly Walk with God in loving fellowship. One day the "mysteries" will all be solved! We shall "know as we are known" when we all arrive at home!

Our Father's Children

Did you ever try to tell a small boy that you knew his father better than he did? If he is a normal boy with an attentive father you will get a prompt and spirited rebuttal! Can't you hear him now: "You do not so know my Daddy better than me!" Just ask such a boy anything about his daddy and you will get a definitive response. He promptly tells you what his daddy can do and will do. He will tell you about his job, what he knows and what he thinks, about his dreams and aspirations. **But just what does a small boy really know about his father?** He knows so little of his father's burdens, plans, frustrations, hopes and fears. He has only very vague ideas about his daddy's work and the problems he has facing him. Why then does that little boy **respond with such confidence**? His response is **prompted by what he does truly know from experience**! He knows that his daddy loves him! If he is hungry, his daddy will find something for him to eat. His daddy will clothe him sufficiently to protect him from the elements. If threatened, his daddy will defend him. If it is dark and they are far from home, he is confident that his daddy knows the way. He just reaches up, takes his daddy's big hand, and walks confidently even though he cannot see where he is going; and he is **very proud to be walking with his dad**!

Theologically, most of us, especially if we are teachers or ministers of the Gospel, will bristle at even the suggestion that those of another persuasion know **our Heavenly Father** better than we do. We often respond defensively or even offensively! Here is where many **doctrinal controversies** have their genesis. **Like that**

little boy we are often prompted to launch into contentious, fervent expositions of our postures and beliefs. We are unwilling to admit there is anything vital that we do not understand. Actually, like that little boy, **there is so much we do not understand!** In fact, such a young boy, as pictured, has a more complete concept of his earthly dad, than we do of our Heavenly Father. Unfortunately, because of such challenges we often find ourselves committed to winning theological arguments instead of the winning of souls! **Most tragically of all, we fail to reflect our Father's love!** If this be true we will fail as soul-winners, for it is **His love that draws all men to Himself.**

It is wonderful, however, that like a small boy with all his limitations, we can have full assurance of Our Heavenly Father's love and care! We have learned, through experience, that He does love us, provides for us, protects us, walks with us in all of life's journeys and we are confident He knows the way home. He has assured us that wayfaring men, though fools, need not be lost on the way home! It is very reassuring to remember that **He does possess absolute knowledge!** He will tell us **everything we need to know** to do everything He wants done in the way it ought to be accomplished, if we but **learn to listen** and be led by His Holy Spirit. He will never call upon us to do anything He will not enable us to do! Like Paul, of old, we need to simply ask, Lord what wilt Thou have me to do?

Jesus did pronounce many blessings upon our lives and service before Him. However, **more than to bless our works**, He came to perform **His blessed works** in us and through us! **In us He moves!** True humility has its roots in the recognition of our human limitations. In John 15:5, Jesus teaches, "Without Me ye can do nothing." Failure to realize our human limitations and be totally dependent upon God, exposes us to the horrible danger of self-sufficiency; and we find ourselves doing our own "thing" in His name. There has been an epidemic of tragic failures among prominent leaders across Christendom, because of their egocentric life styles. Their tragic moral failures have brought great reproach upon the cause of Christ, and caused untold thousands of God's "Little ones" to stumble. We need to pray with truly humble, broken hearts, "Thy Kingdom come, Thy will be done on earth as it is in Heaven." My heart's desire, as I write this book, is that God will be able to communicate through it; and the reader will receive "light" as God speaks confirming truth, deep within themselves. Only then will they have the light that brings true conviction; and know God is speaking to them person to person.

These writings come from deep convictions and sincerity of heart. There has been much prayer that God would guide in editing out anything He would not say amen to, and that I might be inspired to write everything He would have others read. My main purpose in writing the book is to share with others what He has blest me with. Every effort is being made to distinguish between my personal opinions and God-given convictions. I would not die for my own opinions, let alone those of someone else! However, I believe I would lay down my life for a conviction. How important then, that I should know the difference! Failure to distinguish between mere belief and opinions on the one hand, and our God-given convictions on the other has tragic consequences. This failure is directly responsible for many inconsistencies and outright contradictions in the lives and witness of many professed Christians. Mere opinions and beliefs are like weather vanes, they shift with the prevailing winds of change and circumstance; and are totally inadequate to provide dependable guidance systems that determine eternal destinies. They lead to the unwitting acceptance of moral relativity as a system of values. We may be always changing our minds, but God is not changing His! His truth is absolute and His words yea and amen. We understand His truth when He gives **light**. When God speaks to us intuitively through His Spirit, His Word, another's witness or by some crucial event: a **conviction** is born! We cannot properly quote someone unless we have been in direct communication with him! So many professed Christians lack convictions simply because they have not been in direct communication with God! A God-given conviction is like a **compass, consistently and constantly pointing us in the right direction**. I am unwilling to have my eternal destiny hinge on mere human opinions or beliefs. Remember Jesus saying, "I am the Way, the Truth and the Life?" God has ordained that through our Lord, under the anointing of His Holy Spirit, we could walk and talk with Himself! Remember, God's adopted sons are those led by His Spirit. *Romans 8* Of course, those living by true convictions will be out of step with those who live by mere opinion or belief. One is being led by the reaches of the human mind, the other by the mind of God! Those who lack God-given convictions are quick to accuse those with deep, abiding convictions of being legalistic. The **true legalist** is the person locked into his own mindset rather than being led by the Holy Spirit who is, according to the Word, "The Mind of Christ."

What does differentiate opinions from convictions? This question bothered me for some time. I believe God helped me understand the simple answer. All convictions are introduced to the mind as opinions that are strengthened to the point of beliefs. They only become convictions when God's Holy Spirit speaks; and His light confirms them as such. It is the Holy Spirit who convicts of sin and declares what is right in the sight of God. Speaking of the Spirit, Jesus said, "And when He is come, He will reprove the world of sin, and of righteousness, and of judgment." *John 16:9* If God confirms a conviction, **live by it**! Genuine convictions are not always changing with the customs, styles and the opinions of men.

How to Walk with God

So many professed Christians cancel out the witness of much of their own lives, because they have failed to continue walking in the light of earlier convictions. Others may well question what other part of their witness will be next abandoned. God does give unfolding light and deeper insights that provide clearer understanding of truth as a whole. We should walk in that light as a new conviction; but never cancel out the principles of truth established when God had spoken in earlier confidences.

The thoughts in this book will come to you as just my opinions and beliefs until God's Holy Spirit confirms them as truth to you. Fellow humans can share the content of their own minds; but the convicting power of light comes only from the Lord!

Beginning to Walk

My walk with God, in Christ Jesus, began at my mother's knees. Mother made the Lord and His love very real to me; because she had learned the secrets of an intimate walk with God while still in her teens. Attending an independent Bible school on a hilltop in Durham, Maine, she realized the wonderful joy of personal, vibrant fellowship with Jesus. It was there that she met and married my father, Ralph Emerson Gleason. He was a strictly fundamentalist minister and they served together as staff members of that Independent Movement.

Father and mother were assigned as missionaries to Israel while it was still under Turkish rule. Tumultuous events both at home and abroad, brought about their return home. Mother never lost her love for the Holy Land. She carried a great prayer burden for the peace of Jerusalem throughout her entire lifetime; and was homesick for the land she loved until God took her home to **His** Jerusalem. She prayed, continually for the restoration of the Jews to their promised land. I can still "hear" her admonition, "Son, don't you ever get caught in anything **anti-Semitic**! Remember, they are still God's chosen people and heirs of God's covenants with Abraham." She believed the Jewish people were being disciplined by God for having rejected the Lord, as their Messiah. Her firm belief that one day the Jewish rulers would retry Jesus and reverse the verdict of rejection, never wavered. In warning against any personal satisfaction at their discomfort under chastisement, she would say, "Do you remember what I do to any of you who seem to enjoy my punishment of another?" We remembered! For she gave us the same punishment with perhaps even greater severity!

Mother, not only **told** me how to walk with God, she **showed** how! She did teach us by **precept**, but she showed us how by **example**! Her consistent, constant Christ-like walk in the face of heartbreak, suffering and a life of poverty left an indelible imprint upon my life. "How beautiful are the feet of them that preach the gospel of peace, and bring glad tidings of good things." The beautiful feet that brought God's glad tidings of good things to me, **walked in my mother's shoes.** My **first glimpse of my living Lord came when I saw Him walking in my mother's shoes**! I could not have doubted the reality of God's presence, even if I had wanted to!

Among the earliest words that I spoke were that lisping prayer, "Dear Jesus!", as mother taught me to pray. Indelibly stamped in memory, is that first prayer of confession of sin. At about four years of age, I stood at mother's knees asking God to forgive me for being such an awful sinner. Though limited in my range of options, the sense of conviction of guilt never felt stronger. Ashamed and sorry for my sins, I knew then that Jesus had died to forgive sinners and "make them feel all better!" I knew the joy of sensing peace of heart and mind.

The first experiences of public worship, recalled, came when attending Sunday School with my sister, Phyllis. This Sunday School was conducted by an Adventist Congregation over Sheridan's Grocery Store in the little town of Sabattus, Maine. The memories of those precious times come flooding back when hearing the singing of such songs as: Love Lifted Me, Dare To Be A Daniel and Brighten The Corner Where You Are. The example of Daniel and the lessons learned from his life have inspired prayer, that I too, might "**Refuse to defile myself**"; and live victoriously in a filthy, pagan world.

Rev. A. A. Walsh, a traveling Baptist Evangelist, came to our Community Church near the center of the square in Sabattus when I was eleven years old. During those revival services, both Phyllis and I went forward to a public altar for the first time reaffirming our faith, confessing our sins; and seeking reconciliation with God. The following Sunday afternoon we were baptized in Sabattus Lake.

After baptism, when walking across the sandy beach, soaking wet in knickers and sneakers, one of the little street urchins from our alley mocked, "I'd do it too but you can't live it!" Something arose from deep within my heart and I vowed, "By God's grace, I **will live it**!" Suddenly, Jesus **stepped in**! I became **as aware of His presence as I was of anyone else**. How I would treasure a video recording of the expressions that must have been on my face! I was approaching my mother when the Lord witnessed of His presence. Abruptly turning on my heels, I headed down the railroad tracks that passed the foot of the lake and walked the tracks back to our alley, went into the house and straight to my room. There was this awful fear, that if anyone spoke to me, Jesus would go away. From that day to this, **Jesus has been just as real a presence as anyone else about me.**

No one had ever suggested such an experience. There had been no psychic patterns for it, and I had no reason for expecting such an event to take place. They say, "You can't stand on the promises of the Bible if you don't know what they are." When I was but eleven years old, God fulfilled a promise I did not even know existed. In love and obedience, the **conditions** of the promise were met, and the **promise received**. That promise is found in John fourteen, twenty-one, "He that hath My commandments, and keepeth them, he it is that loveth Me: and he that loveth Me shall be loved of My Father, and **I will love Him**, and **will manifest Myself to him**!" Thank God! He could deal with me as a trusting child who had not yet learned such "couldn't be done"!

A few years ago, I visited the beach with our son, Carlton Jr., and pointed out the washed out railroad tracks that marked the start of a wonderful journey. I thrill to the wonderful words of the song, "Friendship with Jesus, fellowship divine! Oh, what blessed sweet communion! Jesus is a friend of mine."

Just when could I say I was saved? I used to be troubled when folk would say, "Unless you can name the day and the hour, you have not been truly converted." For those living Godless pagan lives, the day they turned around might well be fixed in memory. However, I do not know of a day in my life when I did not intend to be a Christian! There were a lot of days when I did not perform like one. There have been many days I would like to live over again. Was I truly **born-again** that day at mother's knee? Could it have been when so moved by the challenge of Daniel and determined that I would "Dare to be a Daniel"? Did my public stand and baptism, at eleven years old, simply reflect **reaching an age of understanding**? Thank God! I do not have to understand everything for He surely does. I find such comfort in the First Epistle of John and in the first chapter, "If we walk in the light, as He is in the light, we have fellowship one with another, and the blood of Jesus Christ His Son cleanseth us from all sin!" Firmly established, is the belief that each of us must be convicted of Sin by the Holy Spirit, repent of that sin, ask forgiveness and be forgiven that the sin barrier separating us from God be removed! We are then reconciled to fellowship with God. How wonderfully God worked through mother! Although not saving grace in itself, I believe there is a wonderful way in which a small child, walking along with his mother and holding her hand, senses the presence of God, if that mother, at the same time by faith, is holding the hand of her Heavenly Father! It is so vital that Dads and Mothers realize what it means to their children when they themselves walk with God. He does love through those who are in love with Him!

Memory often recalls precious moments walking down tree lined country roads in Chelsea, Maine with Mother. One special evening, when in my late teens, Mother expressed her joy and confidence because of my commitments as a Christian. My brothers were not living as Christians then, and she worried about what they might be doing. She went on to say, "I worry only about your safety!" Then, as a seeming second thought, added, "You too must be tempted to do wrong at times." It was necessary to confess that frequently there were severe temptations. There had been so many times when my human nature demanded fulfillment contrary to His established guidelines. Then the question: "Do you feel such temptations when in my presence?" It seemed an almost preposterous question! Upon my assertion that such temptations were not even suggested in her presence: she presented the truth she really wanted me to understand. "Even now, we walk different pathways most of the time and I cannot be with you. The day will come when I will be taken home and we will no longer be able to walk in fellowship. However, God has provided a **Companion** with Whom you may have constant, unbroken fellowship everywhere, all the time. Jesus knew that His disciples would be confused, fearful and lonely when He should return to the Father. On the night before His crucifixion, He promised He would not leave them comfortless; but would ask the Father to send another Comforter. He promised this Comforter, the Holy Spirit, who was then **with them**, was to be **in them**; and they never needed to be truly alone again."

That Comforter, from the Lord, had already come into my heart and life. He came in His fullness one night at the altar in my home church at Lynn, Massachusetts. In those years between my awareness of Christ's presence on the beach at Sabattus, and that special night in Lynn, a civil war had raged within my heart and mind. I was like the double-minded man of the Book of James, "unstable in my ways." I stood constantly committed to walking with the Lord, but my human nature, with its fleshly desires, contended so often with my Christian value systems. Tempted, torn and troubled, I had even prayed, "Lord, I don't want to live like this. If you cannot give constant victory over myself, clean me up and take me home!"

Total Surrender

One Sunday evening, during the altar call, God invited me to accept His **Gift**, reserved for His children, **the Comforter, His Holy Spirit** in His fullness. Fortunately, no over zealous altar worker interfered with the "**Wonderful Counselor**" **and I was** able to talk it through with Him! That night I totally surrendered all that I was or ever would be, all that I had or ever would have to God. From that night to this very day, the will of God as revealed by His Holy Spirit has been the **benchmark** of my life. It was the common expectation of many of our fellow worshippers that the fullness of the Spirit would be indicated by some great surge of emotion; but nothing seemed to happen when I felt I had prayed out all that was in my heart. It seemed that the Lord asked, "Just what happened when you invited Me to come?" In my heart, I responded, "Lord you said you stood at my heart's door knocking, I opened the door by surrender and you did come in!" I remembered then that I was the one who had to open the door. Then it was up to Him to keep His word and come in. He seemed to say, it's just that way in making room for the Holy Spirit. I had been assuming He had not kept His word. So I thanked Him for keeping His word regardless of how I felt emotionally. The only change I sensed was of great peace. The battle was over! We do not **believe because** we have some sort **of feeling**. We **have feeling because** we **believe**! First the faith, then the feeling. Until faith becomes operative, there is nothing to feel. After the altar service at our church, it was customary to have a time of praise and the opportunity for those who had found victory to testify to what God had done. I began my testimony telling what I sought and my stand of faith. I started to say, "I don't have any special feeling" when suddenly it seemed I was standing under a cascade of God's glory. Goose pimples broke out from head to toe, and it felt as though something was flowing through me, wave after wave. There was no urge to shout or demonstrate in any way, just great peace, joy and the realization it was well with my soul! God clearly witnessed to His presence.

Crucified with Christ

From that night on I could say with Paul, "I am crucified with Christ, yet I live, yet not I but Christ liveth in me." *Galations 2:20* Gone was my perverted carnal spirit that had a tendency to flirt with the world. (It is the love of self and for the world that dies when self is crucified!) God, the Father; and God, the Son came to this **temple** in the person of God, the Holy Spirit. If you correctly understand the **unity** of the Trinity you will understand how this must be. From that moment, the will of God as revealed by His Holy Spirit, became life's **Benchmark**. Those familiar with the engineering term, benchmark, realize it is a fixed point of reference to which all grades, elevations and positions must relate.

It did not take very long for me to realize the truth in Second Corinthians four, seven that, "We have this treasure in earthen vessels!" Our carnal spirit may be crucified, but we must live this life in our fleshly body with all its sensuous demands and weaknesses. However, we are assured that His strength is made perfect in our weaknesses. Our human frailties become His opportunities to demonstrate His grace is sufficient to make us more than conquerors!

When we receive the fullness of His Spirit we may then truly walk in the Spirit. He is God's Executive Administrator! He is our direct contact with God the Father and God the Son! He is our channel of communications. Through Him we are in unity with the Trinity.

Fruit of the Spirit

It is totally impossible for human hearts, minds or lives to produce the fruits of the Spirit through human resources. The fruits of the Spirit are just that, **fruits of the Spirit**! We but present our redeemed, totally surrendered **hearts and lives** as the **climate and soil in which the Holy Spirit produces His fruits**. We can never boast of our holiness, our righteousness, our good works or anything else! All these are **His works, the fruits of His Spirit** produced in and through us. Although we have nothing of which to boast: we have **so much to praise God for**. The disciples had seen Jesus heal the sick and cast out demons on many occasions. One day, while Jesus was on the Mount of Transfiguration, a man brought his demonically tormented son to the disciples; but they could not cure him. When Jesus came, He rebuked the demon and the child was delivered from his awful bondage. Later, the disciples asked Jesus just why they had failed. They asked in effect, why couldn't we do that? He sharply rebuked them, "O faithless and perverse generation, how long will I be with you? How long will I suffer you?" *Matthew 17:14-21* He said, in effect, "Are you ever going to 'catch on'? What am I going to have to do to teach you faith?"

Working the Works of God

The Lord must be just as frustrated with us today; because of our inability to permit His release of miracle working grace in and through our lives. Jesus told His disciples at that time, "This kind goeth not out but by prayer and fasting." At His ascension, the Lord told His followers, "Tarry at Jerusalem until ye be endued with power from on high". How long? **Until empowered**! This is what happened to me that night in Lynn, Massachusetts! Too often we fail to fast and pray until God does move. Then, like King Saul of old, we presume to make things happen according to our own notions and through our own resources seeking to **simulate** fruits of the Spirit. Those who are aware of the presence of God in their own lives can often discern whether a ministry is egocentric or Christo-centric.

Preachers and musicians reflect many backgrounds, abilities and techniques and have different appeal to different folk. The real test, however, is not whether we do, or do not appreciate them; but can the Lord **use** them to communicate **His** message? Can He reveal His presence to those in the congregation? It is my belief God seldom works through people He cannot get to, except in judgment. How can He talk to us unless we learn to listen? How can we quote Him if we have not been in communication with Him? "Her prophets have daubed themselves with untempered mortar, seeing vanity, saying, thus saith the Lord God, when the Lord hath not spoken." *Ezekiel 22:28* We are to be His witnesses, His ambassadors! **Unless He speaks**, giving instruction, we have **no message,**

nothing to witness to! "In us He lives and moves!"

Fulfillment of Calvary

There is that wonderful sense, also, that "In us He has His **being**!" Nearing the end of His agony on the cross, Jesus cried, "It is finished!" The ransom price had been paid for the redemption of the world! The **blood of the Lamb, ordained to be sacrificed before the world was created, had been shed.** Although the sacrifice had been made, the redemptive plan completely finished, the mission of Calvary had not yet been fulfilled. That mission will not be fulfilled until the last soul to be redeemed, is won! The fulfillment of Calvary's mission became the responsibility of the Church under The Great Commission! We have been commanded to go and teach all nations and to baptize believers in the name of the Father, the Son and the Holy Ghost. *Matthew 28:19* A very trite saying is also very true, "**Without Him, we cannot: without us, He will not!**"

Jesus Christ, our Savior and Lord, now depends upon us to lift Him up to a dying world that they might be drawn to Himself. We have been given a vital, key role in the mission of Calvary! Can a doubting, confused, fearful world see Jesus alive in us? God forbid that the light in us should be just more darkness. Can we, like Him, love the unlovely and really care about their salvation? Are we living clean, victorious lives in a world of filth because He is at home in our hearts and lives? Do we honestly pray for those who oppose us and despitefully use us? Can we see in the worst of offenders the greatest need for a Savior and dedicate ourselves as intercessors for their redemption? If they, too, really knew the Lord would they not be as we are? Can we sing in the shadows of life and praise Him in our suffering? If we can do these things, we will demonstrate a power and a presence that cannot be explained by just human good will and the mere benevolent works of a human life, however disciplined! We are to "**Glorify God in our body, which is His**!"

J. Basil Smith

I recall one precious memory of an experience in Toronto, Ontario. God was glorified and a soul was redeemed when as a local pastor, I visited a patient in a convalescent home. He was an ex-Nazi storm trooper who knew little or nothing about the Lord, so I told him what the Lord was to me. I told him of the lifting of my burden of sin, of the peace, the joy, the strength and of God's love for me that made every day special. I read a passage of Scripture and prayed for him. As I turned to leave a man called from a nearby bed, "Padre, may I talk with you!" As I approached his bed this very distinguished looking man, of middle age, said, "I am J. Basil Smith. I have believed from my youth that if religion were real then it should bring joy, peace, love and meaning to one's life. It should remove one's sense of guilt and make God real. I was raised Roman Catholic. I have been to all manner of churches; and tried Unity Thought. I have studied the religions of the East. Nowhere have I found what I was looking for. But just now, I heard **you describe perfectly what I had been looking for all my life**! Will you tell me how I can find what you have?

    I remember, so clearly, saying, "The only difference I know between myself and anyone else is that I have met Jesus as my Lord and Savior!" A troubled look swept across his face and he said, "But Jesus is just a myth to me!" After explaining the Gospel to him I said, "Unless you can believe that Jesus was the Son of God who died for the sins of the world, then you will never find what you say you are looking for." He assured me, he would like to believe Christ to be the Son of God and Savior of the world, but had too many doubts. I then said, "God will give you faith to believe if you sincerely seek Him and learn to listen." He affirmed he would do anything suggested. He was advised to read the Gospel of John and the First Epistle of John at least twice. I asked him to pray as he read, "Lord talk to me from your Book. Help me to understand what I am reading!"

    When I returned later to continue ministering, he had been transferred to another hospital and they did not tell me where he had been taken. It was three weeks before I found him in St. Luke's Hospital in Toronto. What a beautiful reunion that was! He informed me that he had indeed read all the assigned passages. He had also read Luke and the Book of Acts. He said, "As I have been lying here I have been studying that crucifix on the wall. I have been asking myself, Who was He? What did He do? Why did He do it? Pastor, I can now say, **I believe He was the Son of God who died for the sins of the world, that we might be saved!**" (Thank God for that crucifix!) I told him, "Basil, if you believe that, you can be saved right now!" I was embarrassed as Basil, true to his Catholic training concerning confession, openly confessed the sins of his life. All the barriers were swept away and he then thanked God for his deliverance from sin.

    On the next visit, Basil seemed quietly subdued. I was concerned. Had he truly found peace with God? After a few moments of greeting, he went on to say, "Pastor, I am so glad you came when you did the last time you were here. They have informed me that my problem is terminal. Had I not accepted Christ as Savior when I did, I might have questioned my own motives. Since finding what I had searched for so long, I was looking forward to coming to your church to testify what God had done for me. Now that will not happen unless God works a miracle!" Later he said, "A man died in the next bed, and as they were wheeling him through the door; I thought, unless God works a miracle they are going to wheel me through that door too. It really won't matter though, for **I will al-**

ready be in Heaven!" They did wheel J. Basil Smith through that door and I firmly believe he is now in Heaven. I expect to meet him there and relive the joy of the moment when he first met the Lord! How wonderful to be a "Worker together with Christ," in fulfilling the mission of Calvary!

We hold the balance of power when energized, empowered by the Holy Spirit. "Greater is He that is within you than he that is in the world." According to Romans 8:4, the righteousness of the Law is **fulfilled** in us when we walk, not after the flesh, but after the Spirit. "Let Jesus be Jesus in me" is more than a beautiful sentiment. It is both a possibility and a necessity. There is nothing, absolutely nothing, we cannot be, or cannot do if God wills it so, and we trust and obey. In us **He does live, and move and have His being**! What a beautiful sharing in love is ours when we learn how to walk with God in a companionship of obedient trust!

In the evening after the last supper, Thomas was troubled and said, "We know not whither thou goest; and how can we know the way?" "Jesus saith unto him, **I am The Way, The Truth,** and **The Life**; no man cometh unto the Father, but by Me. *John 14:6* "Christ in us" is not only "our hope of glory," it is the hope of others we meet along life's journey. We are reminded of what God says are "Beautiful feet upon the mountains of earth" as their owners' publish peace, and say, "Our God reigneth!" How wonderful it would be if we could see everyone, over whom we have influence, won to Christ! This seems very unlikely, yet, I pray almost every day, "**Lord, don't let me miss anyone that could be won.**" I have no idea how many have been won through my life and witness. I have never tried to keep count of those we have introduced to the Savior. Only God truly knows what has transpired between Himself and a professed seeker of His salvation. There have been those who seemed to give every evidence of praying through, only to have the fruit of their lives deny that assumption.

I recall one man, with whom we frequently prayed, who just could not seem to get consistent victory over self and sin. Nearly twelve years later, I met this man at Keswick Campgrounds on Lake Rosseau in Ontario, Canada. He was then, a radiant, Spirit-filled, faithful layman in his church. I was so delighted that I, impulsively called him by name and asked, "When did you become so established in the Lord?" He looked rather shocked and almost offended by the question, then replied, "You ought to know, **you were there**!"

Vicky Allison, as a Spirit filled teenager, in Trenton, New Jersey, attending high school, was informed that dancing was a required subject and she would be given an "F" should she refuse to take classes. She insisted that would be a violation of her conscience and it was contrary to the beliefs of her church. After several sessions in the Principal's office, the Principal asked that she have her Pastor visit the school to explain the objections. They seemed to believe our church to be negative, legalistic and very much behind the times.

At that meeting with the Principal and the Vice Principal, the reasons were given as to just why the church objected to dancing from the positive rather than negative point of view. The church should not be known for what it doesn't believe, but what it does stand for. Then I asked them questions. "How would you like to have a school where: no student lied, you could leave the room during exams knowing no student would cheat, you could leave a purse or money laying around and it would not be stolen, there was no profanity, drugs and no girl had to leave school because of pregnancy?" They exchanged startled looks and said, "That would be like Heaven!" How wonderful that Vicky had lived such a Christian witness: I could say, with confidence, "If all your students were like Vicky Allison, you would have such a school!" They were asked, "Why then do you want to force her to violate her conscience?" They promptly assured me Vicky would never be penalized for living according to conscience in their school.

Many folk fail to understand that verse in Titus, two: "Who gave Himself for us, that He might redeem us from all iniquity, and purify unto Himself a **peculiar** people, **zealous of good works**." By peculiar people, God was not thinking of funny bunnies, odd balls, out of this world negative characters. He was speaking of those who were **particularly His**, purified and zealous of good works. Vicky stood out because she believed in holy living and filling her life with good works. Vicky was raised by her devout, paternal grandmother, Mrs. Allison, and Vicky was a good student. Thank God for people with strong, clear-cut convictions who live so that others may know what they positively believe by the way they live! The real secret of Vicky's witness, however, resided in the fact that God's Holy Spirit could produce His fruit in her life!

Vicky married David Bailey, under God's guidance and approval. They have never wavered in their witness of God's love and power and have faithfully served the church, even to this day. They are precious members of our family in the Lord; and just thinking about them brings us joy. ✥

5 Walking in Love

Learning to Communicate

Learning to communicate is absolutely vital to genuine communion and fellowship in any relationship! My Mother had a saying, "Take an Irishman for what he means, not what he says!" At first I reacted, "Let the Irishman say what he means!" I have learned that many people **do not** say what they really mean or think! Others, trying to sincerely communicate what is actually on their minds, and in their hearts fail to be understood. Our terminology, or glossary, may carry different connotations. Much of what we say reflects our background and cultures not shared by those addressed. Heart to heart, mind to mind communications are essential if there is to be the bonding necessary for intimate fellowship. True interaction of personalities, is the very essence of friendship. Jeremiah 33:3 is one of my wife, Joyce's, favorite Bible verses: "Call unto Me, and I will answer thee, and shew thee great and mighty things, which thou knowest not."

Many people have asked, "Just what is the will of God for me?" His written Word is a text of His commandments, instructions and promises. Others may counsel us and be used of God in doing so, but **only God** can tell us the **specific details** of His will and purpose for our lives. He alone can tell us what **we must know** to effectively walk with Him and accomplish the tasks He has assigned to us. **If we ever know His will we will have to learn to communicate with Him.**

Early in my life, Mother told me that God gave us intelligence and conscience through which He would guide us; and she believed it her duty to challenge me to live, guided by them! I have done my best to pass this on to our own children; and our children in the Gospel. God deals with us one on one, through direct communication. "There is One Mediator between God and man: the Man, Christ Jesus!"

When still a very young teenager, our daughter Joanne told of a pastor's daughter with whom she was acquainted. This girl, a very attractive twelve-year-old, looked to be sixteen. She confided to Joanne how she was putting it over on her father by dating boys behind her father's back. We were on a long trip to visit a grandparent, and I had the opportunity to teach a vital lesson. We discussed her newly found acquaintance with regard to her behavior. Joanne was asked what she saw wrong with it all. She finally came up with the conclusion the girl wasn't getting away with anything simply because she had deceived a father, who trusted her. God, who would one day judge her, knew all about it. This was followed with the question: what to do with such a child? Joanne said, "You cannot spank a twelve-year-old!" This was an awaited opportunity.

She was informed, "Honey, don't get that idea. If you are still under my roof at twenty-one; and have not learned to behave: I will paddle you. My responsibility, before God as your father, is to bring you to the place where God takes over the direct leadership of your life. When you have learned to know the will of God and be directly led of Him, through your own intelligence and conscience: my days of discipline will be over, regardless of your age! When that day comes we can be buddies and friends." That trip marked, to a great extent, **that day** when she realized she was responsible to her Heavenly Father for her behavior, above that to anyone else. To my knowledge, she was never rebellious, defiant or deceitful after that lesson. Except for minor instances of differences of opinion, we developed a beautiful relationship of trust, loving and sharing that exists to this day. Now a grandmother, herself: she is in constant touch with God's own appointed Mediator!

Heart felt prayer is, essentially, two way communication with God. Too often when praying **in the presence of others**, we are **more aware** of others **about us** than we are of the **invisible God above us**. As pastor, when praying before others and leading them, too, in prayer, I would have to fight the tendency to talk over the shoulder of God, giving sermonettes to the people. How offended we are when someone, pretending to engage us in conversation, is talking in effect, to some others present and trying to impress them. **Prayer must be heart to heart, mind to mind conversation directly with God!**

Praying in Jesus' Name

Jesus told the disciples in the upper room, "Whatsoever ye shall ask the Father in My name, He will give it you." *John 16:23* This most precious of promises was followed by the comment, "Hitherto have ye asked nothing in My name: ask and receive that your joy may be full." **Failure to understand** just what constitutes **praying in Jesus' name** has resulted in failure to bring the miracle working power of God, as an effective force, into the lives and experiences of professed believers.

Until that hour in the upper room, the disciples had asked nothing in Jesus' name. They, as the Master, had worshipped and prayed in the temple, according to the Law, through blood sacrifices of animals as administered by an earthly priesthood. **What had changed?** Jesus was about to be crucified! He was to become the ultimate and eternal sacrifice, for all sin, for all men, for all time. He, as God's High Priest, was to sacrifice Himself, the veil of the temple was to be rent in two, and all mankind would have access to direct communication with God, through Christ, by His Holy Spirit! It is my belief the veil of the temple was not rent that we too might go where only the High Priest had been permitted to go. It is **my conviction**, the Holy Spirit left His place in the temple of stone: to live in the hearts and lives of God's **reconciled children**, who would serve as His temples. Praying in Jesus' name became the avenue of approach to God, and the assurance our prayers would be answered; because of the death, burial, and resurrection of our Lord, Jesus Christ.

Secret of Praying in Jesus' Name

Praying in Jesus' name is not just a **tag** we place as an addendum to our prayers, neither is it spiritualized **name dropping** inserted to impress God we are personal friends of His Son! What then is the **secret of praying in Jesus' name**? Praying in Jesus' name involves **two crucifixions**! His! And our own! It was the shedding of His Blood that atoned for our sins; and provided our access to God! It is our **self**-crucifixion that makes it available to us! Prayer that moves the heart and hand of God was made possible by the supreme surrender of our Lord, Himself. **We too, must be totally surrendered** to the will of God, as we understand it, to experience the benefits of His crucifixion. In James 5:16 we read, "The effectual, fervent prayer of a righteous man availeth much." Also in James 4:3 we are warned, "Ye ask and receive not, because ye ask amiss, that ye may consume it upon your own lusts." What was wrong with the prayer of those asking amiss? **They had not experienced their own crucifixion!** They were not living a crucified life. They were **selfish**! David, the psalmist in Psalm 66, said "If I regard **iniquity in my heart**, the Lord **will not hear me**." God will not, in compassion and wisdom, answer prayers that are not for our good; and His glory!

So often my prayer has been, "Lord, I am not trying to be deceitful, you know what I want. You know my heart's desire, my request, but only you know whether or not this is consistent with your will for me. If this request is not in keeping with what you know is best, then I don't really want it to be." God has honored many such prayers with **positive answers**. Other times He has left me to wait and trust. However, He has frequently taken away all interest and desire for that which had seemed so important to me! We are not wise enough to know exactly what is best unless clearly stated in His Word or we are given direct assurance through His Indwelling Spirit. God always responds to sincere prayer from our hearts to His own. He may answer in the affirmative or the negative. He may test our faith by delaying the answer to suit His own time frame. We may be certain, when we pray through, surrender the matter to Him, trust and obey: all Hell cannot prevent His loving response!

As in most situations, there are ditches on both sides of the road. On the one extreme, there are those who believe **praying in Jesus' name** obligates God to give them everything they ask for, if their faith is strong enough. Prayer requests, made consistent with the will of God are no problem to them. **Tragedy occurs** for such folk when God, in His love, wisdom and mercy does not grant the request. Their friends, holding similar interpretations of the promise, chide them for their lack of faith. Their confidence in themselves, and even in God, is undermined. Jesus prayed in the garden, "If it be possible, let this cup pass from Me!" The cup was not removed, yet He did not lose confidence: for He had prayed, "Not my will, but thine be done." Not my will, but thine be done, is the prayer of the crucified life!

In the ditch on the other side of the road, we find those who pray with such a lack of confidence and assurance: their prayer is hardly more than mere wishful thinking. Their faith, undermined by the possibility God might not answer their request, their prayer is ineffectual. "Not my will, but thine be done," should never become a conditioning for defeat, nor an excuse for unanswered prayer. We can stand assured that when we pray according to the will of God, He hears and will answer. David also said in that 66 Psalm, "But verily God hath heard me; He hath attended to the voice of my prayer. Blessed be God, which hath not turned away my prayer, nor His mercy from me." Nothing but unbelief or disobedience can prevent our receiving what God has in His will for us if we truly pray in Jesus' Name!

Praying with Confidence

How can we know when to stand in faith on an issue? How can we entertain the possibility God might not grant our petition, as we prayed it, and yet not lose confidence? The secret lies in our own crucifixion! When we die to self, in total surrender to God, we lose our shallow, humanistic self, and find our true Christ-centered self. He enthroned within us, His Spirit then directs our thoughts, monitors our prayers, and we find ourselves praying the prayers God wants to answer. We then have this assurance of Romans 8:26, "The Spirit also helpeth our infirmities: for we know not what we should pray for as we ought: but the Spirit, Itself (Himself), maketh intercession for us with groanings that cannot be uttered." We are further assured in verse 26, "The **Spirit makes intercession for the saints according to the will of God**." Such a wonderful relationship in communion and communication with our living Lord is not just the prerogative of a privileged few. It was meant to be the norm for all born-again believers. Our Heavenly Father is, always, just a whisper away! We have a **direct, open line** to our Father, **in Jesus' name**!

Many have been accused of giving God their talking **time**; and reserving their **listening time** for Satan! We often are guilty of pouring out our hearts and minds concerning what we want or think; and fail to wait upon God in quiet meditation until He can communicate what is on His own heart and mind. Remember, it is those "who wait upon the Lord whose strength is renewed." May we, like young Samuel, of old, be quick to say, "Speak Lord, Thy servant heareth."

"Pray, without ceasing?" Of course! I believe I am in constant conversation with My God, as I walk in fellowship with Him, everyday! It is as natural as it would be talking to anyone else, I was walking with!

Learning to Listen

Learning to listen to God is one of the most vital lessons ever brought home to me! Listening that I might know His will and be instructed by Him as I faced the problems of life, day by day. We often feel so terribly alone simply because we do not communicate with those about us. Many husbands and wives, as well as other members of family and friends, endure years of failure simply because they do not understand one another. They lack a proper understanding of each other and what they individually believe or feel. **They have not learned to listen!**

God often seems to be so very far away, even though He is always near. He is everywhere present and seeking to communicate with all His created children. The Lord tells us in Revelation three, "I stand at the door and knock: **if any man hear My voice**, and open the door, **I will come in to him**, and will sup with him, and he with Me." He is constantly, knocking, calling! **Are we listening?** Most of us are very familiar with the assurance of Jesus, "My sheep **know My voice**." Have we learned to discern His voice above the many voices clamoring for our attention and response? God created us for a one on one personal relationship with Himself. We do not have to depend upon other secondary sources of information. We need more than the opinions of others providing secondhand information. In Romans, we are informed that "As many as are led by the Spirit of God, they are the sons of God." No other human can, assuredly, say, "This is the will of God for you," unless they are quoting some universally applied truth of the Scripture! If you ever truly know the will of God, you **must learn to listen**!

In the dark days of national depression, I lost my job in a shoe factory because of the intrigue and lies of a fellow worker. In those days men were literally unable to **buy** a job. The only job I could find was washing dishes in a restaurant across the river from where a loved one was hospitalized. There were mounting hospital bills and I was hardly making enough money to buy food for the family. I was not reacting very well in that situation. One day, discouraged and somewhat disillusioned, I complained, within myself, "It isn't **what you are** or **what you know** that counts; its **who you know** that really matters!" Thank God, He was not offended because **I did know Him**! There in that restaurant, in the midsection of Main Street, Augusta, Maine: **God spoke directly to** me! "Look not to the East, nor the South, nor to the North. **Promotion cometh from the Lord**, whom He will He setteth up and whom He will He putteth down." I knew **God had spoken directly to me**! Immediate peace and joy flooded my soul and I began to sing choruses of praise. He reminded me that He was indeed the **right one to know**! He also spoke through a passage of Scripture that I **did know**. "Whatsoever ye do in word or deed, do it heartily as unto the Lord." Instantly, God became my Boss and I started washing dishes for Him!

Those assurances of promotion sounded like Scripture, even though, to my knowledge, I had never read them. Certainly the truth of that verse had never registered in my conscious thought. I went home, got out my concordance; and sure enough, there it was! In **Psalm** seventy-five, verses six and seven: "For **promotion** cometh neither from the east, nor from the west, nor from the south. But God is the Judge: He putteth down one, and setteth up another." Here, again, **I stood upon a promise that I did not know existed**! Isn't it wonderful that **He did** and quoted it to me?

The owner of the restaurant came into the washroom about three days later and stopped to chat. First, he commended me for my work being done washing dishes. Later, he asked, "Why is a man like you washing dishes?" I frankly confessed, "I could find nothing else to do." He came back, "You can be my new counter man for three times what you are getting now!" My first reaction, Thank you, Lord, for the promotion! Then a sobering afterthought: I asked, "Doesn't a counter man have to draw beer for the waitresses?" His reply, "You don't have to drink it, just serve it!" My hopes sank within me as I testified: "I teach a class of teenage boys in a little church up on the hill. I tell them to avoid alcoholic beverages as though they were poison. How do you think they would react if they came in here and saw me serving them? Would I still have any influence over them?" That man stared at me for a few moments, and as he turned away said, "I have never met a man like you before!" How vivid that scene still is! Later, during my years of study for the ministry, I stopped in to visit him. He was sitting with a group of his friends in the dining area; and introduced me as one who would a respected celebrity.

Within one week of that day, in the washroom, I had a job with the State of Maine for the **exact pay** I would have received as a counter man! **God has supplied all my needs ever since!** There have been a wide range of assignments, referred to elsewhere in the book, but always He has been **My boss**! I am content to let Him handle the promotions! One day, in more recent years, when lamenting my inability to be a greater help on our children's college costs, our daughter, Janice, said, "We all knew you were doing your best for us with what you had." She went on to say, **"I was a senior in High School before I knew we were not rich."** How in the world could children, brought up in a home where we seldom had anything left over from week to week, not know we were poor? Then it came to me: "Why of course, we **never thought poor**!" We thanked God for what we did have and trusted him for what we didn't have! We never hinted of our financial needs to the church membership; even though under God's guidance, many of them were very generous at crucial times. We were always well fed, properly clothed, lived in acceptable quarters; and lacked nothing of necessities. Thank God! Our children never thought of themselves as poor! What a blessing from a gracious God!

One Wednesday night, at our church in Toronto, we had a missionary from England. Thinking of the offering to be taken at the end of the service, I was troubled. All I had was a little change and a five dollar bill. Five dollars then, was like thirty dollars is now. That was our grocery money for the rest of the week! I asked the Lord, "How much shall I give?" He seemed to say, "Five dollars!" My response, "But, Lord, that's our grocery money and you have said if we did not provide for our own we were worse than infidels!" "Five dollars!" I don't remember much of that man's sermon, all I remember was about what should be done with that five dollars. Finally I said, "Lord if you want me to give the five dollars, I'll do it, but I want to be sure it is Your idea, not mine!" "Five dollars!" The five dollars went into the offering plate and I went home in peace! On the way home Joyce and I remembered that one of our very faithful members was not at prayer meeting. We wondered if she were all right. Joyce, knowing nothing about the five dollar deal, suggested we swing by Mrs. Jim Hall's on our way home. When I rang the door bell, the door was opened instantly for Mrs. Hall was standing just inside the door. She greeted me with an outstretched hand and squeezed a **five dollar bill** into my hand; saying, "**I knew you were coming for the Lord told me to give you this!**" I am so thankful that **Mrs. James Hall had learned to listen too**! Not just for the money, but for such a clear witness to His presence and His interest in us. I do not have the nerve to ask Him for more than He has already given. He truly has, already done, more than we can ask or think.

When thinking of such specific, "out of the blue" conversations with the Lord; we could well ask, "**How did He do that?**" How, indeed, does God carry on an intimate, direct conversation with His children. All of His, spiritually alive, children know that **He does speak directly** to them. In the absence of an audible voice, just how does He do it? When leaving service with Dr. Jerry Falwell, for a special assignment by the Lord in Washington, D.C.; I talked with Dr. Jerry about the certainty I had of God's leading during my work with him at Lynchburg. I asked the question, "How many times have I assured you something is so, and it was so, even though I did not know why it was so?" Jerry assured me,

"Over and over again, Carl!" In one instance the Lord revealed something that I took up with Dr. Jerry. Later, Jerry asked, "How could you have known that? Only God could have known that!" It seemed so simple to reply, "But Jerry, He is the One I was talking to!" On yet another occasion, Jerry said, "Carl you were the only one who saw that vital step to be taken. Just weeks later we all saw, it was the only thing to do." I could sincerely, and I believe, with honest humility reply, "I am not that smart! I have only learned to listen!"

There could be no greater confidence at such times if He had written it on the wall, or sent an angel in white to visibly and audibly relay the information! It had become very important to me to better understand just how He did communicate so effectively. I asked my Lord to explain to me, in simple terms, just how He made me to understand His will for me. Because of my limited understanding of psychology and the science of the mind: I believed God taught me a deeper understanding of the more complex, from the obvious! Most of us accept the fact that the normal, healthy brain has stored all of its data input in our memory banks. If we have consciously, sometimes even subconsciously, processed data, it remains stored in memory. In many, if not most cases, we can focus our mind and call upon it to recall specific data. Even when there is a malfunction of our recall system, psychologists have been known to access that data for us under hypnosis.

King David said, "Thy Word have I **hid in my heart** that I might not sin against Thee." We all know that Scripture, stored in memory; is often recalled by the Holy Spirit to sustain and guide us in a time of crisis and need. **I believe, when God's Holy Spirit has free access to our inmost being: He can plant God's clear communication, directly, into our subconscious mind, and raise it to the level of conscious thought just as data we had stored in memory by our own conscious thought processes.** He is not limited to what we know, but can explain to us what He, alone, knows! I see no other reasonable explanation. It is all I need to set the issue at rest for me. I asked Him for a **simple** explanation. I think He gave me a simple answer. Isn't it nice He understands our limitations?

Another incident comes to mind during our construction days at Liberty University. J. O. Renolds, our Director of All Field Operations, Bill Maitland, Al Fleming and I were discussing a problem one morning after dismissing the supervisors to their activities. It soon became apparent that all four of us were reading the problem differently and heading off in four different directions. The differences of opinion began to sharpen. As Chaplain of the unit, I suggested: "Let's ask Someone who knows!" For a moment they may have thought I was suggesting myself. I clearly recall saying, "Not me, Him!" (While pointing a finger to the ceiling. Then added, "He is smart, if we learn to listen, people will think we are smart, too, for we will have the right answers. Only, let us not forget just who is the One who is smart or we are all in big trouble. Failure to give God **all the glory** hinders the revelation of Himself and sets us up for a tragic ego-trip." The four of us stood in a circle in the office that morning, our hands on each other's shoulders and each of us prayed for God's instructions concerning the matter. A beautiful sense of peace flooded the room and the problem disappeared. To this day, I do not remember what it was all about. Perhaps the Lord sensed we were not sufficiently consulting Him, and wanted us to remember, we too, "must be about His Father's business." God may also have been preparing us for a test of faith, just days ahead. We were to be challenged regarding a water supply vital to our Summer Youth Programs just ahead.

Water from the Rock

The floods of eighty-six wiped out the Thomas Road Ministries' Youth Camp on Treasure Island in the James River. The bridge went out and practically everything was totaled. There was almost a state of panic as youth leaders sought to establish a new complex for their work. Dr. Jerry had succeeded in purchasing Camp Hideaway, a small resort complex, right in the heart of Liberty Mountain. This was designated, among other things, to be prepared for youth outreach. Water was our biggest problem! The existing sources had been condemned and a new source of water absolutely essential before the camping program could begin. This became our responsibility in Field Operations. We brought in a well-drilling crew and proceeded to drill, high on the mountain. The drillers became skeptical about finding water after going just over three hundred feet, finding no water. In mid May we tapped a flow of three gallons per minute at three hundred and sixty-five feet. That was not near enough. At four hundred and eighteen the drilling company served notice, "You are wasting your money, there is no water down there. It is a dry mountain!" We urged them to keep going; but at about four hundred and thirty feet they became insistent. Bill Maitland called from Hideaway saying the drillers were going to quit. J. O. Renolds, our Field Operations Director, and I left to go over to the site. We met Bill Maitland and Al Fleming, one of our managers, on the Candler's Mountain Road, overlooking the campus of Liberty University. We stood together beside the road discussing our problem.

Time was running out and the camp program was impossible without the water. No water, no camp! Bill Maitland, our Assistant Director said, "I asked the Lord to tell us just where to drill; and not let us drill where there was no water!" We discussed just how far we would go down. Each of us had a suggestion. Then J. O. said, "Let's drill down to about four hundred and fifty feet." Suddenly a song flooded through my mind, "Water from **that rock** is what is needed!" We again stood in our familiar prayer circle and joined in prayer: "Lord that's your mountain, you know what is at stake. If there is no water, there will be no camp program. You know exactly where that water is! Lord, don't let us stop one foot short of that water! Please God, give us water from **that rock**!"

The drilling crew, very reluctantly, began work the next morning. At about nine thirty in the morning, Bill called to say the drilling crew was quitting. We urged they continue until noon. At about eleven thirty, Bill Maitland walked into the office almost speechless. I asked, "What happened, Bill?" In a voice, husky with emotion, Bill said, "We just struck water!" Eight gallons per minute at **four hundred and forty-nine feet**! They had tapped a subterranean flow that provided an abundance of water. God had given water **from that rock** as needed! There were four of us involved in this special effort, and all can testify to the facts. Three of us recently checked our notes and memories for the exact details. During the last seven years, hundreds of children and youth, every year, have been "Drinking from the Springs of Living Water" on that mountain! They are up there, right now, drinking water from that rock in the heart of Liberty Mountain; and **living water from the heart of God**!

How awful it would be to fail to give Him glory, honor and praise! There is no possibility of coincidence here; and one need not exaggerate the truth to magnify the Lord.

Our Father's Business

When but twelve years old, Jesus sensing His destiny said, "I must be about My Father's business!" We too must be about our Father's business! Just what constitutes the Father's business for you and me? Remember, we do not know for certain that Jesus is Lord until the Spirit witnesses to His identity. We have already considered the fact that, as natural men, we cannot access the mind of God apart from the moving of His Spirit. We can, however, know everything we need to know if we but ask Him.

My own extrovert, impulsive nature has betrayed me too many times in my life! I have missed so much I could have known had I learned to listen better to others about me. This has resulted in saddling myself with my own opinions, when I could have been blest by the input of others. We do well to remember, truth, that multifaceted diamond must be examined carefully, if we are to expose all of its prisms to light for maximum understanding and true evaluation. How wonderful that we finite, limited creatures can be instructed by His infinite wisdom! How thankful I am to God that He has permitted circumstances, so traumatic, I have been forced to listen to Him! There are so many things He can share and teach once He has our full attention. I have learned to pray, "Lord if heartbreak, adversity and testing are necessary for my development and to bring a closer walk with Thee, so let it be!" Yet, I have also prayed, fervently, "Lord don't let me, or others about me, suffer because I have been inattentive or disobedient." May God help us all to use our intelligence to access His mind, and our moral sensitivity, or conscience to access His heart! He has provided a wonderful system of communications! May we learn to listen and make full use of them.

God Speaks Clearly

There are three major ways, through which, God speaks to us. **First**, there is the Bible, "It is written!" What The Bible teaches is true, absolutely correct, if we correctly understand it. This is possible, only, when the Holy Spirit is our Teacher! **Second**, we have the direct witness of the Holy Spirit. Romans eight, six: "The Spirit, Itself (Himself), beareth witness with our spirit that we are the children of God." Isaiah twenty, twenty-one assures us, "And thine ears shall hear a word behind thee saying, this is the way, walk ye in it!" **Third**, John, in his First Epistle nineteen, twenty-one observes: "Beloved if our heart condemn us not, then have we peace toward God; but if our heart condemn us God is greater than our hearts." Those who have learned to walk with God, and to listen, know almost immediately when they have disappointed Him. We can sense when He stops talking to us! I have become familiar with **these three major methods of communication** throughout my life. They have provided assurance of His guiding Presence in virtually all major decisions of life.

By **praying through**, we mean praying until assured that God had **picked up** on the other end of the **prayer line**, and the situation is now in His hands. When this assurance comes, praise flows from a grateful heart. There came a time in nineteen forty-one, that for nine months, I could not seem to pray through. There were no apparent changes, **I simply lost the awareness of His Presence**! It seemed He did not listen when I prayed. Nothing happened. Nothing changed, there was no peace or joy. My isolation and loneliness became intense. Finally, the estrangement became unbearable. One Sunday afternoon, alone in my brother, Ralph's house at 66 Pacific Street in Lynn, Massachusetts, I went to my room determined to pray until the answer came. The details of that room are still vivid in memory, especially the place where I knelt in prayer. I prayed with David, "Search me, O God, and know my heart, try me and know my thoughts and see if there be any wicked way in me!" To this day, I can remember verbatim what I prayed that afternoon. I asked the Lord to talk to me that I might understand the matter. I promised if He found wrong doing, I would quit it. If there was something He wanted me to do, I would do it. If there was sin, I would put it under the Blood, realizing, no matter what the problem, the same cure was required. I reaffirmed my total commitment of all that I was or ever would be; all that I had or ever would have were still His to command. Pleading the blood of Calvary, I thanked Him for His grace. There were no flashing lights, no surging emotions, just quiet peace as it had been when the Spirit came in His fullness many years before.

Arising from my knees, and going down the stairs, I froze on the landing in mid stairway: **I was singing!** Without a second thought, my heart was singing again! I still did not know what the crisis was all about! All I knew was, the battle was over! I had prayed through and God was in control.

Dr. G. B. Williamson, President of Eastern Nazarene College, was guest speaker at our church the next Sunday morning. There is no memory of anything he said, but the Spirit kept urging, "Speak to him!" Why should I speak to him, what did I want to talk to him about? At the door I asked the only thing I could think about: "Do you have evening school at the college?" His reply, "No, but why don't you enroll in the day time?" It seemed my work made that impossible. He countered, "How much do you pay for room and board?" Upon receiving the information, he replied, "That will pay for room, board and tuition at school, come and see me next Tuesday!" He still had not told me how I was going to work when going to school! That following Tuesday, we met in his office at Eastern Nazarene College. I learned that it was also registration day for the Fall Semester. Enrolling that day I started classes the following Thursday, carrying a full load of college studies until graduation. The F. A. Bartlett Tree Expert Company, with whom I was employed, paid my salary fifty-two weeks a year until I resigned to take the first pastorate. The only exception was of that period spent in the service of my country.

When that special burden of unanswered prayer dropped on me, there was no way of knowing God was preparing for decision at one of the most vital crossroads of my life. **He was calling me into the ministry!** How happy I was that I had learned to listen! He has also taught, the more time spent in the **secret place** of prayer, the less time spent in His **woodshed**! God's timing was perfect. Had I not prayed through that day, I would have missed Dr. Williamson; and not gone to college. The Japanese struck Pearl Harbor that December and we became a nation at war. Had I not gone to college, I would have gone directly into the service and probably never would have gone to college or into the ministry. **No wonder the Lord turned on the pressure!**

God also led Dr. G. B. Williamson to speak to a young Canadian girl at Toronto, Ontario urging her to come to E.N.C. She arrived on campus in the fall of Forty-two; and we met briefly before I went into the service. God had arranged that too, for **Joyce Brooks**, was to become my wife and partner in the ministry. He has things all figured out, yet we often make it so difficult for Him to explain it all to us. How grateful I am that we let Him work out His will! None of us can even imagine what God has in store for those who truly trust Him.

Is the **mind like the computer** or is **the computer like the mind**? The mind is God's creation. The computer, the creation of man. In the understanding of computer systems: we are also coming to a better understanding of our own minds. Once again, God is providing insight into the more complex through an understanding of what is more obvious. God created His earthly computer when He made man in the Garden, giving us mind and spirit! It was His purpose, I believe, that His **Holy Spirit should program our inmost being**; and communicate with us and through us! There are soft disks at work within this computer upon which I write. They were empty, vacant disks, quite useless in themselves. One of those useless disks was inserted into this machine, and initialized! This process of initialization, programed the disk to read the mind and heart of this computer. It was given the power to receive data directly from the computer, store it; and use it, becoming a vital factor in the production of this manuscript. We have the privilege of being **initialized and energized by the Spirit of the living God**! When our God-given potential is submitted, in total surrender, to the God who created it, we may then become programmed and empowered, enabling us to become vital factors in promoting the will of God on the earth!

It was mankind's most horrible tragedy, that **Adam permitted Satan to program and contaminate us with the virus of sin**. When men today are spiritually reborn: they open their hearts to the programming intended at creation. However, when the Spirit does come, He must contend with a mind and spirit already programmed! He is confronted with the necessity of reprogramming our frames of reference, mindsets, values and personality shaping influences. The computer feeds back what is programmed into it. So does the mind. The **content of the data banks is determined by the programmer**. The contents of our **subconscious minds** is determined by what has been programmed into it through our responses to information, experiences, people and many other sources of data input. Our **value systems** are largely **determined** by such programming. You may also conclude, what we refer to as **personality**! Proverbs twenty-three, seven: "As a man thinketh in his heart, so is he!" Therefore, "Keep thy heart with all diligence for out of it are the issues of life." *Proverbs 4:21*

In teaching us to listen, the Holy Spirit must set us free from the prejudices and preconditioning of the past. He must help us overcome false premises of truth, now stored in the subconscious mind He would use. He would teach us to honestly, openly analyze new data, by **reason**, and refuse to **rationalize** old conclusions into the new data. He would also help us guard against Satan's efforts to **program in his "viruses"** again. We will address these issues in detail later in this book.

Our **Walk with God** is a companionship of sharing. Love and communications flowing both ways. We need to pour out our hearts to God; and then listen attentively until He speaks. We will study more carefully the guidance of our Father by His Holy Spirit in later chapters. Unless the Holy Spirit Who **inspired** the Bible, **explains** it, you will never understand just what God is trying to tell you! The Bible will be, to a very great extent, a closed Book to you! If you have totally surrendered to God and His Spirit indwells, you may understand everything essential to your salvation; and your service before Him!

Relay Beacons

The Space Administration has provided satellite tracking stations at strategic locations around the world. Mission Control uses these stations as monitoring sites, aiding the command center, and providing beacons for reference by spacecraft. Similar guidance systems: such as radio, radar and light beacons are also used by airplanes flying in earth's atmosphere. **God has His tracking stations and beacons of light to aid in communications** with His children, while on their way to successful lives, and safe arrival home! How I thank God for those **lights in the dark places** along the road He has led me! There have been many more than may possibly be detailed within the confines of this book. However, let me tell of a few of them.

Poverty and the difficulty in finding adequate housing for our large family led to my living away from home for the first time, just after my thirteenth birthday. I went to live with a farmer in Durham, Maine working for board and clothes. Early adolescence was a crucial period of life to be suddenly separated from my mother. It did not take long to learn, few people shared mother's values, hatred for sin and love for God. I had thought if you told the truth, did not steal, did not use profanity nor develop sinful habits: everyone would admire you. How shocking, when such virtues set one up for ridicule and mockery. The farmer, with whom I lived, was a good man and truly Christian, but so many others about me, were trying to find excuses for sinful failure. Their basic argument: "You can't live as the Bible commands!" The last thing they wanted was someone proving God's grace sufficient to make one, "more than a conqueror"! The invectives of "mother's boy", "sissy", "holier than thou", "prude", and "puritan" were frequently applied with scorn. A vibrant, genuine Christian was, not only a rebuke to the sensuous, but a threat of their exposure. They dared not tolerate someone not as guilty as themselves.

Above this storm of darkness, God lifted up a beacon of light! Leola Jordan, arrived to teach at the Soper school, in Durham from her home in Brewer, Maine. This dark-haired, vibrant nineteen year old turned our little, one room, country school into a light house! Her love for and devotion to the Lord were clearly evident. She also made it very clear that we were expected to follow her example. (Thank God, no Madilyn O'Hare anywhere in sight!) Suddenly, out of the surrounding spiritual darkness, Leola Jordan had appeared as a living embodiment of the virtues and ideals mother had taught all of my life! She was living confirmation the Bible was true, God's love was real and we can all share that love. Only God, Himself, knows how many lives were touched by His light and love revealed through the prism of the life presented by that Spirit filled young school teacher. Her love for God and us kids, still maintains its afterglow! Leola Jordan had taken a place along beside my mother, presenting an ideal standard to which all womanhood would be compared, through the years to follow! Leola Jordan became Mrs. David Marstaller, and together, they continued to be "lights set on their hills," wherever they have been. I know of no couple more Christ-like than they. Now in their late eighties and early nineties, they are still wonderful inspirations to me; and deeply loved. Few people are as precious, even now as I write. Had it not been for that beacon of light God planted in the old Soper school, this book would probably never have been written! Children, grandchildren, great-grandchildren, along with vast numbers of school and church children have shared my love for Leola and David.

God knew my need for special help during a later critical stage of my journey. In later teens, He brought me under the influence of Rev. Ira E. Miller, then pastor of the Lynn, Massachusetts Church Of The Nazarene. He was the first person in remembrance whose presence you could sense, without turning your head: because of the intensified awareness of the presence of the Lord within the room. No one could doubt his love for God and others. It was evident that he waited on God until God spoke and then carefully repeated what He had revealed. I know this to be so for God would whisper, "A-men" to me as he spoke, seeming to say, "That is what I said!" This was the period of preparation, preceding the coming of the Holy Spirit in His fullness. Pastor Miller was a loving counselor, a sensitive encourager, but he could gently rebuke when necessary. I recall him saying one day, when he thought I was too obsessed with tennis: "Carlton, be not drunk with tennis wherein is excess, but be filled with the Spirit." He was very vital to my maturity as a Christian. Ira E. Miller probably provided the embodiment of what the ideal pastor should be and do.

Dr. Mel-Thomas Rothwell, chairman of the Department of Philosophy at Eastern Nazarene College, shone as a beacon through the mental challenges and confusion that marked my college years. Here my simple faith was confronted with the skepticism and materialism of so-called liberalism. I had been challenged to total commitment and had a deep and abiding faith. Dr. Rothwell helped provide "reasons for that hope that dwelt within me." He challenged me to use the intelligence God had given and to seek after wisdom. He underscored my belief that God is truth, and no scientific **fact ever disproved God**! Each new scientific fact, law or force, scientifically verified by correct data, was just one more revelation of my God's creativity.

In graduate studies, at Brown University, the many philosophic principles and values drawn from the teaching of this brilliant and Godly man, were invaluable in maintaining a Christian perspective. Dr. Edger Brightman, chairman of the Department of Philosophy at Boston University, called Dr. Mel-Thomas Rothwell "one of the most brilliant philosophers of his day." To we students, he was a courtly gentleman, inspiring friend and wonderful example. At Brown, I came to the realization that I could learn all the genuine facts the skeptic might know; but he could not enjoy the advantage of what I knew, unless he, too, came to know my Savior! God maintains a network of beacons and relay stations all the way from earth to Heaven. Were this book an autobiography, I would pay tribute to many others who contributed so much to make my journey one filled with precious memories. All of us should be available to God that we might be used of Him in aiding others. How wonderful to be able to improve the quality of life for others, just because we loved God so much, He could love others through us. We have a great challenge to make this world a better place, just because we lived in it! God help us to continually pray, "Help me to help others, whether I realize it or not! Don't let me miss any one I could help, or win!"

Praise God for Leola Jordan, who confirmed my mother's teaching by being an example of the Christian ideals she had taught and for Rev. Ira E. Miller, who became such a wonderful role model revealing what a pastor can and should be. Thank the Lord for Dr. Mel-Thomas Rothwell, with his challenge to seek after wisdom with an understanding heart, and an unknown engineer, blowing the whistle of his steam engine hauling a railroad train along a wilderness valley, sending a message on the night winds, as an in course correction communique.

Call in the Wilderness

One early spring evening of 1934, a young man stood alone beside a huge pine tree on the forest slope, just above a tar-papered lumber camp where the orange glow of a kerosene lamp could be seen in the window. He was thrilled to the very depth of his being by the scents of the forest, the smell of pines, balsam and of pungent scents of earth and humus. Soft breezes gently ruffled his hair and caused a slight sighing in the pine branches overhead.

How to Walk with God

The call of night birds and the hooting of an owl added magical qualities to the night. Below the cabin, the East Branch of Medunkeunk sounded its bubbly, gurgling laughter, as it swept to the dam where it plunged with subdued thunder to the pool below. Out in the dead water, a beaver slapped the water with his tail, sounding an alert.

That young man, in lumber camp jargon, was tending the wanigan! The log drive had been recently completed; and loggers had not yet come back for the year's new cutting operations. He was there to provide care for the horses and security for the property, until logging activities resumed. He was very much alone, but not lonely! Intense love for the wilderness was so real and vibrant, he felt himself a part of the wilderness setting rather than merely an observer. There were no thoughts, whatsoever, of ever leaving what was so much a part of his life. His dreams were of being a woodsman, eventually heading his own logging operations. Total contentment flooded mind and spirit. He longed for nothing else, for he loved the wilderness.

Then a strange, life altering, thing happened! The low pressure system, preceding an approaching storm, trapped the sound of a steam engine railroad train of the Canadian National Railroad as it passed through a valley, twelve miles away. The tranquility of that idyllic moment was broken by the low, mournful wail of that whistle. I am convinced, **God communicated with me through that sound on the night air**! God spoke as clearly to my mind as if addressing me through my ears. "There are people out there who need your help! I have work for you that cannot be performed where you are." Almost immediately I felt out of place and no longer content. I still loved the wilderness; but now it seemed a selfish indulgence to remain in it. A restless mood increasingly robbed me of the sense of fulfillment I had known. That fall, I returned to my home in Chelsea, Maine.

This was, probably, my first clear call to the ministry of the Gospel. God began using me as a ray of hope to others in the surrounding darkness, during their hours of need. He began working on me to be an effective beacon and relay station. This period of preparation involved poverty, family tragedies and heart break. There was college, graduate school and three years of military service in World War II. Only God really knows what has been accomplished during forty-eight years of ministry. God has faithfully taught me how to walk with Him, and permit Him to minister to others through my heart and life. Four church buildings have been constructed by the congregations God has called us to lead. Three of these were completed church sanctuaries. Church congregations have been organized and scores of young people called to full time service as ministers, missionaries, educators and Christian administrators. The last major assignment was to serve the Lord as an administrator assisting in the construction of Liberty University with Dr. Jerry Falwell.

During that period, when content with the wilderness, there were many exciting, stimulating experiences. I had deep respect for most of the men with whom I associated. With all their faults and weaknesses, they were loyal courageous and having a sense of personal integrity. They were quick to respond to another's need and for most of them, a handshake was a binding contract. These woodsmen were a special group of men. Hard working, independent and willing to share. In those days men did not lock their camps or sit guard over their belongings. If you were truly in need, "help yourself," but be man enough not to exploit and willing to pass it on by helping others. I missed them after leaving the woods and was often homesick, longing to return. When working out of a temporary camp, seven miles up the East Branch of Medunkeunk, I snowshoed across wooded ridges to pick up a country road that ended at a farmhouse where friendly, hospitable folk waved at the passing stranger or even invited him in. That country road led to the ferry, where we crossed the Penobscot River to the general store at Medway. It was at this store we obtained the necessary supplies to be packed back to the lumber camp. All this is deeply etched in memory.

The wilderness and its folk did draw me back, year after year. Many years have been spent fishing; and big game hunting in the forests of the Medunkeunk watershed. A few years ago, while camping, alone, on a hunting trip, a trapper passed the campsite and openly wondered how a man from Virginia had found his way so deep in the Medunkeunk wilderness. He reacted immediately to my explanation of many years along the Medunkeunk, including being on the last log drive down that stream. That trapper was Eddie Stanley, a retired stationary engineer, from the mill at East Millinocket. He was also one of the young people who used to play in that farmyard I passed through on my way to Medway more than fifty years before! That was the Stanley farm! Eddie also informed me that his brother, Otho, was on that last log drive! We established the fact, later, that Otho was that eighteen year old kid who slept **in the next bunk** to me on that log drive! What thrilled me most, Eddie turned out to be one of those true woodsmen, I had been missing for so long. Through Eddie, I was to meet Ray Pasanen, another of that clan of men of the forests.

Many years ago I followed a huge wounded buck for two days around the forest near the confluence of Medunkeunk main stream and the Buffalo. He circled again and again to bring me back to the place where the chase had started. Having met other members of the Stanley clan, brothers, sons, nephews, and found them all so much like the woodsmen I used to know. I realized that like that old buck, **I had come full circle**!

How to Walk with God

Why should this family seem so important to me? Was it because of boyhood memories and nostalgia for the past? Were they simply typical of the people left behind whom I had missed so much? I have come to believe there is much more involved than just precious memories from my youth. There is a growing sense of destiny, almost to the point of conviction that God, having led me halfway around the world, in His service, has brought me full circle again. This confidence has been reinforced by meetings with Otho's brother John and his sisters Clara and Norma, his sons Otho Jr., Charles and Dwayne, and his daughter Charlene. There are members of the family who obviously love God and are praying for God's blessing on the family. My strong focus on this family, and their folk, could very well have come because God has responded in answer to somebody's prayer! When I finally make it home to Heaven, I hope to meet that mother who brought up such a family on a wilderness farm. **My love for God took me out of the wilderness** I loved. **My love for the wilderness brought me back** to share His love with those once left behind!

Fred and Grace Lee were subcontractors working with John Willette in 1934. Renewing my acquaintance with Grace Lee has been a precious privilege. How precious to relive good memories; and to know that Grace experiences the joy of friendship with Jesus our Lord! Joyce and I highly value her friendship.

Meeting Otho Stanley again was of great importance to me. He was the only Stanley I really knew when I left. Meeting that old bunkmate again, after so many years, gave us so much in common to talk about. However, my greatest concern for Otho was that when we wake up in eternity, he will be in the next "bunk"! When we were vacationing at Lake Millinocket, Grace Lee told me how sick Otho really was. We had two visits that will always be precious memories for me because we talked honestly and freely about what lies beyond earth's horizons. I shared with him what wonderful things the Lord had done for me. In the familiar terminology of the woodsman, I told him of my "honey hole"! It has always seemed incongruous that men should be so interested in where I had shot big bucks and made nice catches of fish and not be interested in the best things I have ever found. When trying to tell friends and loved ones of the freedom from the burden of sin and of joy, peace, hope and a sense of eternal destiny, I had found many reacted as though I were trying to impose something upon them. God gave us the right and the responsibility to choose our own destinies. He will not impose His will upon us; and none of us should presume to make another's decisions for him. We, alone must respond to the leading of His Holy Spirit through intelligence and conscience. Otho assured me he was talking it over with the Lord as he sat alone in his room. He was encouraged to pray through until God gave him witness all was well with his soul. I shared many of God's precious promises of forgiveness and prayed with Otho before leaving. Eddie called telling me of Otho's passing, even as I was writing this chapter relating to our friendship! Now I can end the chapter. I do not know just what went on between Otho and the Lord, I was not there. However, the Lord was and I have great confidence in Him! I had asked God, in Jesus' name, not to take Otho until he had prayed through to peace. Otho told me he was sincerely seeking that peace. Knowing my Lord, I do not believe He would see some one trying to make it home and cut him off before he got there! I did carry a spiritual burden for Otho, but now have the assurance of peace! **I am confident that I will see him in the morning!** There is firm belief God sent me back to communicate His love to Otho during the darkness of his time of crisis, permitting me to serve as one of His beacons. God is trying to communicate with all of us! May we all take the advice, Eli, the priest, gave to the child Samuel. "And Eli perceived that the Lord had called the child. Therefore Eli said unto Samuel ... if He call thee, thou shalt say, speak Lord, for thy servant heareth!" *I Samuel 3:9* May we too, learn to listen as God seeks to communicate with us. There is nothing in this world nearly so wonderful as being reconciled to God! ❖

6. Walking in Holiness

His Presence Necessary

Jesus was very much aware of the problems His disciples would face when His physical presence should be taken from them. We are all greatly influenced by the witness of our five physical senses. It is also difficult to know the reality of things beyond the scope of the sensuous. Paul in his second letter to the church at Corinth, addresses these problems in chapter four. He, recognizing how what we can see, touch, or smell seems more real than things of a metaphysical or spiritual nature, informs us that those physical things seen now are but temporal. Everything we can taste, touch or smell will pass with time. It is the, as yet **unseen** realities, that are eternal.

The **phenomenal**, that which is verified by our physical senses, always seems more real than the **noumena**, the unseen causative factors that produce them! Actually, the converse is true. As we have stated, the **law of adequate causation** posits, the **lesser** cannot produce the **greater**! For example: if ten pounds of matter is lifted, at least ten pounds of lift or thrust has been exerted. **This world**, this **universe** and **everybody** and **everything** in it did not just happen! All creation is the effect of an adequate cause. God did indeed, create the world and everything in it. Personally, I have greater proof! Through faith, I have been reconciled to God and have learned to walk in fellowship with Him. When fellow students at Brown University tried to prove Jesus, my Lord but a myth: they were told they were too late! **I had already met Him!** The Lord Jesus Christ is as real to me as are my earthly friends. I am no more aware of them, than of Him! He has been a personal friend since eleven years of age. I can sense His approval and disapproval and am aware of the joy, peace and love His presence brings.

Not many important people of earth even know I exist, let alone care for, or desire my friendship. That the Creator of the universe, and all that is in it, should not only know who I am, but love me, is beyond human comprehension!

He Cares

Believing God big enough to create so vast a universe is not nearly so difficult to believe as it is that He would pay any attention to anyone as small as man! How could it be that He who designed and created the world should know about me and truly care? God witnessed to His personal care for me one Wednesday night at prayer meeting, early in my ministry in Providence, Rhode Island. While still a student at Eastern Nazarene College, pastoring a small church, we were completing construction of a new church building. A group of volunteer painters and I had painted late into the evening, trying to prepare the basement chapel for our first prayer meeting. All the helpers had to go home before midnight. I continued to paint alone, until after three in the morning. It was February and, thoughtlessly, we had left the windows closed. It was a minor miracle that I was not fatally overcome by the fumes.

My system was so saturated by the fumes from that special kind of paint, severe hiccupping developed. This continued unabated for about seventeen hours. We tried every cure we could possibly think of. Nothing brought relief! After three meals and two sessions of sleep, the fumes still caused my body to be wracked. As service time approached, consideration was given to having my wife, Joyce, bring a devotional at the first prayer meeting. It seemed the Lord rebuked me by imprinting upon my mind, "I have given you the message I want delivered!" During announcements and the song service, I tried to make communications between hiccups. Frequently I failed, hiccupping with my mouth open. The church folk, though very considerate and understanding were laughing and finding the whole thing very humorous. They had my hiccups timed and you could see they anticipated the next one. I laughed with them, poking fun at my own performance; until it came time to read the Scriptures! While opening my Bible to read, protest suddenly arose from deep in my soul. I prayed, "Oh, Lord, No! It is one thing to laugh while making announcements or singing; but the reading of Your Word must not be an exercise in humor, please touch me and let me read your Word with reverence!" **Instantly God stepped in! My hiccups abruptly ceased!** After reading several verses, I noticed the people were on the edge of their seats, watching for the next hiccup. How vividly, I remember that night! People now living remember me saying, "You may relax for God healed me of the hiccups so that I would be able to read His Word with reverence!" Suddenly, the awesome fact struck home to me. The Lord God Almighty had looked down into a little basement chapel where a young preacher asked to be cured of the hiccups! **God did work a miracle** and heal him! Why would I not believe He knows all about us and truly does love us?

He Loves Us

Many years later in the ministry God, again, spoke of His great love. I had fallen about eighteen feet, from a ladder and had landed on the flat of my back on macadam. Our, then teen-aged son, Carlton Jr., initially saved my life at the scene for he had the presence of mind to detect I had swallowed my own tongue and was choking. He was able to pry my mouth open and pull the tongue free. Later, in Mercer County Hospital in Trenton, New Jersey, doctors discovered I had a massive brain concussion, the right elbow was shattered, my back was broken in two places; and most of my body functions, below the waist, had been shut down. The doctors questioned my chances for survival. In those many hours of darkness, suspended between two worlds, one question dominated my mind: "Why should God love me?" As I recall, there was no doubt of His love. I simply could not comprehend why He should love me! I thought of the years of ministry and its successes but I also remembered the seeming failures. I recalled miracles of grace when God had healed but then there were those who were not healed. There was the memory of those led to the Lord; yet there were those I had seemed to fail. There had been so many unmistakable answers to prayer. Then there were those times of unanswered prayer! I could think of no legitimate reason why the God of Heaven should love me.

There was a man in the next bed whose Spirit-filled wife kept vigil at his bedside. In those horrible hours of my darkness, I must have been calling aloud, "Why should He love me?" Later, when the crisis had passed, Judy Sorter came to my bedside and quietly said, "Mr. Gleason, **He loves us simply because we are His children**! He created us. We belong to Him. He is our Father!" Here, the Holy Spirit, speaking through that young wife and mother, burdened with her own heartbreak, had echoed the truth spoken in Romans eight, sixteen, "The Spirit itself beareth witness with our spirit, that we are the children of God!"

God did miraculously touch my body. Now after more than nineteen years, I walk miles of wilderness, climb mountains, build stone walls and climb trees, with ropes, performing tree surgery. However, most precious to me, was that assurance that I was His child and very much loved! "Blessed Assurance!" It should be great comfort to everyone that God loves all of us! He is no respecter of persons. There are no unimportant people in all His creation!

A few years ago our daughter, Janice, flew in for a few precious days of fellowship. We discussed such things as how God had provided the means for the children to attend college and other meaningful things. As we discussed how these problems were seen through eyes of the children, there were second thoughts about the handling of life's priorities. Concern was expressed lest, burdened by the needs of church people and limited in material wealth, our own children might have felt neglected. Upon my voicing this fear, Janice, just walking through the door into the dining room, turned and said, "Daddy don't you know that each of us girls grew up thinking we were someone **very special** to you?" They were all special to me but I did not know how successful I had been in letting them know that to be true. Could any father ask greater emotional fulfillment than to know his children realized they were special to him? How I thank my Heavenly Father for the many times He has revealed I was **special** to Him! He is wonderful! **All His children are special to Him too!**

Mind of the Spirit

We have already spoken to the fact that mankind, limited to the **data base** of human reason, cannot comprehend the mysteries of God! "The natural man receiveth not the things of the Spirit of God: for they are foolishness to Him: neither can He know them, for they are spiritually discerned!" *I Corinthians 2:14* In John six, forty-four, Jesus said, "No man can come to Me except the Father which hath sent Me draw him." The Book of Romans, chapter eight deals directly with God's provision, **opening access to His heart and mind**. "To be carnally minded is spiritual death; because the carnal mind is enmity against God: cannot possibly be subject to the laws of God." However, we are not limited to sensual verification if the Spirit of God lives in us!"

This familiar truth was vividly illustrated while we visited the Holy Land. Joyce and I joined a Dr. Norman Vincent Peale pilgrimage group with our daughter, Janice, and her husband. We were privileged to have fellowship with Dr. John Peale, who headed the party for his father. We frequently discussed significant events recorded in Scripture as related to specific places of interest. While at Ceaseria Phillipi, Dr. Peale asked, "What stands out in your mind as significant about this place as recorded in The Bible?" Nothing seemed to have special meaning for the moment. Mentally I had confused Ceaseria Phillipi, capital of Upper Galilee with Ceaseria, the ancient Roman seat of authority, on the sea coast. Just moments later our son-in-law asked, "Dad, what is there about this place that would suggest keys? Jesus always had a purpose for leading His disciples to specific places, where He could teach object lessons." Then it came to me, it was at this place Jesus asked His disciples who men thought Him to be. After they reported the speculation of others, He pointedly asked, "Whom do ye say that I am?" Simon Peter, always the impulsive extrovert, declared, "Thou art The Christ, Son of the Living God!" It was no rash impulse this time! Jesus said, "Flesh and blood did not reveal this unto thee, but My Father which is in Heaven!"

We were standing by a series of pools of water made by a stream flowing from beneath a cave in Mt. Hermon. This stream is one of the major sources of the River Jordan. You cannot travel in that land and not hear people repeatedly say, "Water is life! Where there is water there is life. Where there is no water there is no life!" Our Lord had brought His disciples to this place to bear vivid testimony, "In Him was life and His life was the Light of men!"

Keys to the Kingdom

Our Savior had **another truth** to drive home. Many people have grossly misunderstood the significance of His statements, "Thou art Peter, and upon this rock I will build My church; and I give thee the keys to The Kingdom." Moments later, Jesus said of this same Peter, "Get thee behind me, Satan!" It was not Peter upon whom the Lord would build His church nor who held the "keys to the kingdom"! It was God's **revelation, through the Spirit, that Jesus was indeed the Christ, the Son of the living God, that constituted the keys to the Kingdom! Peter's confession of faith**, based upon God's revelation of Jesus as Lord, is "**the Stone upon which the church is founded!**" Jesus is "The Corner Stone" ... He is "the Rock of Ages"! Mere mental belief, and acceptance of the concept, Jesus is the Son of God", will not bring us into personal relationship with Him. We are told that Satan believes and trembles, yet is not saved! We do not arrive at the conclusion, "Jesus is Lord", by **reason**; but by **revelation** as God speaks! We read in First Corinthians, twelve, "No man can say that Jesus is the Lord, but by the Holy Ghost." "**With the heart man believeth unto righteousness**; and with the mouth confession is made unto salvation." Romans 10:10 We know Jesus Is Lord, when the Holy Spirit speaks in revelation. Jesus said, "He shall speak of Me!"

Comforter Promised

There, after the last supper, Jesus assured His disciples He would not leave them without divine guidance and comfort but would provide for the abiding presence of the Holy Spirit. He promised that when He got back to the Father He would ask the Father to send God, the Holy Spirit, not only to live **with them,** but **in them**! The Lord also said, "If a man love Me, he will keep My words: and My Father will love him, and **we will come unto him, and make our abode with him**." verse 23 God the Father and God the Son dwell within us when we have received God the Holy Spirit **in His fullness**! Born of the Spirit, filled with the Spirit, we may now be led by the Spirit.

The Trinity is one spiritual unity; yet there is an apparent order of authority within the Trinity. Jesus clearly states a Father and Son relationship exists. He said, "The Father is greater than I." There is also the statement, "The Father dwelling in Me, He doeth the works." When speaking of the end times, the Lord said, "Only the Father knows." It would seem that the Son has primacy over the Holy Spirit. In John chapter sixteen, verses thirteen and fourteen, Jesus said of the Holy Spirit, "He will not speak for Himself. **He will speak whatever I have said and will glorify Me**."

One may well question, "If the Son has ascendancy over the Spirit, and the Father has ascendancy over the Son, why then is blasphemy of the Holy Spirit said to be the **unpardonable sin**? Jesus made that assertion in Matthew twelve, "All manner of sin and blasphemy shall be forgiven unto men: but the blasphemy against the Holy Ghost shall not be forgiven unto men." We are warned: "Quench not the Spirit! Grieve not the Spirit!" This is true, simply because the Holy Spirit is our direct contact to the Godhead!

Without the Holy Spirit we would not even know Jesus is Lord and Savior. Only the Spirit can cause us to understand spiritual realities. It is He who witnesses to our spiritual birth and the fullness of His presence. Do not be quick to condemn sinners because they do not believe! Earnestly intercede for them in prayer, that the Spirit of God will give light that they may believe. Jesus flatly stated, "It is the Spirit who convicts of sin, instructs in righteousness, and tells of judgments and blessings to come." We have pointed out, He is God's Executive Officer representing, and presenting God, the Father and God, the Son. Jesus said the Holy Spirit should be our Teacher, Comforter, Companion and our source of wisdom and power.

Unpardonable Sin

The Bible lists Esau, King Saul and Judus Iscariot among those who could not repent because they had not received God's Holy Spirit or that he had been taken from them. One of the most somber passages in the Scripture, to me, is found in Second Thessalonians chapter two, "Because they received not the love of the truth, that they might be saved; God shall send them a strong delusion, that they should believe a lie; and be damned who believed not the truth, but had pleasure in unrighteousness." Such people, rejecting the Holy Spirit and His message of truth, were damned while still living. When we blaspheme the Holy Spirit and the truth, because we love the world with its unrighteousness we have rejected the means by which a loving God planned to save us!

Many people, through the years, have expressed fear they had sinned away their day of grace and had committed unpardonable sin. My personal belief, perhaps even my conviction, is that anyone so concerned has not done so! Their sorrow for sin, their revulsion of it and their longing for God's approval all speak of the Spirit of God working within them! I have met very few people whose attitude and conduct led me to believe they had been rejected by God because they had rejected Him, once too often. We are warned, however, "My Spirit will not always strive with man! *Genesis 6:3* For this reason we are cautioned not to "grieve" or "quench" the Spirit.

Coming of the Spirit

Because we are **finite**, God is **infinite**, truth **absolute** and we **cannot absolutely** understand it: there is often much confusion in doctrinal explanations. Sincere, intelligent, Spirit-filled men often expound contradictory theories concerning the same biblical truths, as they are, subjectively, influenced by their own theological backgrounds; and the consensus of their peers. **Only God knows perfect doctrine!** The rest of us, "Know in part and prophecy in part." We do, "See through the glass darkly." How gracious, then, we should be to others who can see no better than we do. We are especially limited in vision when approaching the nature of the Holy Spirit's involvement in the lives of men. Some sincere Christians think they are **born of the Spirit** and **filled with the Spirit at the same moment of time**. They would affirm the Holy Spirit **does not come in parts**! They flatly state, they got all there was to get the first time! They believe they receive all of Him there is to receive when He comes effecting the new birth. The real question is, **not how much we have of Him** but **how much He has of us**! Much depends upon the degree of light we have and our responses to that light. These measure our spiritual maturity.

The Holy Spirit is **with us** in **prevenient grace** from the **moment of our physical birth**. Were it not for His presence Satan would so dominate us that we could not be saved. It is understood that new born infants have natural antibodies in their systems. Built-in protection from diseases until their bodies can develop their own immune systems. The Holy Spirit, through God's prevenient grace, provides **spiritual immunity** for the newborn human baby as protection. Without such grace Satan could destroy us before we came to an age of decision. Upon reaching the age of personal accountability, faced with the light of God's truth and convicted of sin by the Spirit, we accept or reject that protection. If we reject the Holy Spirit, we also reject a great measure of God's protective immunity and expose ourselves, unnecessarily, to Satan's attacks. **It is terribly dangerous to say no** to God! The Spirit of rebellion and rejection of God's Spirit, in these days, has produced a revival of Satanism and the occult! So many people are "giving place to Satan" in these days! The earlier in life one accepts the Lord, the more sensitive he is to spiritual things. The less light of truth rejected, the less we give "place to Satan". Created to be indwelt as a temple of the Holy Spirit, some spirit will dominate our inmost being. All nature abhors a vacuum! Fortunately, we have the deciding vote in a choice of masters. We do **not choose whether or not** we will have a master, it is simply the **question** of **which master**?

The Holy Spirit is **with us** as God's "midwife" at our spiritual rebirth **when we become new creatures** in Christ Jesus. We are created to be living temples for the Holy Spirit, thus providing the Lord with a body **in which** He may live. Now we may present our bodies as a **living** sacrifice, wholly and acceptable unto God as our reasonable response. *Romans 12:1* Before our new birth, we are dead in trespasses and sins and have nothing worthy to present to God. We were created to be an habitation, a temple, for His Holy Spirit. God's dwelling in the Tent Of Meeting in the wilderness and later in the temples at Jerusalem were temporary dwellings, or places of meeting; where His presence could be made known to His people. Our **God** not only wants to **walk with us**; but to **live in us**!

My mother held the strong belief that the rending of the veil of the temple occurred, not to permit all men to enter the Holy of Holies, where only the high priest could go, but to permit the Holy Spirit to exit the temple, and **enter into all men**! At Pentecost, God's promise to the prophet Joel was fulfilled when His Holy Spirit was poured out upon all believers. In Jesus' own words, "And I will pray the Father, and He shall give you another Comforter, that He may abide with you forever; Even the Spirit of Truth; **whom the world cannot receive**, because it seeth Him not, neither knoweth Him: but **ye know Him**; for **He dwelleth with you, and shall be in you!**" *John 14:16-17* Jesus also said in Luke eleven, "If ye then, being evil (or human), know how to give good gifts unto your children: how much more shall your Heavenly Father give the Holy Spirit to them that ask Him." The Holy Spirit is **The Gift** of the Father to all **His children who ask for Him**!

    The period of time lapsing between our becoming newborn children of God and the receiving of the Holy Spirit in His fullness depends entirely upon our light, understanding and our submissive obedience. **It could be five minutes or five years.** We must become His children, understand the nature and the need of His "gift"; and ask for it! God sends the Holy Spirit only to totally submissive hearts. It is concisely and correctly said, "We must die to ourselves to be filled with Himself!" **We too, must be crucified!** This may sound terribly judgmental, but I honestly do not believe any self-centered person can be filled with the Holy Spirit. If Christ is to reign as Lord, within, self must be dethroned! We cannot be self-centered and Christ-centered at the same time. Our life would then be like a wheel with two hubs!

    These sequential steps in receiving the Holy Spirit in His fullness are illustrated in the Samarian revival under Philip's preaching. The people believed and were baptized. The sick were healed and unclean spirits were cast out. It was days later that Peter and John were sent down from Jerusalem. When taught the truth concerning the Holy Spirit, the Samaritan believers **asked for and received** Him. If being born of the Spirit and filled with the Spirit were all part of one work of grace they would have received the Holy Ghost when they believed and were baptized. The Holy Spirit does not need our **instructions** to fill us; but He does need our **consent** and comes in when invited. Let us state this fact! God does not do one work in a Calvinist and yet another in the Armenian! He does not need our instructions on how to redeem and reconcile. All He requires of us is total submission and trust. He has promised to keep what we commit to Him!

    We are often confused by the differences in definition and explanations concerning the coming of the Holy Spirit to **live in us** as they reflect some doctrinal bias, or preconditioning. It is a **conviction** to me that if we "walk in the light" of God's Word and the leading of the Holy Spirit, we will be filled with the Spirit! If we **just**

keep saying yes to God, as we understand His will, we "yes" ourselves into the fullness of His presence; and He will be in control of our lives. It has been said, often, "it doesn't take much of a man to be a Spirit-filled Christian, but it does take all their is of him!" Remember the Scripture, "A wayfaring man, though a fool, need not err therein?" How many want to plead ignorance in the light of that biblical passage?

Walking in the Light

There have been countless occasions when men were filled with the Spirit and yet not sure of when and how it happened. They had been taught, perhaps, that it took one, two, three or even four "experiences" to receive the Spirit. Many believe certain phenomenon or ecstatic gifts mark His coming. The faith of many seekers is undermined as they wait for some proof, or forecasted phenomena to take place. They may even attempt to simulate what they think should happen. (Priming a spiritual pump!) There is nothing to see or feel until faith has brought the victory. Remember, first the faith; and then the phenomena!

God confirmed my **conviction** that walking, obediently, in all the light one had, brought the fullness of His blessing. On Yerba Buena Island, in San Francisco Bay, stationed at Treasure Island, and while making up my bunk that first day, the sailor in the next bunk was also getting his gear in order. We struck up a conversation and it did not take long to get to the subject of our love for the Lord, for both of us were totally committed Christians. In sharing what the Lord had meant to me through the years I testified to receiving the Holy Spirit in His fullness. David Gentry's face reflected disappointment and longing as he said, "I wish I, too, had been filled with the Spirit!" Shocked, I replied, "David, I cannot believe you have not been filled with the Holy Ghost! From the moment we began our conversation, my spirit has been witnessing with your spirit that we were one in Him!" I asked that he tell of the high points and crises times in his Christian walk. He told of a clear-cut moment when he surrendered to Christ and was born-again. Then he added, "There was one other time that stands out rather vividly in memory. I had been struggling with my personal weaknesses, while longing to be all that God wanted me to be. I remember that I prayed, "Lord take everything out of me that displeases you and give me everything I need to be what you want me to be. I will do anything you say and will do nothing that I know displeases you, if you will only help me!" He went on to say, "Nothing really happened; but I sensed a great peace, a greater hunger for His Word and perhaps an even greater love!" With full confidence I assured him, "David, **that was when you received the Holy Spirit in His fullness**!" His response; "But I didn't speak in tongues!" I was happy to assure him, "Most of my friends and my

Spirit-filled Mother did not speak in tongues, neither had I!"

There is no intent to reflect against the spiritual integrity of those who believe they were given that special gift when they received the Holy Spirit in His fullness. It is, however, in error to believe this a criterion for measuring or indicating His presence. Paul poses the rhetorical question, in I Corinthians, twelve, "Do all speak with tongues?" The implication is, "Of course not!" There is so much concerning this glossolalia that I do not understand. Some of my finest and most deeply spiritual friends profess to being so gifted. If God gave me such, I would praise Him for the anointing. However, I see no need for such. I can fellowship and commune with Him in a language clearly understood. This is another one of those areas of truth, "Seen through a glass darkly." I am certain that such a gift is not evidence, or proof of the Spirit's coming in His fullness! In fact, God's Word states it to be the **least** of the gifts. Please remember, not everyone has all the **gifts** of the Spirit. However, we are told, **all must have the fruits** of the Spirit. In Matthew seven, Jesus tells us we are **known by the fruit produced** in our lives! Some critics have declared this spiritual phenomena to be a counterfeit of Satan. I have seen unmistakable evidence that certain such demonstrations were demonic. Satan has counterfeited most of what Christ has done. He is anti-Christ and a master counterfeiter. No smart counterfeiter would create a counterfeit unless there was an authentic object, of value, to be copied. There must be a genuine gift of tongues somewhere, past, present or future or Satan would not counterfeit it. This is a good time to remember we are not to judge others; but keep our own hearts and minds open to the leading of the Spirit!

Tabernacle for the Spirit

Some believe the baptism of the Spirit occurs at the new birth; that we are baptized into the family of God. Many who hold such a belief take the position that the Holy Spirit comes in His fullness at a later date as an enduement for service. The Holy Spirit is indeed, involved in our new birth and there are many anointings for service. However, there is a distinct time in the life of the new born child of God when he presents himself in total surrender of self to God and receives God's Gift of His Holy Spirit as an indwelling presence. **I do not believe God sends His Spirit to abide in a heart still bound in servitude to Satan.** When we become new creatures in Christ Jesus, we **now have a life to surrender**; and a **clean heart for His habitation**. We need instruction in preparation for His coming that cannot be received by one dead in trespasses and sin. At the last supper, Jesus said of the Spirit, "**Whom the world cannot receive.**" Remember, the Holy Spirit is **God's Gift to His children**! The sequential steps leading to the Comforter taking residence within are not ordered by time, but light!

How to Walk with God

These steps are explained in chapter fourteen of John's Gospel. Jesus said if we loved Him, obeyed Him, He would pray the Father to send another Comforter. He, the Spirit of Truth, the Gift of the Father could not be received by the world for they did not know Him. Our Lord said His disciples knew Him for He dwelt with them and should come to live in them. Jesus makes it emphatic in verse twenty-three, "If a man love Me he will keep My words; and My Father will love him, and we will come unto him and make Our abode with him." Jesus told His **disciples** and followers to tarry at Jerusalem until they were endued with power. He assured them they would receive power to be His witnesses when the Holy Spirit came to live within them. How long to tarry? Until endued with power from on high!

God gives **the Gift** of His Spirit to all His children who ask for Him. **The Holy Spirit gives gifts to those He indwells, according to God's purpose for their lives.** Gifts are given severally, according to need and purpose and no one has all, or even a great many, gifts. Let us take note of our instruction in God's Word: **Not all** receive the **same gifts**, but **all must bear the fruits of the Spirit**! Each of us must permit the Holy Spirit to produce His fruit in our lives! These issues are clearly dealt with in Scripture, especially, the above mentioned passage in Corinthians.

The church attended in my teenage years believed there were two special works of grace, two crisis experiences, the new birth and entire sanctification, or the infilling with the Holy Spirit. I believed, and still firmly do, in these sequential stages. First, by being born-again we become new creatures in Christ Jesus. Now, being made alive to God, we may present our bodies as "living sacrifices" to be habitations of His Holy Spirit. When the Holy Spirit comes in His fullness to live in us as His temples: we have established a very **personal, living relationship with God**.

Problems arose, for me, because of an emphasis on two works of grace or two **experiences**. When I failed and became conscious that I had displeased God and sinned, what happened to my experiences? Did I then have to follow the one-two sequence all over again? When restored to fellowship: how many **experiences** did I have then? I now refuse to play the numbers game! How many past experiences are no longer important. It is my relationship with my Lord, right now, that is of supreme importance. King David, in the Fifty-first Psalm, cried out in his moments of failure, "Create in me a clean heart; O God and renew a right Spirit within me. Cast me not away from **Thy presence**; and **take not Thy Holy Spirit from me**." We are **not** born-again or filled with the Spirit **by** an **experience**; but by a **presence**! We are born of the Spirit and filled with the Spirit, when **personally** led by the Holy Spirit to accept Jesus Christ as Savior and Lord; and to receive the Gift of the Father. God, the Father, God, the Son, in the person of God, the

Holy Spirit have taken up residence in us, as Their temples and we are **personally reconciled to God**! These steps in personal reconciliation **are experiences**! We are not saved **by** an experience! Being saved **is** an experience! We are saved by the personal intervention of God in our lives. Please do not dismiss this as a **play on words**! I am not eternally secure because I **have had** an experience. I am eternally secure because I **have a Savior right now.**

When we backslide, or break fellowship with God it is not a matter of having another experience or being saved again. Our prayer should be, like David's, "Restore unto me the joy of Thy salvation and uphold me with Thy Free Spirit." This is a prayer for the **restoration** of a **Personal Presence**!

Many years ago, my wife and I became engaged; and then we were married. Those were precious experiences treasured in our memories. However, I do not go around today rejoicing because of those experiences of yesterday! I rejoice today for the gracious, lovely Christ-centered companion who has walked with me throughout the years. We have a very warm and personal fellowship that has grown more precious with the passing of time. I can truthfully say: I know my wife better, understand her more completely, admire and depend upon her more fully, love her and need her more than ever before in my life. Why should not my Lord and Savior be even more precious as time passes and eternity approaches?

Born of the Spirit, filled with the Spirit and led by the Spirit of God we are enabled to **Walk with God in the most precious and personal of all relationships known to mankind!**

Holiness

Concepts of holiness have their genesis in the character of God. Stated doctrines of holiness are but **concepts of holiness** as viewed by men. However, holiness is not a doctrine born in the minds of men! The true nature of holiness is resident in the character of God Himself. God has flatly stated, in His Word, **"I am holy!"** God is the very essence of holiness and love. Jesus, God's only begotten Son, came to earth as an example of God's love and holiness, in the flesh. When God created man in His own image, **He created man holy**! Everything created by God was holy! He looked upon it all and said, "That is good!"

Because man was holy at creation he could walk with God in holiness! The Bible teaches that it is **the presence of God that makes persons, places or things holy**! It was the presence of God on Mt. Sinai that made the ground, about the burning bush, holy ground! God said, "Take the shoes from off your feet, for the place on which thou standeth is holy ground!" It was the presence of the pre-incarnate Jesus, outside the walls of Jericho that made the place where Joshua stood, holy ground. Again the command, "Take the shoes from off your feet for the place whereon thou standeth is holy ground." No angel, walking with man, was ever recorded as making the place holy; because he was there! It was the **presence of God's Holy Spirit, on the Mercy Seat, that marked the Holy of Holies**. I have the conviction, asserted before, that at the rending of the veil, the Holy Spirit departed the most holy place to indwell redeemed mankind: who would function as His temples. **It is the abiding presence of the Holy Spirit that makes man holy!** Adam and Eve, in the Garden, were holy, not only because they were created holy, but **they were in the presence of God**! When Adam **surrendered dominion** to Satan because of his sin of disobedience: **he surrendered his holy standing** also. He was now separated from God!

This would be a good time for me to reaffirm that I am **not** trying to present the negative, that which I do not believe. My purpose is to state as clearly as possible, those convictions **I do believe** and consider vital to happiness and spiritual well being. Reference will be made to distaff points of view, only when necessary for clarity. It is my purpose to light the candles which I believe my Lord has given me in dark places. For many years, I have had the blessed assurance that He knew all the answers and would share them with me when necessary for my good or His glory. It is my desire to pass on, the best I can, these assurances, born of faith and verified by experience.

Everything written in this book will come to the reader as my opinion or belief. You will share my convictions, only, when God has confirmed them with you. It is not only your right; but your responsibility to have it so! In writing, or speaking, I have prayerfully asked the Lord what He wanted others to hear and that I might listen prayerfully to pass on only that which He could whisper amen to. I wish to write only what He has revealed under the anointing of the Spirit. I have frequently stated, "What I say doesn't amount to a hill of beans! It is what God says to others as I speak that constitutes light!"

An amusing experience comes to mind at this point. Early in my ministry, a man mocking my calling to preach God's truth said, "So you think you are God's mouthpiece! Why should God tell you what He wants me to know? Let Him tell me himself!" In those days I was tempted to share his skepticism. Why indeed? God is so nice! Knowing this bothered me He gave needed assurance. He directed my attention to the twenty-second chapter of Numbers where God spoke through Balaam's donkey. Peter, commenting on the incident said, "The dumb ass speaking with a man's voice forbad the madness of the prophet." *II Peter 2:16* This was so comforting to me! Surely, if God could use a four-footed jackass as a "mouthpiece" to rebuke a great prophet who was not listening very well, He could use me too! God has instructed us, in His Word, not to waste time trying to teach mocking skeptics. It seems God, Himself, has difficulty prying ideas into closed minds! Learning to listen is so important! We should always keep our minds open to truth. Like the Bereans, we should prayerfully search the Scriptures to verify truth. We are urged, by God, to "Try the spirits to see whether or not they be of God." There is so much to know that will make our own lives beautiful and make us a blessing to others.

When God made reference to "the foolishness of preaching," He was not referring to **foolish preachers**! If I were to, knowingly and with sincerity, attempt to introduce you to your own father, you would think me an idiot. How pathetic that mankind had become so estranged from its Creator, while living in a world that speaks so much of His presence and power; we need someone to introduce us to Him! One day that will no longer be necessary. God, our Father, assures us, "And they shall teach no more every man his brother, saying, know the Lord: for they shall all know Me, from the least of them, even unto the greatest of them, saith the Lord: for I will forgive their iniquity, and I will remember their sins no more." *Jeremiah 31:34*

Conflicting Concepts

Few issues divide sincere believers more sharply than their concepts of **holiness**. How holy does God expect us to be? How holy can we be? By holiness do we mean Christian **perfection**? What constitutes holiness for the Christian? How can I be holy? When can I be holy? Can I live a holy life in a world like this?

Too often we approach these questions from a prejudiced, biased point of view. Our mindset almost always presents barriers to the Holy Spirit shedding God's light on the matter. We tend to mock the approach of others to truth about holiness. One extreme laughingly says of another, "They are holy mackerel one day and deader than a mackerel the next." Critics from this school of thought also charge such folk, "Feel themselves over every morning to see if their salvation, their holiness, had leaked out, over night!" Those believing you can live holy lives are thought to be modern Pharisees and thoroughly self-righteous perfectionists.

Those who believe it possible to live holy lives retaliate on their detractors by accusing them of getting saved that they might go out, "raise Hell" and still get to Heaven. Such theological mockery and name calling must truly grieve the Heavenly Father. Very often the beliefs of one group are grotesquely distorted by those of opposing beliefs; and the distortions presented for ridicule. They create theological mock-ups, pick them to pieces and then feel very smug about their own superior concepts. No beliefs, or value systems, are beyond the scorn of those who would mock and ridicule! Psalm One tells us, among other things, "Blessed is the man that does not sit in the seat of the scornful." They are very much like children, name calling across the road, from the ditches on either side, shouting, "My pop can lick your pop! He is wiser and stronger than yours!" If truly born-again we all have the **same Father**! Every person born of the Spirit of God is a brother or sister whether they are pleased with each other or not! They may feel "stuck with one another", yet they are siblings. How desperately the Father wants His children to live in family unity, the unity of the Trinity, bonded by His love.

Let us seek to approach these questions with honest, open hearts and minds! Please do not misunderstand my position. I do not make a pretense of wisdom that supplies the definitive answers to all theological questions. No one knows everything about anything. I do not even know what I need to know to make the decisions which effect my temporal and eternal destinies! How can I have adequate answers to questions relating to absolute truth? Jesus said, speaking of the Holy Spirit after the last supper, "When He the Spirit of truth is come, He will teach you all things, **whatsoever** I have spoken unto you!" Does Our Lord understand the issues of personal holiness as related to God's children? Does He want us to understand what He expects of us, of what we can be? We can surely know the truth that sets us free! He will tell us if we learn to listen, and to be instructed by His Spirit. We can know all that we need to know, to be what we ought to be, do what ought to be done, with a Christ-like spirit: if we but learn to be led by His Spirit!

The Holiness People

Those folk commonly known as believers in holiness, believe the blood of Jesus cleanses **from all sin**. They believe you can obtain and maintain victory over sin! It is their confidence: the blood goes deeper than the stains have gone, and that God sets them free from the world, flesh and the Devil. I, too, believe this! However, Satan has a very effective snare for such folk and only the presence and power of God can keep them out of it.

Phariseeism

The specter of self-righteous Phariseeism, haunts the devout believer of holiness. Because of the emphasis on holy living, there is a tendency to focus on their deeds of righteousness. They very often identify themselves in negative terms of what they do not believe or do not do! This places the focus on self and good works! It also invites criticism of others not professing to believe as they do. The door is opened to legalism. They may even appear to be boastful of **their** holiness. Pharisaic judgmentalism interferes with God's ability to love through us. Legalism becomes the letter of the law that quenches the Spirit and destroys fellowship, not only between men, but between God and man.

Saul of Tarsus, zealous Pharisee, sought to **fulfill the Law**

of God, by **persecuting and destroying the followers of the Son of God**! There he was, **trying to do the will of God** while **destroying the works of the Son of God**. No wonder this man in his wretchedness cried, "That I would, I do not! That I would not that do I! Who can deliver me?" We can readily see why Jesus confronted him on the way to Damascus, saying in effect, "Paul, why are you doing this to Me?"

Legalistic attitudes still hinder Christ's projection of His love through the church. I have known legalistic folk to say, "People will not now endure sound doctrine." The unfortunate facts: it was, the manner in which truth was being presented, being rejected! "The letter killeth; but the spirit giveth life." *II Corinthians 3:6*

The true secret of a life of holiness does not rest upon what we do or don't do, but upon Who He is and what He is doing within and through us. Legalism will often drive folk from the church before they ever have a chance to truly meet the Lord. May our love for the Lord create an atmosphere where the unsaved and the spiritually needy may find comfort and feel loved. Let us be very careful not to force others to reject us, before they accept Jesus as Savior and Lord!

As a teenager, I was often embarrassed to explain the code of Christian ethics as taught by my church. When asked "What does your church believe?" I would respond, "We believe the blood of Christ cleanses from all sin, and that He can keep us from evil and help us to live victorious lives in a daily walk with God!" Then the embarrassing part: "Are you an example of what your church believes?" What could I say? "No I am not an example!" They could then say, "If it does not work for you, why would I want it?" On the other hand I could not say, "Sure, look me over, see what a wonderful job the Lord has done on me! If you will listen to what I say, do what I do, you could be just like me!" All this deeply troubled me for I could not respond, conscientiously, to either alternative. One day while praying about the problems involved, it seemed the Lord offered a solution. He reminded me that when questions concerning man's ability to live a holy life in a filthy world surfaced, I had been given the perfect opportunity to testify to the **sufficiency of His grace** and the power of His love! Dare anyone say, "His grace is insufficient, He can not keep, or that He can; but does not want to?" A precious, familiar hymn became a great assurance; "Praise the Lord for sins forgiven! God still rules upon the throne, and I know the blood still reaches, deeper than the stains have gone!"

Dangers of Legalism

Jesus dealt directly with the problem of religious legalism in Luke eighteen. He spoke to the problems of their pride in themselves; their scorn for those considered their spiritual inferiors, and the judgment of God's rejection. In verse fourteen He compares the prayers of the Pharisee and the publican. The one, self-congratulatory and self-centered, did not reach beyond the sound of his own voice. Jesus said of the humble, penitent publican confessing his sins, "He went down to his house justified."

We need to keep in mind that the Pharisees were the holiness people of their day. They held for rigid adherence to the Word of God. They looked for a coming Messiah, and believed in the resurrection of the dead. We see their conflicts reflected in Paul, who recognized, that in his zeal, he was going about serving God in the wrong way. He was trying to force conformity to his own beliefs! This is the problem of the legalists today. They may well be correct in their cry against sin and in their call to holiness. But, they too are going about it in the wrong way. They demand that others accept their beliefs and opinions as their own convictions too! They are calling for conformity rather than a transforming relationship with God. We are instructed, "Be renewed in the spirit of **your** mind; and put on the new man, which after God is **created in righteousness and true holiness**." *Ephesians 4:23-24* The **triumph of legalism over love** has haunted the professed holiness movements because many have become obsessed with their own holiness. One of the distinctive characteristics of a cult is the feeling they have exclusive qualities or beliefs not shared by others beyond their constituencies. We are cautioned, "For we dare not make ourselves of the number or compare with some that commend themselves: but they measuring themselves by themselves, and comparing themselves among themselves, are not wise." *II Corinthians 10:12* So many feel they are quite all right if they are not as bad as somebody else. Some criticize because others do not appear to be as righteous as they. We should not attempt to be like, nor different from, one another. We should all be dedicating our total being to be like Jesus. We are warned in Timothy to turn away from those who have a form of godliness but have not been energized by the Spirit of God. *II Timothy 3:5* Holiness is not measured by what men do or do not do, but by what God's Holy Spirit does in and through us!

Non-Believers in Holiness

Many devout Christians do not believe we are truly cleansed from all sin. They believe we are doomed to sin in thought, word and deed every day, because of fallen human nature! I have known countless thousands of such who live far above their stated doctrine, simply because they do truly love God and are filled with God's Holy Spirit! Such folk **live up to God's standards**, through His grace, rather **than down to the level** of their own doctrinal profession. I am reminded, again, of the promise in John concerning those who walk in the light! These folk differ from my position, only in their concepts and definitions concerning doctrine. Especially their definition of sin! We are experiencing the same relationships with God through His Spirit. It is my confidence that their definitions do not matter. **They are eternally secure!** Not because of a professed experience of salvation, but because of the **abiding presence of God** through His Spirit, made possible by our Lord's sacrifice! I, personally, do see **absolute, eternal security in the love of Christ**! I see **no security in sin**! Mother told me, when I was very young, **The Blood of Jesus is God's antidote for sin.** It is His cure from all unrighteousness. Just **as long as you see symptoms of the disease, take the medicine!**" Our daughter, Judy, when a child, had a severe and persistent rash. Our doctor prescribed a medicine, with instructions on the label, "take every four hours." But it did not say for how long. We gave Judy the medicine as prescribed; and after a little while the rash disappeared! We stopped giving the medicine and the rash reappeared. Once again, we followed instructions and again the rash cleared up. These procedures continued until the infection disappeared, never to return. We still had more medicine in the bottle!

Jesus spoke to the principle of forgiveness in Matthew chapter eighteen. Peter had asked how many times should he forgive a brother who repeatedly sinned against him. Our Lord replied, "Until seventy times seven!" There is no magic in that specific number. Jesus was simply saying, there should be no limit to forgiveness. If your brother repents and asks forgiveness, forgive him! Truly, he was assuring us there are no limits to His own forgiveness of the truly repentant that asked him to forgive. In First John, He stated, unequivocally, "If you confess, I will forgive!" We have peace with God, **when He forgives us**. We have peace with others **when we forgive them**! Jesus flatly stated that our refusal to forgive others endangered His forgiveness of us.

My concern for those who believe God overlooks a sinning life style, is that they base their future security on presumption rather than faith. This subject will be taken up, in depth later in the book. We are told in Luke thirteen that many will seek to enter the kingdom and face a closed door. Even though they professed knowing Him and living a life of many good works: He said, I don't know you! The five foolish virgins had no oil. They were not anointed by God's Holy Spirit. In the crisis hour at the gates, they were turned away. They could not use another's merit, and had no time to obtain their own. They were waiting for the Lord and expected to be admitted but awakened to the realization, the light within had become darkness. Were they ever ready to meet the Lord? Had they, like the church of Ephesus, as mentioned in Revelation two, lost their first love? Two things are certain: they thought they were going to get in and they were turned away, heartbroken. Our eternal destinies are at stake; and we can make our calling and election sure!

Let's make certain it is truly well with our souls. We have

such assurance provided. In I John 4:13, "**Hereby know** we that we dwell in Him, and He in us, **because He hath given us of His Spirit**." Don't settle for the assurance of earthly counselors. **Get personal confirmation from the Wonderful Counselor!** His Spirit will witness with our spirit that we are children of God, or He will convict of sin and call for repentance! God will speak to you, one on one if you will but learn to walk with Him!

Many believe that holiness comes as an **experience** through a work of grace subsequent to the new birth. I have come to view **holiness** as the **consequence of a relationship**! One of the **fruits** of the Spirit! As stated before, it is the **presence** of **God** that **makes** any person place or thing **holy**! If the presence of the **Holy Spirit indwells us, we are holy**, regardless of how we may define doctrine. If He does not abide within us as His temples, I do not believe we have holiness of heart. "Know ye not that your body is the temple of the Holy Ghost which is in you, which ye have of God, and ye are not your own? For ye are bought with a price: therefore glorify God in your body, and in your spirit, which are God's!" *I Corinthians 6:19-20* We are assured, in chapter three of First Corinthians verse seventeen, "For the **temple** of God **is holy, which temple ye are**!" We never should boast of **our** holiness. **We have nothing of which to boast.** We may, properly **praise only God** for the life giving power of His **Presence, that makes us holy**!

When the Holy Spirit, upon our total surrender of self, comes to indwell His human temple, He does not perform one work in a Calvinist and yet another in an Armenian! He performs His perfect work in both! The only difference lies in the definitions and explanations each would give expressing his theological bias. People born of the Spirit, filled with the Spirit and led by the Spirit are redeemed, restored, reconciled to God. The very presence of God, in the Person of His Holy Spirit, enables us to **walk with God in soul-satisfying fellowship**.

Hung Up on Perfection

We seem to have so much difficulty understanding that word, **perfection**. What perfection? Whose perfection? How perfect? Human perfection? Christian perfection? Sinless perfection? Faultless perfection? God's perfection? Absolute perfection? The word is bandied about too loosely! It is often used as an alibi for failure: "Nobody is perfect!" Pointed, verbal attacks may be launched with, "Do you think you are perfect?" How can we defend any concept of **perfection** when in reference to finite human beings?

When the Holy Spirit abides, with purifying presence, in our hearts and lives: **are we perfect**? Only the Godhead is **absolutely perfect**! We cannot ever know even **Adamic perfection** for the whole human race is burdened by the consequences and scars of Adam's sin. Each of us is often reminded of our human limitations and must say, "We have this treasure in **earthen vessels**." *II Corinthians 4:7* I have no wisdom of which to boast: no strength to glory in, no holiness to take pride in. I can only praise God for "The Gift" of the Father, the Holy Spirit who does teach me what I must know, strengthens me in my weakness, and purifies by His presence! There is truly nothing about which I may feel exalted; but I have so much to praise the Lord for!

We are commanded in Hebrews, chapter six, "Therefore leaving the principles of the doctrine of Christ, let us go on to the **perfection**!" Jesus, Himself, said in Matthew five, "Be ye therefore **perfect**, even as your Father in Heaven is perfect. "Perfection of the Father?" When we read First Corinthians thirteen, we can be certain it is not a **special kind of human love** being described. This is a description of **God's love**! Faith, hope and **love** are all **gifts** of the Father. God **is** love! His Holy Spirit is the very **essence** of love! When the **Holy Spirit abides in us: He loves through us!** First Corinthians thirteen is a description of **God's holiness** expressed through, Spirit-filled, human lives. **God** actually **loves others through the Spirit-filled**! He wants to love the unlovely through us! He wants us to love our enemies that hate us: that He might win those lost ones through us.

The First Epistle of John is a gold mine of truth concerning the subject of love. In chapter four let's capsulate verses eight through twelve: "He that loveth not knoweth not God: for God is love. Behold if God so loved us, we ought to love one another. No man hath seen God at any time. If we love one another, God dwelleth in us, and **His love is perfected in us**!" If God cannot love someone through us; we are useless to Him as a soul winner for that particular person. Remember, His love is pure, spiritual energy flowing to us and through us!

Christian Perfection? Only Jesus Christ is **perfect**! How could finite beings ever attain the perfection of the infinite? God sent His only begotten Son into the world to redeem us and provide an example of what He expects His children to be like. To be like Jesus, is the goal of all who seek Christian perfection. We learn in Romans eight, "God predestined that we should be conformed to the image of His Son!" The Spirit-filled Christian, seeking **perfection** is simply seeking **Christ-likeness**! My desire is to be like Jesus! How much like Him? All that I can be by His grace! We sing prayerfully, "Stamp Thine own image deep on my heart." May God help us that we, His created, finite children, may so reflect the Family Image that we feel at home in the presence of the Father. How wonderful it would be, if those studying us, could recognize, we too, "Had been with Jesus!"

Is it possible for me, with all my finite imperfections, to love God with my total being? Jesus said I must! Jesus said unto him, "Thou shalt love the Lord thy God with all thy heart, and with all thy soul, and with all thy mind. This is the first and great commandment. The second is like unto it, Thou shalt love thy neighbor as thyself. On these two commandments hang all the law and the prophets." *Matthew 22:37-40* Our ability to live in conformity with Bible standards and be able to live in loving relationships with others depends entirely upon our loving God with our total being and walking, obediently keeping His commandments. In the second chapter of John's First Epistle we have this assertion, "And hereby we do **know** that we know Him, if we keep His commandments. *I John 2:3* Who so **keepeth His Word, in him is the love of God perfected**." *I John 2:5* And in chapter three, this assurance, "And he that keepeth His commandments dwelleth in Him, and He in him. And **hereby we know that He abideth in us, by the Spirit which He hath given us**."

Our obediently walking in the light we have in Christ brings cleansing **from all** sin, through His blood. In chapter one, John states, "If we walk in the light, as He is in the light, we have fellowship one with another, and the blood of Jesus Christ His Son, cleanseth us **from** all sin." *I John 1:7* Let God speak to you from His Word as found in Ephesions three, fourteen through twenty-one: "I bow my knees unto the Father of our Lord Jesus Christ, that He would grant you to be strengthened with might by His Spirit in the inner man; that Christ may dwell in your hearts by faith; that ye being rooted and grounded in love, may know the love of Christ, which passeth knowledge; and you may be filled with the fullness of God. Now unto Him, that is able to do exceeding abundantly above all that you can ask or think, **according to the power that worketh in us**." God also said, "**Be ye holy, for I am holy**." He has made full provision that we might be holy! If we are not holy it surely is not His fault.

It seems I can still hear Mother's voice, when we were children, "There, I have provided warm water, soap, washcloth and a towel. When I come back I expect to find you clean!" May we follow our Lord's instructions and be **"clean"** when He returns! *Romans 6:22* "Now being **made free from sin**, and become servants of God; ye have your **fruit unto holiness**, and the end, everlasting life." It is also recorded in Scripture, "Without holiness, no man shall see the Lord!" I am convinced, as Paul was, "His grace is sufficient; and **His strength is made perfect in my weakness**." Do you question this? Then, ask Him! Ever hear anyone say, "I was just dying to have you ask that?" **Our Lord did, indeed, die that you might ask such a question!** He will give you all the light you will walk in. "The path of the just is as a shining light that shineth more and more unto the perfect day." *Proverbs 4:18*

At Pentecost, God fulfilled a promise made to Ezekiel in chapter thirty-six, verse twenty-seven, "I will put **My Spirit within you**, and **cause you to walk in My statutes**, and ye shall keep My commandments and do them!" When God promised Ezekiel the Gift of His Spirit, He also said, "And I will take away your stony heart out of your flesh, and I will give you a heart of flesh." *Ezekiel 36:26* God in speaking of a changed heart was not referring to the physical organ that pumps life-giving blood through our veins! He was using the known and the familiar to teach the unknown and the intangible. This object lesson was given to help us understand the significance of our spiritual rebirth when we become new creatures in Christ Jesus. *I Corinthians 15:40-44* In this message to us, God tells us there are both physical and spiritual bodies that differ in their God-given properties and functions. First of all we are natural, physical men born in sin and spiritually dead; the natural descendants of Adam. After receiving physical life we may receive spiritual life through the blood of Our Lord! When we confess our sins, forsake our sins and are forgiven, the sin-barrier is removed; and we are reconciled to God! This spiritual resurrection from our death in trespasses and sin makes us "new creatures" in Christ Jesus, spiritual children of God.

We must never forget we know in part and that we prophecy in part. At best, we see imperfectly and find it very difficult to understand the many mysteries of Godliness. There are probably no perfect, identical examples of the spiritual to be found in the realm of the physical.

The physical heart of man pumps the very lifeblood of the physical body. Our dictionaries tell us, "Blood is essential for life, providing necessary vital ingredients." The life-blood essential for our spiritual life was provided for us on Calvary. Through His death, we may become, eternally, spiritually alive! "If any man be in Christ he is a new creature: old things have passed away; behold, all things are become new." *II Corinthians 5:17* The spiritual heart promised to Ezekiel is among those new things. In Psalm fifty-one, David claimed that provision of God's mercy before it was given as a promise to Ezekiel when he prayed, "Create in me a clean heart, O God; and renew a right spirit within me!"

We are assured that our eternal spirit will return to the God who gave it when this physical body dies. In physical death our eternal spirit separates from its temporal accommodations and our bodies go back to dust, including the physical heart.

One day while fishing in Maine, a man, who is very close to me, confided: "Sometimes I give you a bad time; but I really respect you. You have what it takes to live a Christian life; but I don't! Believe me, I have really tried yet cannot make it." In all sincerity, I could say: "I, too, discovered as a young Christian, I didn't have what it takes to overcome sin either!" We both came to the same realization. Satan had tormented me, "Give it up, you don't have what it takes!" In that he was telling the truth. (Imagine Satan telling the truth?) However he also told me that, although there was true deliverance for some special people, I wasn't one of them. He urged me to give it up and admit I had blown it anyway. Go ahead and live it up! He was lying this time! I have found out through the years that he has used that line on about every Christian I know! How thankful I am for that beatitude "Blessed are they that hunger and thirst after righteousness for they shall be filled!" That hungry yearning for a clean heart and a right relationship with God was, in itself, **assurance that I could find what it takes**! No promise of God was more vital in bringing about my salvation.

    The difference between my companion and I lay in my belief that if Christ were to really live in me, **we** could make it! When I could say with Paul, "I am crucified with Christ", He did indeed live in me! The life I then lived was by faith in the Son of God and in His love. God truly did give His only begotten Son that whosoever believed in Him should not perish but have everlasting life. *John 3:16* How thankful I am that "**whosoever**" included me! **No one is excluded!**

    One day mother said, "Son you will not live to be very old before you will realize your heart comes in by express, your head on slow freight! Long before you understand love, you will fall into it. You never will understand the love of God; but you can experience it. With all your getting get understanding. Pray for the reason of the hope that dwelleth in you; but never let your head get in the way of your heart! With the heart man believeth and with the mouth confession is made unto salvation. Very often you **will know** something is right or wrong but will **not know why** it is right or wrong. You can't go wrong doing right and you can't be right doing wrong! If you die doing it: do right!" Only God knows how many times, through the years, that advice has guided me through the dark places, where all I knew was the consciousness a course of action was right or wrong! If it is right do it! If it is wrong leave it alone! ✣

7 God's Love is Sufficient

Believing love to be pure spiritual energy flowing from the heart of God: we can understand why Jesus told His Disciples not to leave Jerusalem without it. For He instructed them, "Ye shall receive **power** after that the Holy Ghost is come upon you; and ye shall be witnesses unto Me both in Jerusalem, and in Samaria and unto the uttermost part of the earth." *Acts 1:8* Love as a gift, comes in the Person of the Holy Spirit. The totally surrendered hearts and lives of the followers of Jesus became the climate and soil in which the Holy Spirit would continue to produce the fruit of God's love! Now, loving God with all their hearts, minds and spirits: they could love others as themselves and become witnesses to that love. Having received God's love: Christ's followers could now reciprocate that love and communicate it to others. God could now love others through them! If we are to be effective witnesses to the truth of John, three, sixteen, we must reflect that love! We who are genuinely Christian may do nothing that is not done in love for it is "God's power unto salvation." *I Timothy 5:2* God's love must not be confused with human passion and physical desire.

Many of us are afraid to love. Loving, often misunderstood, makes us more vulnerable to rejection and exposes our inner and most private self. There is also an element of mystery to loving and we tend to fear the unknown. Love is often equated with mere physical desire and we are conscious of the implications involved in such a confusion. When we equate love with lust, we are severely limited in our scope of loving without feeling a sense of guilt. Most of our problems in learning to love center in our ignorance of what love truly is! I have presumed to believe **love is a positive flow of spiritual energy from the very heart of God**! The presence of God's Holy Spirit creates a **spiritual force field** at the inmost depth of our being. God may then express Himself through the hearts, minds, spirits and lives of those He has created in His own image for just that purpose. I believe God gives love to hallow and sanctify every human relationship; as well as our relationship with God himself! Marriage to legalize relations between a man and a woman, when they do not have a spiritual love for each other, comes very close to legalized prostitution. Marriage without genuine love; and not arranged according to the leading of the Lord, is a very hazardous undertaking. Too many professed Christians marry for the wrong reasons. Their convictions guard against promiscuity and premarital sex and they will not submit to sexual union outside of marriage. Tragically, in this sex-crazed society and because of prolonged intimate relationships, sexual desire may be aroused to such intensity: a couple may marry just to justify physical union. When their passions subside: there is little left to bond them for they lack that true **tie that binds**. It requires love as a God-given spiritual force to create a bond that grows stronger with the years as physical desire wanes. An alarming increase in divorce among professed Christians attests to the magnitude of this problem. If lust and desire determine our decisions: we may easily become intimate with just about anyone who appeals to our sensual nature! However, if we reserve our physical bodies for those alone with whom we share spiritual love, we will have established vital guidelines for our social conduct.

I confess, this does sound very judgmental; but without expressions of spiritual love, women often feel degraded and used in the intimacy of physical union. These roles may also be reversed. It takes spiritual love to hallow physical union and make it something beautiful. Unless hearts and minds are bonded by love, sexual sharing is reduced to mere animal behavior, an exercise in physical desire.

During the pastoral ministry, many young women came to me with the question, "How can I know if my boyfriend really loves me?" I believe God provided the answer. Love and lust are two four lettered words beginning with the letter L and having symptoms that are often difficult to distinguish. When physical emotions have been deeply stirred, the distinction between the two is difficult to make. There is, however, one telltale distinguishing factor! **Lust says, "Give me!" Love says, "Let me give!"** Lust seeks self-gratification as its primary objective. Love, "seeketh not her own." True love places the welfare and well-being of another above self-interest and personal desires. True love will not intentionally exploit nor degrade the loved one, either physically or spiritually. Love cannot flourish in the presence of physical desire unless love flows as spiritual energy.

When our daughters were in their teens, boys in the church would tell newcomers, "Don't bother with the Gleason girls, they have been brainwashed!" They had been! Early in life they were warned that boys would come along and ask them to prove their love by giving the boys what they had no right to ask for. They were instructed that when such propositions were made; they were to respond with questions of their own. First, ask the boys if they thought they were ladies. No boy trying to impress a girl would answer in the negative, Second, ask them if they were thought to be a nice girl. Again an affirmative response could be expected. They were then to reply, "Then why don't you **prove your love** for me by treating me like a nice girl, who is a lady?" I assured them, the wise guys would immediately start looking for easier prey. Nice young men, who were being unwise, would respect them and realize they were the kind of a girl they would like to marry some day! Years later, Judy would say, "Dad we didn't even know what you were talking about but years later, the 'alarm buzzers' would go off and we knew exactly what you were talking about!"

One of the major problems of courtship years is to know just where to draw the line regarding intimacy. Many folk have a wide range of ideas concerning what is proper and right. My response to young men seeking guidance was, "I can tell you **exactly where** to draw the line! You will probably go out with many girls before you will marry. The date you are then out with may well **not** be your future wife. She may be out with another young man. **Don't do one thing, or take one liberty you do not wish the young man to take who is out with the girl you will marry!**" There is a very real sense in which you betray your future wife: by dishonoring the girl of that evening. I believe if we live with honor, God will honor us by giving special protection to the girl of our future.

Levels of Loving

One of our greatest problems in loving lies in our failure to recognize there are various levels of love! There is the love of a mother for her child. God used this love to illustrate His own. In Isaiah sixty-six, He states, "As one whom his mother comforteth, so will I comfort you." There is a special love of parents for their children and children for parents. There is the love of brothers, sisters and other members of the family. We may also experience the love of brothers and sisters in the Lord. However, there are two kinds of love that are exclusive! The love for God that He shares with none other and the love of husband and wife that can be truly experienced by but one man and one woman, as long as they both shall live or the marriage vows are broken by adultery.

Parents may love all of their children equally. They need not deprive one to love another. Children may love their parents with all their being and deprive no one else of love. Brothers and sisters may love one another without conflicting loyalties. We can love every member of the Christian fellowship with beautiful transcending, outgoing, self-forgetting, transforming love. Each of these manner and levels of love must be responded to, or expressed, with great care lest we **shift levels** in our loving. We must love no one as we love God! Nor may we love another man or woman as we love husband or wife. These levels of love call for exclusive and total commitment! We must guard against shifting of levels in other areas too. A shifting of levels in our types of loving could result in homosexuality, lesbianism, incest and other types of forbidden perversion. Great care and discipline is vital in all expressions of love. The tragedies of broken homes, lives, marriages, bodies and ministries attest to the **horrible consequences of shifting levels in loving**. Yet, without genuine love for any given relationship, we find it **impossible to function unselfishly**; and permit **God to love others through us**.

Many pastors and church workers, aware of the dangers in

loving, often erect barriers as safeguards against compromise. At times an overly conscientious pastor may fail approximately fifty-percent of his congregation, simply because they are women. They may think of him as disinterested, distant, indifferent and not truly caring. I came to the realization, none were going to bare their soul sufficiently to have their spiritual needs met, if they did not trust me and sense my Christian love. If people are not comfortable with their counselor, they will usually talk about almost anything but that which lies at the heart of their problems. Much time was spent before God, seeking a flow of His love that others might be aware of His presence. Only then could I preserve love as a sacred trust and prevent it from degenerating to lust. I honestly realized, that in human frailty, this could happen but was determined, before God, it would not! Satan constantly seeks to exploit our human weakness. Failure to stay close to God and keep our hearts flooded with His love, exposes us to great danger! We are warned in the Word, we sin when we are "drawn away by our own lusts and enticed." Satan does everything within his power to turn our hearts and minds to lust. It is impossible for us to live victorious, Christian lives, in this sin-cursed world, **unless energized** from above! That positive, spiritual flow from the heart of God **is "The power of God, unto salvation**!" If we blow our spiritual fuses, the lights go out; the energy of pure loving is lost! However, if we heed the admonitions, "Quench not the Spirit, Grieve not the Spirit", His love will continue to flow! It is impossible to live the Christian standard, as taught by the Bible without this purifying, life-giving flow!

Love is not something we can demand! No one can force us to love them, nor can we force ourselves to love another just because we think we ought to. Although we may have the capacity to love and the desire to do so: love is born only when it has been inspired. Too often we demand the love and devotion of family members and expect them to love and respect us when we are not loving, lovable nor respectable! Only God can enable us to love the unlovely. God often does enable us to love some unlovely family member, **simply because He does**, having even died for them. Only the flow of His love, through us, enables us to love, even when our love is not reciprocated.

If we would be loved in our proper relationship: we should pray to be truly loving. If a man wishes to be treated like a king in his castle: he should not treat his wife and children as though they were peasants! He should enthrone his wife beside him as queen and give his children the status of royal princes and princesses. A man wise enough to do this will be honored above measure by a wife and children of character. I have often said, "If my wife and children treated me with greater honor or respect, I probably couldn't handle it. It would go to my head: pride and an inflated ego would take over!" So many times, we unwisely seek to insure our status by being demanding. That may engender fear and force conformity but it is totally counter productive. It will deny us what we really want, love and respect.

True, God-inspired love knows no boundaries in time or space. It will defy all barriers, temporal and eternal. I am confident all our loved ones, who have died in the faith, are in His presence right now. They are loving Him and still loving us. We have more than just a memory of their love. We too are living in His presence every day. He is present everywhere! I see God, as a loving Father, walking between two children in the darkness, holding each by the hand. They may not be able to communicate directly with each other but they can whisper, touch or squeeze and He will pass it on! We can know anything, He wishes to share, if we but learn to listen. We may be separated from our loved ones by thousands of miles on earth; or by death, yet still united in His love, holding His hands!

Truly Loving God

While still a teenager, I heard many talking about loving God. Folk testified of such love and spoke of it in sermons and Sunday school lessons. Gospel music brought challenges to share His love. Doubts arose in my mind. I began to question, "Do I truly love God, or just have religious sentiments?" My heart cried out for an answer. I had no doubt God loved me, but did I honestly reciprocate that love? Did I truly love Him more than self or others? Reading my Bible, I asked the Lord to speak to me from its pages. If His Holy Spirit had written communicating His love and will: would He please have that same Holy Spirit help me to understand what He wanted me to know? Make Himself real to me? I asked that He remove every barrier to my loving Him according to the great commandment. He has been removing those barriers throughout the intervening years. In times of crisis, bereavement, sickness and seeming failure: He has become established as first in my love!

It was that experience in The Church Of The Nazarene, in Lynn, Massachusetts, when the Holy Spirit came in His fullness, that my love, responding to His love, gave assurance that I **truly did love God**! That greatest of commandments, witnessed to by the Lord Himself was fulfilled in my heart that night. I have been determined, ever since, to keep Him in first place; and never lose my first love!

God's Grace

This better understanding of what love is, has suggested a solution to another mystery: what constitutes God's grace? The Bible teems with references to God's grace bestowed upon helpless mankind. I have heard many explanations of what grace does; but nothing seemed to clearly define **what it actually is**. Some have said it is God's unmerited favor. Surely we do not merit it but what is this favor? We speak of saving grace, healing grace, enabling grace and, of course, amazing grace. John in his Gospel, chapter three, says, "The wind bloweth where it listeth, and thou hearest the sound thereof, but cannot tell whence it cometh, and whither it goeth." He was saying, the wind is real, yet you do not see it: you only see what it does. You feel the wind, hear the sound of it, mark its passing through surrounding vegetation, know it is a real force; but cannot see it nor predict its coming or going. God's grace is very much like that! We do not see His love, we see what it does. I have come to believe **God's grace is His love in motion**! Jesus was referring to God's saving grace that brings about the new birth. **He used the wind to illustrate the unseen movement of the Holy Spirit operative in the lives of men**. You cannot see love, even though you can feel it. When you see manifestations of God's grace, I believe you are seeing evidence of God's love at work, blessing mankind. God's grace is a positive flow of creative, spiritual energy, from His own heart: expressing itself in the redeeming, cleansing, enabling, healing and transforming of mankind. Through acts of grace, He becomes visible; and speaks of His constant presence and loving care!

Loving Like God

The call to love in First Corinthians thirteen, presents a tremendous challenge to the sincere Christian, who wants to fulfill the total purpose of God, in and through, his or her life. It is intimidating to read that our love should be so great as to overcome envy, resentment, discouragement, bitterness and all impulse to retaliate. Refusing to take offense, we are to be genuinely sorry when our enemies suffer reversals and tragedy. Humanly speaking, we could well become discouraged by these seemingly impossible standards. It is a great relief to understand: God is not speaking of our human love but His own! Only God can love like that! Are we then, off the hook? Certainly not! It simply means, if we **truly love God**, we will **love like God**! When God's Holy Spirit abides in His fullness: we have the fullness of His love. We have those inner springs of living water, Jesus spoke about in John. "If any man thirst; let him come unto me and drink. Out of his inmost being shall flow rivers of living water. This spake He of the Spirit." In I John, four, we find our instructions on how to love like God. "He that loveth not knoweth not God; for God **is** love." We have the very essence of God, the energy of His person, when His Holy Spirit is enthroned within. Now from our inmost being there can flow rivers of living water. We are told, if God so loved us, in spite of our sins, we should love one another in spite of our human faults. This must be factual in our lives if we are to safely pray the prayer Christ taught His disciples! We can pray, "Father, forgive us as we forgive others." If we remember correctly, **He did not forgive us because we were so nice** but **because He was so loving**! We have peace **with God when He forgives us**: we have **peace with others when we forgive them**! Because we have been forgiven we can **lovingly** forgive others!

In the sermon on the mount, Jesus makes it very clear, "Love your enemies, bless them that curse you, do good to them that despitefully use you, and persecute you." He goes on to say, if our love is limited to nice people who love us, we are of little use to Him in loving a sinful world back to Himself! It startled me recently, to be reminded, **He has already, provisionally forgiven the sins of others against me**! He died that they might be forgiven for sins against me, yet I am reluctant to forgive. He has flatly stated, "Forgive them, or I won't forgive you!" He has called upon us to help Him redeem lost mankind. **To forgive like Him,** we **must love like Him**!

Song in the Night

The truth of this message from the mount, came home to me as a **song in the night**! I learned, early in life, praise was the most direct route to victory, firmly believing God would permit nothing, not subject to His permissive will, to come upon me. When tragedy, heartbreak, suffering or abuse came: I would pray it through and then praise Him. If I could not praise God with sincerity, I had not yet prayed it through! I was convinced: if He did permit bad things to happen, He had His purpose and my first concern was to accomplish whatever He was trying to work out by permitting the misfortune. A tremendous test of faith became a challenge to my wife and me just recently.

I cannot remember going through so intense a period as the innocent victim of half-truths, innuendoes, false witness and slander. All this caused yet more and more time in prayer that I might rise above the disappointments and prepare my heart to present the truth under the anointing of His Spirit. Upon learning of this campaign of backbiting and slander: I sincerely prayed for the man, at the source of it all, committing him to the Lord, making him God's own problem. I praised God for whatever He was trying to accomplish by permitting all this to happen. This period of abuse came abruptly, after one of the greatest periods of victories, under God's anointing, in many years. Throughout this terrible testing time, there was an under current of joy flowing like a subterranean stream. The positives of God's recent blessing were considered to be the source of that joy. One beautiful night when praying for guidance, peace and further instructions: **God revealed the source of my joy**! It came as a **song in the night**! God spoke through the beatitude, "Blessed are ye when men shall revile you and persecute and say all manner of evil against you, falsely, for

My sake. **Rejoice and be exceedingly glad**: for **great is your reward in Heaven** for so persecuted they the **prophets which were before you**!" God assured me right then, **the positives were not my source of joy at all**! My joy unspeakable, my peace in the midst of the storm **had its genesis in the abuse of my enemy**. The Holy Spirit lifted up the words, "Blessed are ye," and then "Great is your reward in Heaven!" Those abuses by my enemy were but "brownie points" building up in Heaven! As if that were not enough, the Spirit lifted out, "So persecuted they **the prophets**, which were **before you**!" I would like to think God, Himself, called me a prophet! I never dared to class myself as one. I haven't even classed myself as a preacher. It is uncertain that anything I ever preached in my whole life could have been called a sermon. What I have delivered has always been considered to be messages from the Lord to be passed on. How blest! How honored, I feel! Even now, I truly praise God **for** the abuse of my tormentor. I know what it is to hear beautiful songs in the night! Intercessory prayer is offered almost continually for my tormentor. I continue to praise God **for** him: lest I think of him in the negative and lose my joy.

Praising Your Way Through

the Lord began my lessons on praise when about four years old. Mother was standing at the kitchen sink weeping, one day, as I entered the room. She had many frustrations and burdens and never got over her disappointment caused by her abbreviated missionary service. That scene: of watching her as she wept, is vivid in my mind today. She comforted me so often as I wept over some childish hurt but I watched, helplessly, while mother wept in her heartbreak. It was a traumatic experience for a four-year old. Abruptly, mother turned from the sink, leaned back against it as she dried her hands on her apron and began saying, "Praise the Lord!" For minutes she said nothing but, "Praise the Lord!" Her voice seemed broken and there was little that sounded like rejoicing in her words of praise. A lilting quality crept into her voice; and then the words of praise sounded like shouts of triumph. Moments later she turned to her work again, singing a favorite hymn. She had praised her way through when she could not pray through! I do not believe she ever knew I was in the room! It is my simple belief, that the Lord led me into the kitchen that day to teach a vital lesson on the power of praise.

"Rejoice in the Lord, **always**: and again I say rejoice." *Philippians 4:4* God wants to teach us to praise Him **right now**; not in spite of our problems but **because** of them! Heartfelt praise is a vital key to immediate victory. Praise voices our confidence in God's wisdom and care: knowing He would not permit unnecessary suffering to those who love and trust Him. Paul and Silas, in the Philippian jail, provide an excellent illustration. Abused for Christ's sake, beaten and fastened to the stocks in prison awaiting possible execution the next day: they prayed through, then began to sing hymns of praise. That was when the Lord shook the prison, set them free and made possible the conversion of the Jailer and his family! "Let all those that seek Thee rejoice and be glad in Thee: let such as seek Thy salvation say **continually**, the Lord be magnified." *Psalms 40:16* When we, from the depth of our hearts, praise the Lord: He is magnified! When we complain and curse the darkness it is our enemy and our problems that are magnified! Who wants their problems and heartbreak to get bigger and worse?

Want to break the heart of the Devil? Then just praise the Lord! And the more severe his attacks, the more you praise the Lord. He would just have to ease up on such counter productive methods. Can you imagine how differently the history of the Children of Israel would have read had they gone through the wilderness praising the Lord instead of murmuring and complaining? All Hell cannot defeat a child of God who **praises in everything**! Just don't let the Lord catch you praising the Father for Our Lord's suffering on His cross; while complaining and fussing about the one we are called upon to carry! You cannot honestly praise the Lord unless, in total surrender, you have prayed through. If you cannot praise Him from the very depth of your being, you have more praying to do!

Action or Reaction

We are controlled by what we react to. If Satan can cause us to react, vindictively, to the abuse by an enemy, **he will keep the woods around us filled with them**! It is not an instinctive, honest impulse to want to hug someone beating up on you! However, we must not react in kind but **positively act** in Christ-like response. The best way to avoid reacting to the enemy is to pray through, then just praise the Lord! Hatred, resentment, and negativism are all forces that negate love. They are negative forces. God's love is a positive force: the only force that can conquer hate! Let us be careful to keep the heart and mind as clear channels for a full, free flow of His love. Let us be conduits for power! We must turn to God in commitment, prayer and trust. **He will then act through us!** He wants to be involved and engage the enemy for, "The battle is the Lord's." Our Lord knows very well, the **real enemy is not that human foe** but the Devil who is using him as pawn in the struggle. Our Lord does not want us beating up on our human foe; He wants to defeat Satan, the real enemy, through us. "We wrestle not against flesh and blood; but against principalities and powers of darkness!" That is why we must never resort to carnal methods nor weapons. Don't react directly to negative stimuli but take the shock, go to prayer, and let God act through you.

Overcoming Evil with Good

Those who stand for Biblical righteousness are now confronted with the most vicious and best organized phalanges of evil ever assembled. Satanic forces have infiltrated all elements of our society: governmental, educational, informational media, entertainment, health programs and even some religious organizations. These forces are rewriting history in our text books, eliminating positive teaching of established values; and replacing them with instructions to the perversion of normal human functions that would ensure the disintegration of our society, both morally and socially. Those persons, programs and institutions that would promote Judeo-Christian ethics are being singled out for open, vicious attacks. Such persons are the only ones today who can be openly and publicly abused without great outcry against that abuse. They seem to be the only minority without constitutional rights. Persons under such attack have every right to feel threatened and to react defensively. However, those who do react directly to such vicious assaults, will find themselves controlled by those inimical forces. **We are controlled by what we react to!** Everyone of us is capable of hatred because of our inherent **human nature**. If we react emotionally to hateful stimuli, we will respond according to our fleshly nature and the cycles of hatred intensify to the defeat of everything that is positive and good. We must take the shock of inimical assault and go quickly to God for grace to respond under the anointing of His Holy Spirit. We do not naturally feel like loving someone abusing us. We overcome evil with good when God's Holy Spirit is permitted to channel **His love through us**!

Many zealous Christians are made to appear hateful because of their direct responsive reaction to hate. In Proverbs we are told not to reprove the scorner, lest he hate you. Stirring up hatred only pours oil on the fire. When we react to evil and confront it personally and directly; we impose ourselves between God and the problem. We have permitted Satan to choose the weapons of combat and fight carnality with carnal weapons! We are no match for Satan. We dare not take him on with even the best of **human** resources! We are told to overcome evil with good. **Love is the only force that can safely rebuke hatred!** Those motivated by satanic hatred, desire responsive hate. This makes those who oppose them reveal their own resentment and animosity; and makes themselves feel the justified victims. The repetitive accusation of the Christians' hatred is vital to the justification of their own conduct. This accusation may not be true but it is vital to their own peace of mind to convince themselves it is so. When we respond with love, as Jesus commands, we deny them this evasion of truth and create the atmosphere under which God may convict them of evil. If they repent, surrender to God and are reconciled to God, the greatest of victories has been won. When **we accuse** one of wrongdoing, we incite his wrath; but if **God convicts** he may repent. "He that reproveth a scorner getteth to himself shame: and he that rebuketh a wicked man getteth himself a blot. Reprove not a scorner, lest he hate thee." *Proverbs 9:7-8* Spreading hatred and animosity accomplishes nothing but evil. His love within us is our light to the world. We read in First John two and ten, "He that loveth his brother abideth in the light, and there is none occasion of stumbling in him." (Remember: God's Word forbids our hating anyone, even our enemies!) "If therefore the light that is in thee be darkness, how great is that darkness." *Matthew 6:23* When Jesus comes and the final battle is over, the only thing that will matter is who has, or who has not been redeemed! The mission of Calvary will be fulfilled, only, when the last soul to be redeemed has been won. **This is what we are fighting for!** Nothing else really will matter! We are not here to **put down our enemies**; but to **help the Lord redeem them**. Remember, "It is not His will that any should perish; but that all should come to repentance." *II Peter 3:9* If we, the spiritual Christians, are not to be His hand extended and provide hearts through which He can love: we abort our mission as witnesses of God's great love revealed at Calvary! We will have failed our "Great" commission!

Three Crosses on Calvary

Three crosses were on Calvary that day Jesus died. The cross of the **Redeemer** flanked by the crosses of the **rejector** and the **redeemed**! One man, reacting with rebellious anger and bitterness to his suffering: died and went to Hell! The man on the other side of Jesus, recognized Jesus as Lord and confessed he deserved to die because of his sins. That moment when the Christ, in the midst of His own suffering, assured that repentant sinner, "Today shalt thou be with Me in paradise," is one of the most soul stirring events in Bible history for me! Our Lord had spoken peace to the first man ever recorded, as being redeemed, after His blood had provided atonement. **That man's cross was redemptive!** Our cross will be either that of rejector or the redeemed. That is our decision as we face our God-ordained cross!

Jesus told His disciples, "If any man will come after me, let him deny himself, take up his cross and follow Me!" No man can be happy and filled with praise because of suffering in any form. He is to lift up his head and praise God with rejoicing, not for the cross itself but whatever it is God is trying to accomplish through permitting it! **All God-given crosses are meant to be redemptive**.

Surely, one of the greatest examples of cross bearing and loving like the Lord, was provided by Betty Elliot and Rachel Saint, after the martyrdom of Jim Elliot and Nate Saint in their effort to reach the Yucca Indians in Ecuador, South America. This is, of course, one of the best known events in modern Christianity. Betty

Elliot and Rachel Saint, accepting their crosses and overcoming bitterness and resentment: determined to give their lives to take God's love to those who had slaughtered their loved ones! They committed themselves to completing the mission for which their loved ones gave their lives. That tribe was won to Christ! I have, personally heard one of the Indians, who speared those men, preach through an interpreter!

Just a few years ago, news came, through another missionary, that **Nate Saint's son and daughter were baptized in the same place, in the same river, by the Indian who speared their father!** I told this story to Rev. Richard Herring, missionary and director of a Bible College in Thailand. He too, thinking this to be the very heart and soul of missions, asked me to verify that report. I did write to Marge Saint VanDerPuy for confirmation. The report was true indeed! When Nate Saint's children, in their teens, gave themselves totally to Christ: they asked that they might be baptized in that river where their father had died! Marge, their mother, arranged the journey that took them to reunion with their Aunt Rachel in Ecuador and the excursion to the river for the baptismal. I am so indebted to Mrs. VanDerPuy for her gracious response, verifying this tremendous witness of **love triumphant**. May this witness to the power of God's transforming love, continue a ripple effect that will result in yet more thousands being reconciled to God!

Language of Love

Love has a language all its own! It is amazing how even an animal can telegraph its own level of affection! We are often deeply moved by the obvious expressions of, and appreciation for, love in a kitten or puppy. They cannot speak a word, yet effectively communicate love. Expressions of love and affection seem to transform the whole atmosphere about them and break down barriers. This transforming influence seems so much greater when the love of God is present.

Love is **the most effective** means of communication! When in the pastorate at Providence, Rhode Island: I served for a time as an assistant chaplain in state institutions. It was one of my responsibilities to make my presence known by visiting all wards; except for those of the criminally insane. One unforgettable day, I visited the ward for children deformed from birth. It was heartbreaking to see those mongoloid, microcephalic, hydrocephalic children and many others with pitiful abnormalities. Few of them could verbally communicate anything. However, **God spoke to them**, through me, **in the language of love**! Deeply moved by this love, I could smile and greet each one; even the most deformed! Their responding smiles and eager, outstretched hands, communicated reciprocal love! What joy to be His hand extended, a human channel for His love! **Love broke down the barriers** of those pathetic bodies and minds to reach the immortal souls of the children trapped within. How thrilling to hear Sandi Patti sing, "**Love in any language, fluently spoken here!**" That song triggers recall of those precious memories.

Most of us want our lives to have meaning, to make a difference and improve the quality of life for those about us. We want to live creatively, leaving something worthwhile behind us that was not there when we arrived to mark our passing. An almost daily prayer, "Help me Lord, today, to make a difference, to do something for somebody else whether I realize it or not. Help me to build your kingdom and be a blessing!"

As I was driving home that morning after visiting those unfortunate children, I was swept by the overwhelming conviction, "I have lived well today!" **Thank God for the language of love!**

Excellency of God's Power

"God hath spoken once; twice have I heard this; that **power belongeth unto God**." *Psalms 62:11* The Corinthians were reminded of their human limitations and dependence upon God's grace. "But we have this treasure in earthen vessels, that the **excellency of the power may be of God and not of us**." *II Corinthians 4:7* That is why the followers of Jesus were told to tarry until they received the power of God at the coming of the Holy Spirit.

We are well informed concerning the necessity for adequate power sources for men and machinery. Tremendous power sources are needed to provide thrust for airplanes, rockets and spacecraft. God had provided abundantly, above all our needs, for successful, holy, helpful living and our walk with Him through time. "My God shall supply all your needs according to His riches in glory, by Christ Jesus." *Philippians 4:19*

It is so important, in all our functions and relationships, that we be spiritually energized from above! God alone can supply the spiritual energy that enables us to love the unlovely, to sincerely pray for those who perform evil against us and to overcome the flood of hate from the world about us. Only God can enable us to hate sin and yet love the sinner. We come back to a recurring theme, "It is not what we do but what God does through us that makes us **lights** in a world of darkness."

The word **energize** has always intrigued me. Some years ago when we were building a new church in Trenton, New Jersey that term took on new significance to me. We had built a beautiful colonial church structure. The lighting had been engineered for special effects. A complete sound system that would permit broadcasting from the church was in place. Intercom stations connected all vital areas and chimes were installed in the steeple. Heating and air-conditioning units were in place to insure the comfort of the congregation. Everything was ready but **nothing worked**! There was no power! The limited light and power came from what construction workers call pigtail hook ups to temporary lines strung throughout the church. These lines had their source of power from an inadequate unit set up near the highway. The power company had erected poles and a huge transformer hung on the pole just outside the utility room. Heavy lead cables hung almost to the ground but they were not "tied in"! **We had not energized!** I kept asking Ed Bailey, our electrical contractor, when are we going to tie in? One day Ed said, "Tomorrow! And you can throw the switch if you want to!" I wanted to! Ed and his men carefully prepared the connection and tied into that cable hanging from the transformer. I closed the circuit and the whole electrical system came alive! Those dead and useless wires and appliances surged to life. The lights came on, the radio system crackled with life and the air conditioners started humming. **We had energized!**

God carefully and completely designed man that he might receive power and become His lights in the world. **He created man with the potential spiritual ability to access His own Mind and Heart and to receive, reciprocate and communicate His love**. God provided all that was necessary to fulfill His perfect purpose and plan on the earth. **Adam sinned**, short-circuiting God's power: and the **"lights" went out**! Because of that spiritual darkness, it was no longer possible for God to walk with man in a fellowship of love. For thousands of years God longed to share His love and power: once more, to be reconciled with His created children. He used temporary means to carry on limited association with His people until He could provide a way to restore that relationship once known in the garden.

In the fullness of time God caused a wooden pole, with a crosspiece upon it, to be erected on that skull-shaped hill just outside the walls of Jerusalem. His only begotten Son was crucified on that cross to become the "Transformer" through which the limitless power of God, Himself, was stepped down to flow once more through human channels: blessing and redeeming the world! As God, **the Father, is reaching down, we must reach up with faith, in total surrender, to close the circuit**. His love, as a flow of spiritual energy, will empower our total being, making us alive to our God, fully restored to fellowship. How terrible, when God cannot move within and love through us because of sin and continued rebellious disobedience!

God does, indeed, sustain the world by the power of His presence! He is also sustaining the realm of the spiritual in much the same manner. As we live and function, guided by what we do know of His truth, new horizons open up to us and we have clearer, new insights and deeper revelations of truth. These **secrets** aid us in our progression to Christ-likeness. "**The secret of the Lord is**

with those that fear Him; and He will show them His covenant." *Psalms 25:14* The longer and the closer we walk with God, the more we will love Him and the more clearly He can explain what we need to know, to be what He wants us to be and to do His will on the earth with the right spirit. Transformed by the power of His presence, we are enabled to understand some of the mysteries of Godliness and be more closely conformed to the image of His Son.

God's Strength Made Perfect

Paul's testimony to the Corinthians has been a great encouragement to me. Paul certainly had his challenges concerning cross bearing! Few people have been called upon to suffer such affliction for preaching the Gospel. God did preserve him through it all and he rejoiced in the privilege of suffering for Jesus' sake. There was something that bothered him more than others, he called it his "thorn in the flesh." We can only speculate as to what it was; but he prayed much that he might be delivered from it. One day, God spoke to him about it. Paul testifies, "And He said unto me, My grace is sufficient for thee for **My strength is made perfect in weakness**." the Lord had said, "I will not take away your affliction; but will give special grace to deal with your problem. Your weakness is my opportunity to reveal My strength." *II Corinthians 12* I believe God is looking for people overwhelmed by their weaknesses and limitations: that He may demonstrate His love and power by coming to their aid! "The eyes of the Lord run to and fro throughout the whole earth, to shew Himself strong in behalf of them whose heart is perfect toward Him." *II Corinthians 16:9* Many folk will not call on God; because they do not think, or will not admit, they need Him. Paul responded, "Most gladly therefore I will rather glory in my infirmities, that the power of Christ may rest upon me." He added, "When I am weak, then am I strong." This is no contradiction. He had simply realized his weaknesses presented God with an opportunity to demonstrate the strength of His love, by doing for him what he could not do for himself. **Our Lord's strength is made perfect in our weakness!** God wants, very much, to demonstrate to a skeptical world: that He is a rewarder of those who diligently seek Him!

This passage of Scripture has encouraged and instructed me during many testing times. I have learned, He will either take away your burden, or make you strong enough to bear it. If, as stated in Psalm four, He enlarges us in times of distress: we will forever be wiser and stronger people! People do not develop strong physical bodies lounging around the TV eating junk food. It takes the challenge of discipline, exercise and hard work to develop strong bodies. It takes times of great challenge to us spiritually, to build character!

Lifting the Cross with Love

We have considered the nature of Divine love that God created us to receive and have learned something of what our response in reciprocal love should be. **We must be very careful to learn how to communicate that love** to a lonely, heartbroken world of lost people. Our Lord died to redeem them too!

The **cross** of Calvary is the **greatest symbol of love** the world had ever known! John 3:16 announces, "God so loved the world that He gave His only begotten Son" to save His created children from their bondage in sin! Jesus, The Christ of God, **loved us so much** that, according to Hebrews 12:2, "He endured the cross, despising the shame." John, referring to this love of Jesus and uplifting the cross as a symbol of that love in I John 3:16 states, "**Hereby perceive we the love of God**, because He laid down His life for us." Those who crucified Jesus, did not, in the true sense of the word, **take** our Lord's life. **He gave it** lovingly! The cross of Calvary became the high altar upon which Jesus Christ, the Great High Priest, offered Himself, The Lamb of God in atonement for the sins of the world.

How unfortunate then, that many well-intentioned Christians often hold the cross up before the world in such a manner as to make it a **symbol of divisive hatred** in the minds of others. Ephesians, chapter two, informs us that His sacrifice made of "**One Blood all people**," breaking down the middle wall of partition between us. Jesus instructs in John twelve, thirty two, He would be lifted up and draw all men to Himself. I believe He was not only referring to the crucifixion itself but in the manner by which we declared the Gospel to the world!

The church, of which I was pastor in Philadelphia, Pennsylvania, opened its doors to a Jewish congregation seeking to establish a synagogue in the community . We did so because we loved them and believed they were **seeking to walk with the God of their fathers** according to the dictates of their own consciences, in the light of their understanding and faith. Lew Lisman, the splendid youth leader of the congregation, and I became warm friends. He sensed the love of Christ that we projected through our relationship though not fully understanding just what it was. When the guest list, for his twenty-first birthday celebration was being drawn, Lew said, "I want my pastor's name added to the list!" His mother replied, "You mean, your Rabbi!" He said, "No! I mean my pastor, I have a Rabbi and a pastor!"

An unforgettable moment had occurred at an earlier date. Lew and I were standing just inside the church doors where he had been preparing the sanctuary for their Sabbath services. He seemed troubled and preoccupied about something. As he turned to leave he said, "Pastor, what do Christians really think about Jews?" I replied, "**They love them!**" He came back immediately, "**Then you**

don't hate us?" I said, "Of course not! Christians are forbidden to hate anyone, especially God's own chosen people!" His face mirrored confusion as he continued, "Then you **really don't hate us**?" Now I had a question! "Why, Lew, would you think that those who loved Christ would hate you?" The reply of that very special young Jew has haunted me ever since. He responded, "All of my life I have been accused of being a 'Christ-killer'! This is especially true at the time of the year when you observe the crucifixion of Christ and tell the world we did it!" Deeply moved, **I thought, My God, have I lifted up the Cross as a symbol of divisive hatred instead of redeeming, reconciling love**?" Jesus said if we **lifted** Him up **with love, He would draw others** to Himself. Are **we lifting** up the **Cross** in such a manner as to **drive them away**? Are we, in unthinking insensitivity tending to indict generation after generation of Jews because of prejudice? On the Cross **Jesus** cried, "**Father, forgive** them they know not what they do." Are we not **forbidden to judge** and **commanded to love**?

There are facts of history that were all parts of God's intricate plan of redemption. We do well to remember the events leading up to the crucifixion and the crucifixion itself, but let us be very careful to **preach the truth in love**. Just **who did cause the crucifixion? You and I and the rest of the sinners of the world crucified Jesus!** Every sinner from Adam and Eve to the end of time **must share that guilt!** "He was wounded for our transgression, He was bruised for our iniquities: the chastisement for our peace was upon Him; and with His stripes we are healed." *Isaiah 53:5* May God give us the wisdom to fully preach the Truth and **lift up the Cross** now, as it was then, a **symbol of sacrificial love**!

It is true, the Jewish leaders did take responsibility for the crucifixion, before Pilate, saying, "His blood be upon us and our children!" Later as He ascended Calvary and saw the women weeping, Jesus said, "Weep not for Me, ye daughters of Jerusalem. Weep for yourselves and your children." There has been great persecution of the Jews and much weeping. **I do not want to add to that burden, I want them to see Jesus "lifted up in love!"** I am reminded again of my mother's admonition, warning against anti-Semitism.

Do you look for the **submergence** of the Jew in our Christian Culture and the loss of **their own identity**? I do not! I look for their **emergence** into the **fullness of their hope inherent in the promises of God for His special people**! A prominent Rabbi was once asked if he thought the Jews would one day find fullness in Jesus Christ. He replied, in substance, "**Probably not before the Christians do!**" Are we telegraphing the love of God to our Jewish friends and to a world dying in its loneliness? We must lift up the Cross, but let us lift it up with love!

It has been my privilege to speak of my Messiah in many

Jewish synagogues. One such occasion comes vividly to memory! It was at a congregation of Jews in Philadelphia, many of whom had escaped the Holocaust. I had been invited to speak at a Brotherhood Week observance service. I spoke of my confidence that my Messiah had come: recognizing that we, if completely open and honest before God, were all seeking the Truth as it is resident in God. It was acknowledged that we sought to **walk with God on different pathways**. However, the closer we came to understand the Truth as God knows it to be, the closer we would be to one another. I prayed the day would come when we were all totally centered in the will of God, and would be one people! Many in that congregation, sensing my love for God, and feeling that I loved them, wept openly. I can see their faces before me now, vividly etched in memory! God help us to open our own hearts to His great love and let Him speak of that love to others through our hearts.

While in Philadelphia, I had a very fine Jewish doctor as my optometrist. I think of him by name, even now, but cannot obtain his permission to use it for he is no longer living. Just about every time I would visit him, he would open discussion about my belief Messiah had come. He seemed intrigued by my confident faith but took his own exceptions. Finally, one day, sensing the moving of the Spirit, I startled the doctor by saying, "Doctor, you and I have opposing views of Jesus as Messiah. You do not believe He was the Messiah. I believe He is. One of us is right. Which one of us is right? Then I asked, "Doctor, do you pray to the God of your fathers?" He replied, "Of course!" Again, "Does He hear you? Does He answer?" When he answered these questions affirmatively, I questioned, "Does God know which of us is right? Does He know whether or not Jesus was His Son?" That startled doctor said God would know. I responded, "Doctor, I challenge you to go home tonight, kneel by your bed and pray, God of my Fathers, I want to know the truth! Was Jesus of Nazareth your Son and our Messiah or was He not? If He was Messiah, I will believe and follow Him!" It was clearly evident that this fine gentleman was deeply moved. Later, after he had adjusted my glasses, and just before I left, he said, "I am really going to do it!" I never saw the doctor again. Upon the next visit I was informed the doctor had a heart attack and could no longer come in to practice. He died soon after that. **I fully expect to meet that Jewish brother in Heaven!** Why that confidence? Because I have confidence in God's wisdom, His mercy and in His love! I believe God was talking to the doctor all the time, witnessing through my love. I believe God, knowing this would be our last meeting brought the matter to crisis and told me what to say. There was affirmative response that day! Had the doctor not found the Lord as his Messiah, I believe God would have given more time. I feel assured that **our divergent paths had met in Christ**! Again that daily prayer, "Lord send someone across my pathway who is lonely and needs your help. Then help me to know that you have sent them and just what you want me to say. Use me to help others and build your kingdom whether or not I realize it at the time." My concern is that I will not be prayed-up to seize the moment or to follow through when the door is opened. I wish we could help and win everyone, but that seems highly improbable. Again that fervent prayer, "Lord don't let me miss anyone that I can win!" If we want others to **open their minds** to what we believe, let us meet them **with open hearts**!

How to Bear Spiritual Burdens

All creation is locked in mortal combat between the forces of Almighty God and satanic power! "For we know that the whole creation groaneth and travaileth in pain together until now." *Romans 8:22* Every one of us is involved in this tidal conflict on one side or the other. "We wrestle not against flesh and blood, but against principalities, against powers, against the rulers of darkness of this world." *Ephesians 6:12* Spiritual burdens, or heaviness of heart, have been symptomatic of this struggle since the dawn of creation! The psalmist speaks of this burden in Psalm forty-two, "Why art thou cast down O my soul? And why art thou disquieted within me?" Daniel, in chapter nine, gives us the perfect example of one who has assumed the spiritual burden of others so intensely as to be identified with their guilt, while interceding for them before God. We need to recognize the difference between mere earthly burdens and the spiritual if we are to learn how to deal with them successfully.

That sense of spiritual burden, or travail of soul, is an alert from God that something needs to be brought to Him for solution. It is an invitation to come and talk something over with Him in prayer! The root cause of spiritual heaviness, or burden, may be difficult to determine at first. There are numerous spiritual challenges God may wish to address in this manner. One. It could be that as a born-again believer, God would alert you to prepare for coming events and provide the wisdom and strength to avoid snares and seize opportunities. Jesus told Peter, Satan has desired to sift you as wheat, but I have prayed for you that you fail not." Two. Someone we love, or for whom we are responsible, may be in great crisis, needing an intercessor. Three. Perhaps we have missed a turn in the road we seek to walk with Him and He wishes to call our attention to the fact, something displeases Him. At just such a time, King David prayed, "Search me, O God, and know my heart: try me and know my thoughts: and see if there be any wicked way in me and lead me in the way everlasting." *Psalms 139* Four. Our burden could be that of unconfessed sin. Sin and transgressions always disrupt our peace with God. We may excuse our failures or merely seek to ignore them, but sin imposes the burden of guilt;

and only God can deliver us from it! Five. Perhaps we are burdened for the sins of another and God is calling us to intercede for Him. It is very easy to confuse the burden for another's sin with guilt for our own. Unless clearly led by the Spirit, when burdened for another's sin, we may be tempted to question our own spiritual standing before God.

When we become aware of a spiritual burden, we should quickly seek a place of prayer where we can be alone with God. In human weakness and lacking wisdom, we often seek to find relief from our burdens by means other than prayer. If we succeed in shrugging off the burden, the problem is buried in our subconscious mind unresolved. We may resort to the beautiful ministry of music and song to feel better; avoiding the responsibility to pray through. We physically hunger and thirst when our bodies need food and water and we are alerted to eat or drink. Spiritual burdens are alerts to spiritual needs and a call to prayer. God cannot deal effectively with the underlying cause of our burdens unless we ask Him to do so.

Standing in the Gap

God's people have a history of finding many ways to avoid the ministry of intercession. Those historical tragedies of the ages are being repeated all about us. In the times of Isaiah, when Israel was in great crisis, God lamented that the seat of the intercessor was empty. "And He saw that there was no man, and wondered that there was no intercessor." *Isaiah 59:16* In Ezekiel, twenty-two, our brokenhearted God cried, "And I sought for a man among them, that should make up the hedge, and stand in the gap before Me for the land that I should not destroy: but found none." Redemption is provided for all mankind, yet vast multitudes will be eternally lost. When God gave man freedom of choice, He tied His own hands of mercy, making it impossible for Him to force men to accept His free gifts. If needy men and women cannot or will not ask for themselves, someone else must ask for them. Someone must stand in the gap, interceding before God for them, extending an invitation for God to step into their hearts and lives. We are admonished, in Galations, six, "Bear ye one another's burdens, and so fulfill the law of Christ." Will others be in Hell because we failed to stand in some gap, interceding that they should not be destroyed?

Jesus said, "Come unto Me all ye that labor and are heavy laden and I will give you rest." *Matthew 11:28* Unless you are so spiritually dead as to be totally insensitive, **you will be burdened**! Now, what will you do with that burden? When sensing spiritual conflict, or burden, go quickly to the place of prayer, preferably a special place set apart for intimate times alone with God. Acknowledging His call to prayer ask, "Lord, are You trying to tell me something? Am I doing anything that displeases You? Is there something You want me to do?" Tell Him you will stop doing anything He condemns and will do anything He asks, if He will but provide the wisdom and grace. You may also ask, "Is there somebody needing my prayer, right now? Is there someone in trouble or temptation for whom I should intercede? If so, help them, in Jesus' name right now!" Such prayer is a matter of daily effort. It is a good practice to try closing a time of prayer with praise. If we cannot truly praise Him from the depth of a grateful heart, we have not as yet prayed through. It is time to continue waiting on God.

We need to be on the alert for false accusations inspired by Satan. He often tries to flood the mind and heart with remorse for sins of the past, now under the blood. He will tell us we are hopeless failures and might just as well give up the struggle, enjoying the pleasures of the world for now. I learned, very early in life to tell him, "My sins are under the blood and I already know, I am unworthy." He simply came too late with such torment! I had peace and the assurance, God loves me as I am, right now! How wonderful to have a personal relationship with God that is so real we can **know** His truth sets us free!

In times of uncertainty concerning the true cause of a burden, pray, "Lord, I don't know just what is wrong, but you do! No matter what the problem, the solution is the same. It is your blood that cleanses **from all** sin, your grace **solves every** problem. I do not have to **understand it**, just **surrender it** to you and **trust you**! I reaffirm my total commitment to you!" Then thank Him for His love and mercy and praise Him! God tells us in the Word, "Cast not away your confidence." You can safely trust Him!

Our Brothers' Keeper

A vital lesson was driven home to me as a teenager, attending a revival meeting. During the invitation I found myself praying in self-examination, then for unsaved friends and back to myself again. the Lord seemed to ask, "Just for whom are you praying?" The reply, "For my unsaved friends and for myself!" the Lord responded so clearly, "I have already redeemed you and I will take care of you. I want you to forget yourself and intercede for others!" During the intervening years I have been best cared for when most completely wrapped up in caring for others. Everyone wants to be blest! We pray so often for His blessings. No one can dedicate their lives to be a blessing to others and not be blest! God will not be out-loved nor out-given.

A friend once shared his heartbreak over the terrible failure of another Christian brother and remarked, "The shock was greater because it was so unexpected." My reply, "It was no surprise to me for I saw it coming!" Immediately, the Lord sharply rebuked me, "And what did you do about it?" God does not give us a spirit of discernment to detect the shortfalls or weaknesses of others that we might criticize, gossip or shun them, but that we might know how to pray for them! **Gossip is an aborted prayer burden!** Under heavy burden, we will talk to someone. If we talk of the sins of others, to other than God, we spread the problem and nothing of remedy is accomplished. However, if concerned by another's failure we intercede for them before God, He will convict and they may repent. **We will have stepped into one more gap for God!** Had I spent time in fasting and praying for that man: God might have stepped in and a horrible tragedy prevented. When anyone in the Christian family or fellowship fails, there is an element of failure by all of us somewhere.

When shocked by scandal we naturally recoil with revulsion and condemn the failure. We must not react to the tragedy; but take it to the Lord. When shocked by another's failure, or we are the victim of their wrong doing, we need to remember, the extent of their sin or injustice measures their need for a Savior. If they were right with the Lord they would not do such things. The worse they are, the more depraved, the more they need redemption and the more they need an intercessor. The most logical, the most effective intercessor is the one most victimized and troubled by the offense. This was so beautifully illustrated by Betty Elliot and Rachel Saint. That is why Jesus told us to pray for those who persecuted us and did all manner of evil against us. There is no human intercessor with greater influence before the throne than those most victimized. We forfeit such power of intercession when we react with animosity toward our tormentors. If we react negatively we are of no use to God in the redemption of the offender. Is it any wonder Satan plays on hate? That is his stock in trade! When we pray through, God acts and channels His love through us. Only God's love conquers sin! Being truly loving is not a mark of weakness, but of the greater strength.

We are horrified by this destruction of innocent children in their own mother's wombs, which we refer to as abortion. Women, choosing to avoid the burden of giving them birth, or taking responsibility for them, permit these unborn babies to be destroyed. The one hope in this national, as well as personal sin, lies in our belief they are eternity bound souls, as yet not contaminated with the guilt of **overt sin**. We believe them covered by God's prevenient grace until the age of accountability. Though denied physical birth, they will have eternal, spiritual life.

There is a proper role for those protesting this carnage through demonstrations, legal action and many other areas of activism. However, if we have failed to carry this to God as a burden of prayer, as energetically as we have through direct human activism, we have limited our impact to only what man can do. Thank God! Many have prayed and are praying! Those opposed to abortion have failed in another aspect. They have permitted those justifying this carnage to take over the high sounding slogan of pro choice. Our God created us with the power, the right, the responsibility of choice. **God is pro choice!** He will not deny us our own right to choose, even to save our immortal souls. We must all choose our destinies! Listen to what God says about it: "I call Heaven and earth together to record this day against you, that I have set before you life and death, blessing and cursing: **therefore choose life, that both thou and thy seed may live!**" *Deuteronomy 30:19* The abortionists are people of choice, but they have **chosen death**! Those opposed to abortion are not in the negative, **they have chosen life**! The choice of the abortionist results in the death of the human seed, the unborn baby and I fear for the adult who made the choice of death. This scriptural reference in Deuteronomy was related to the choices facing Israel at that time and not directly related to abortion. However, all decisions directly related to the will of God are matters of life and death!

We should choose life, also, for those dead in trespasses and sin! God is not moving with revival across the land because His people are not **choosing to pray** for the eternal souls of those dead in trespasses and sin! God wants us to be **pro-life** for them too! Not merely to be for the right of children to be born physically; but for the God-given right of everyone to be **spiritually born-again**. We are not seeing worldwide revival because God's own people have not "humbled themselves and prayed" under spiritual burden and travail of soul until the term of spiritual birth. We read in Isaiah, sixty-six, eight: "As soon as Zion travailed, she brought forth children!" When the church, the Christians of the world, get under the burden for the redemption of the **spiritually unborn**, and travail to term, **God will send revival**! Please remember this: **children denied the right of physical birth will be spiritually alive forever**! Those **denied spiritual rebirth** will remain, **eternally dead** in trespasses and sin.

When we gossip, react in human emotions, fail to carry the burden to pray for the lost: **We have aborted a prayer burden**! We have refused to carry to term. We have failed to tarry, "until"! Paul, speaking to his Galation converts, said, "My little children, of whom I travail in birth again **until Christ be formed in you.**" *Galations 4:19*

If we, of professed Christendom, would turn all gossip time into prayer time, refuse to react to evil's stimuli, take the problem to God and permit Him to pour His grace through us: world wide revival would be inevitable. As it now is there is a revival of the demonic and the occult; because Satan is promoting such through our reactions to his stimuli. God is trying to work through those born of the Spirit, filled with the Spirit and led of the Spirit. May God teach us how to bear spiritual burdens! Every one of us can make the difference between victory and defeat in our own lives and in the lives of others; when we carry everything to God in prayer.

Listen to the words of James, the Lord's own half brother, in James five, "Brethren, if any of you do err from the truth, and one convert him; let him know, that he that converteth a sinner from the error of his way, shall save a soul from death and hide a multitude of sins." The critical, censor's gossip is useless to God in the redemption of his lost brothers and sisters. Our failure to be our brothers' keepers and to bear their burdens before God, is one of the prime causes of spiritual defeat of the brethereen. That second of the greatest commandments is to "love our neighbors as ourselves." I believe He was referring to a love so great as to cause us to agonize before God, bearing the sin burden of others as we had once prayed under the burden of our own sin. I suspect, if we cannot learn to carry burdens of others before God in prayer: He, in His wisdom, will give us burdens enough of our own to keep us on our knees.

Jesus said in Matthew, eleven, "Come unto me all ye that labor and are heavy laden and I will give you rest." He helps with our burdens. He also said, "Take my yoke upon you and learn of Me." He wants us to help Him, help others! We are to become "workers together with Christ!" As He wept over Jerusalem, He now weeps and intercedes, at the right hand of the Father, for those lost ones He died to redeem. In Matthew, He had said, "Please help Me carry My burdens!" How can we love God with heart, soul, mind and strength and not share His concern for others? If we love Him with our total being: we will love our neighbors as ourselves. How proud God must be of soul winners to say, "They shall shine as the stars of the morning, eternally shine as the sun." May every one of us learn the secret of bearing spiritual burdens. How wonderful to hear Him say, "As the Father hath sent Me, so send I you." If we have learned **to walk with God**, we will have learned **to work with Him** too! ✣

8 Walking in Peace

Many honest, hungry, hurting people fail to find spiritual help because they are confused by conflicting doctrinal definitions and explanations. Numerous groups, quoting the same Bible come up with different conclusions, definitions and interpretations of the same passages. They approach the Word from differing backgrounds, viewing Scripture within a frame of reference provided by their peers and personal experiences. Their conclusions are often based, upon the **consensus of men**, rather than on **convictions through the anointing and tutelage of the Spirit**. We may well have perfect peace; and the witness of the Holy Spirit providing assurance; yet lack full understanding! We need to be informed, or to remember, **only God has absolute knowledge and perfectly understands truth as He knows it to be**! The finest, finite minds in the world, "know in part and prophecy in part." They, "see through a glass darkly." No human mind knows everything about anything.

When as a young person seeking to walk with God, I read of the account in Chronicles of Solomon's prayer for wisdom. Overwhelmed by the enormity of his task as the newly crowned king of Israel and realizing his human limitations, he asked God for an understanding heart. God had promised him anything he would ask for. He chose wisdom that he might know the will of God, and wisely lead God's own chosen people. God was so pleased that He, not only granted that request, but gave him everything else he might have asked for. This is a good place to assert, **God did not give Solomon a super brain, but an understanding heart**. Later in life, when King Solomon's heart was not right with God, he did some awfully stupid things! When God could share His own heart with Solomon, he was seen to be very wise. The Book of Ecclesiastes would seem to express much of the conflict in a splendid human mind, when the heart was no longer at peace with God. "Vanity, vanity, all is vanity and vexation of spirit" would seem to be the cry of a man who had lost his spiritual peace! In closing chapters of Ecclesiastes he seemed to have discovered what was missing.

The passage telling of Solomon's wise choice of gifts, made such a deep impression, on my heart and mind, that I prayed, "Lord if you had given me such a choice, I believe I would have asked for wisdom too!" Almost immediately, James one, five came as a promise, "If **any of you lack wisdom**, let him ask of God, that giveth to **all** men liberally, and upbraideth not and **it shall be given him**!" It came to me then, why of course, if God were so pleased that one young man should desire an understanding heart, why would He not be pleased if they all did! He is no respecter of persons! From that day to this I have sought to keep my heart right with God, and learn to listen to what He would share. God did give

Solomon **the access code** to His own heart and mind that day. He will do the same for every one of us! He did, indeed, create us in His own image that we might actually access His own heart and mind.

Please recognize the stance stated early in this book. I am not pretending to be a theologian, philosopher, psychologist or even a scholar! I am speaking, out of my own heart, concerning lessons learned while prayerfully trying to walk faithfully with my God, according to His Word! It is a sharing of secrets, and what I believe to be insights given, in answer to the prayer, that the Author of the Book would explain to me what He had written.

The New Hampshire poet, Robert Frost, came to our college during my student days. He gave a reading of his poem, *Walls*. It was so thrilling to hear that man express what he felt, and what he was trying to communicate through his writings! It certainly made the poem come alive!

When the Holy Spirit comes to us, as our Gift from the Father, we have the Author of the Bible in residence. How I wish, as a Bible scholar, I were familiar with Greek, Hebrew and Aramaic! It would be easy for me to be envious of my scholarly friends. I sincerely confess to them that I must go back to Original Voice when trying to understand difficult passages of Scripture. How I have thanked God for the Teacher, Jesus said He would send to explain all things whatsoever He had said!

We must remember that men provide information and food for thought. They can provide grist for the mind, but it is the Spirit of God that gives the light from which convictions are born! You cannot directly quote someone as a witness unless you have heard him speak. Too many of us say, "Thus saith the Lord," when simply quoting someone we happen to believe. How can you quote someone you have not been in communication with? Hearsay is not accepted in court as evidence. You must actually be a witness! Our Lord told His disciples to tarry at Jerusalem until His Holy Spirit came in personal presence. Only then would they truly be witnesses.

New denominations and schools of thought have arisen because good men, believing the Bible and loving God, simply could not get their heads together with others. The Bible is true! All of it! But, do we have the mind of the Spirit when we interpret it? Truth is absolute, but we, limited to our finite capacities, are not able to absolutely understand it. Were we to posses the sum total of all human knowledge we would still be limited to a fraction of what is to be known.

While waiting for our daughters to come out of a meeting for gifted young people, at a Trenton, New Jersey high school, a group of fathers got into some interesting discussions. One man, a doctor of organic science, made the statement, "Of course we know that truth is **relative, not absolute**!" Believing it important to be sure I understood what he was saying I asked for clarification. He proceeded to explain, "We once believed certain facts to be true, only to have subsequent data prove they were not." This is the **mindset** that gives rise to **moral relativity**. Such persons do not generally believe in a-priori values or principles of truth. I challenged his position by commenting, "Oh! You mean our **concepts** of truth are **relative** and **not absolute**?" Our concepts of truth do change with the introduction of new data and facts in evidence; but truth itself has not changed. What truly is has always been and always will be. There have been many concepts of what the moon is made of and who or what lives on it ever since man first looked at it. Some of these notions have been odd to the extreme, but through it all the moon has not changed with regard to substance or inhabitants!" Since that day our astronauts have been to the moon and we now have samples of the moon's substance; and it has not changed while men were changing their minds!

Denominational covenants are very important to unite people of common persuasion and purpose into a united front to more effectively carry out their convictions and commitments. I do not believe we should all belong to one monolithic earthly church organization. This would only magnify the problems inherent in denominational structures; and their effective administration. John, as recorded in Mark's Gospel said, "We saw one casting out devils in Your name, and he followed not us, and we forbad him, because he followed not us." Jesus replied, "Forbid him not, for there is no man which shall do a miracle in my name, that can lightly speak evil of me!" Each of us must live according to the light that has formed our convictions or we cannot truly walk in fellowship with Him! We must take care that in our different definitions and expressions of our faith we do not cancel out the sacrificial commitment of those that "follow not us." I have often seen the tragic spectacle of good men canceling out the works of other good men simply because they could not get their heads together! Because of conflicts between denominations, or within them, God's work has suffered more from infighting among the brethren than from the external assaults by the heathen! How tragic to win arguments and lose souls! We should be loyal to our covenants and work in harmonious cooperation with our associates to the full extent of our talents, time and resources. However, when there is conflict between the programs of men and what we believe to be the will of God for us we must remember, Jesus did not say, "Follow My disciples" or "Follow My Church". He said, "Follow Me!" We are His ambassadors! There was a crisis period in my life when faced with the choice of conformity to human leadership, or being led of His Spirit. One day in conference with a leader of a denomination, I asked the question, "Why should I fast and pray for understanding of the problems within the church and to know just what God would have me do about them, if someone who does not know the particulars, has not prayed through about them, is going to tell me what to do anyway?" I would be better off not knowing the will of God, were I to blindly follow men. I would never have entered into the ministry had I not believed God called me to **follow Him**!

The great **unity** of the church is not found **through conformity** and the consensus of men! It can only come in answer to Jesus' **High Priestly prayer**; when He prayed for the **unity of the Trinity** to bind His people in spiritual unity. We experience the **unity of the Trinity** when His Holy Spirit provides, "One heart, and one mind!" If **egocentric**, we will have as many minds as we have people! If **Christo-centric**, we truly will be of one heart and mind and we will be one people: **His body** in the earth!

Professed Christians, within and outside of their denominational boundaries, have lost the impact of witnesses; because they are more taken up with conformity to others than a transforming, living relationship with the Lord Himself. We decry the **peer pressure** of the world, but what about the peer pressure in the church? Many sincere folk, even Gospel ministers, under the guise of loyalty to leadership, compromise their personal convictions. Do not let the surrender of your convictions be the price you are willing to pay for acceptance, prestige, power or promotion! Personally, I pray, fervently, that I might avoid controversy and negativism and be loyal and cooperative! However, my conscience has never been for sale. Our secret of power does not lie in human consensus! Why are we afraid of individuals seeking God **first**? This is the secret of our spiritual wisdom and power! Do we not still believe God deals with each of us **personally**? Is He no longer interested, no longer able to instruct, anoint and empower individual men and women? Are there no longer men and women He can trust or use? Let us so live that God, the Father may be able to **answer the prayer of His Son** and the unity of the Trinity may be the tie that binds all Christians as one! Let us not try to be like others. Let's dedicate ourselves to being like Jesus! We will be united as **one Body** when we are **all led by the same Spirit**! **Peace among the brethren is possible in no other way!**

Dr. Billy Graham came to Toronto, Ontario in the mid-fifties for a crusade on the invitation of a group of ministers from many church backgrounds and affiliations. So much of the great success of Dr. Billy Graham has rested upon his ability to focus his attention and that of others on the vital issues of the Gospel! One morning at a prayer breakfast he spoke of the conflicts and the common ground that stood between Calvinists and those of Arminian theology. If I remember correctly he said in effect, "One day, when we no longer see through a glass darkly, we will be amazed to see that the real truth lay somewhere between the conflicting theologies and it will seem so clear, so obvious, we will be amazed that we could not have seen it all the time." May God grant us wisdom, grace and compassion that we may walk heart to heart until the day we shall know as we are known!

In nineteen seventy-seven, God clearly called me to work with Dr. Jerry Falwell in the building of what is now, Liberty University. It was as clear a call to the Lord's service as I had ever received to serve Him in a pastorate. Both Dr. Jerry and I were aware of our differing theological backgrounds; but stood united in what we believed to be the will of God. One day, in a quiet moment after many months of intense activity: Dr. Jerry said, "Carl, you must find some of our preaching a challenge to your way of thinking." I could honestly respond, "Not really! We are actually talking about the same things; but defining them differently!" Jerry continued, "I don't see **holiness** as you do." At that moment, I could honestly say, "Dr. Jerry, I don't know that you understand how I see holiness. I have never been caught up in the numbers game. To me, it is the **Presence of God** that makes any person, place or thing holy. I personally believe that you are one of the best examples, I know, of what I have been preaching about throughout my ministry." Jerry, obviously embarrassed, said "Thanks Carl."

In those days of rather close association, I had confirmation of the conviction that God does not perform one work in a Calvinist's heart and a different one in the Arminian. The Holy Spirit does not need our instructions, nor is He limited by our definitions. I had never seen anyone who loved God and people more, and did more about it at greater personal sacrifice than Dr. Jerry Falwell. I could sense Dr. Jerry's presence in a room without turning my head; by the intensified sense of the presence of the Holy Spirit.

Jesus, as our High Priest, prayed, "Father, I pray that they may be one even as We are one." He prayed that the unity of the Trinity might unite the multiple millions of believers of all ages in a spiritual unity that they should be His church, His bride. I am confident that every born-again believer is my brother or sister in the Lord, whether they want to admit it or not! They are stuck with me! This prayer of Jesus also gives us insight into one of the mysteries of the Trinity. Many have asked, "How can we have three who are God and have but one God-head?" **How can millions of believers be the Church, one body: the body of Christ on the earth? In spiritual unity as that of the Trinity!** If we can come to love the Lord our God with all our heart, mind and soul we can love others as ourselves for He will be loving through us.

We must contend earnestly for what we believe, in the face of differing opinions and definitions. We may maintain our peace while doing so if our hearts are filled with His love and we walk with humility. Too often our witness to His love is lost; because we seem unable to love those who do not share our beliefs. People and churches are **not** truly **divided by issues**, but by **our attitudes** over the issues. Folk who love very much often disagree. Hearts can be at peace even when mindsets differ. There will always be differences of opinions where more than one mind is truly thinking. Only God has absolute knowledge. Our quest should not be to discover **who** is right, rather, **what** is right. How wonderful when we truly do want **His way more than our own**!

Our Lord makes just one distinction between people, those who are for Him and those that are against Him. We either gather with Him in love, or we scatter abroad through our negatives and rebellious conflicts. *Matthew 12:30* Jesus, in Matthew eighteen, also points out that many who have doctrinal and ecclesiastical correctness, may yet receive nothing from God because of spiritual pride and bad attitudes. How wonderful that the sin-burdened publican, in his spiritual hunger and humility should go on his way, justified!

One day, our grandson, Bobby Bartsch, very early in his teens, confided; "Pappy, I am half Christian and half Catholic!" At home, Bobby was attending a Baptist Church, where he had made a decision to serve Christ. On vacation with the family of his father, devout Catholics, he went to church with them. How happy I was to confidently assure him, "Catholics are Christians too, if they really know Jesus! There is only one Jesus. If we know Him as Lord and Savior we all know the same one!"

This experience triggered the precious memory of another Bobby. Rev. Robert Carson, Jesuit Brother, was raised next door to one of our church girls, Vicky Allison. They had played together as children, frequently eating cookies on her grandmother's doorstep. Bobby went to Baltimore, Maryland and entered the Jesuit Seminary. Years later, home for Christmas, Bobby Carson joined Vicky and her husband, David Bailey, for Christmas caroling. We all met in the unfinished fellowship hall of our new church under construction. Since there was no heat or lights, someone suggested we build a fire in the huge fireplace using building scraps. We held the first prayer meeting of the new church by the warmth and flickering light of that fire. Approximately fifty of us joined hearts and hands in a circle of prayer. I remember the simple prayer for I felt it so deeply. "Lord bless this, our first prayer meeting in this your house. Help us to be aware of your presence and your love. Keep us in safety. Flood our hearts with your love and joy that our voices may echo the song of the angels who sang at your birth. Help others be inspired to believe you truly have come with peace on earth for all who surrender to your will!"

Within a week of that night I received a very special card from Bobby Carson. Inscribed across the face of that card, these words: "When I think of you, I thank My God!" Bobby had written a note inside, "I cannot tell you what a thrill it was to meet someone for the first time, outside of my faith, who loves my Jesus the way I love Him! Brother Bobby Carson and I had times of precious fellowship after that experience. We discussed frankly our accepted approaches to truth concerning Jesus. He firmly believed in the primacy of the Pope, the transubstantiation of the elements and his own vows of celibacy. I shared my own beliefs and convictions. However, no one observing us, in those precious moments, would doubt we loved the Lord and each other. I am richly blest each time I recall those hours! What wonderful proof, that God-inspired love knows no boundaries or barriers!

Those experiences may be disconcerting to doctrinal conformists who may think their particular church or faith has "cornered the market," concerning the love of God. How do you explain such a relationship? The question suggests that beautiful song: "The love of God is greater far than tongue or pen can ever tell. It goes beyond the highest star and reaches to the lowest Hell. Could we with ink the ocean fill and were the skies of parchment made, to write the love of God above would drain the ocean dry." Could you have seen us, later joined by a born-again Carmelite priest, you could well echo, again, the song, "Love in any language, fluently spoken here!"

The barriers to understanding between conflicting theologies are very significant between those who class themselves Liberals and Conservatives. If there is not the common denominator of spiritual rebirth then we are not of the same body in Christ. There are instances, however, when the difference is in the definitions. I recall an interesting meeting of Mercer County chaplains in Trenton, New Jersey. We were meeting under the general umbrella of The Council of Churches. During our conversation, a professor from Princeton Theological Seminary responding to something I had said replied, "That is a John Bircher's idea!" I replied, "I did not know the man or anything about his ideas. Oh! I had heard him spoken of, but knew little more." The professor proceeded to say, "The Liberal position is..." I interrupted with, "Please hold it right there for a moment! When you draw the bottom line and add up the columns and defend the conclusion, you become a conservative! You are conserving a fixed position. True liberalism and conservatism are not positions; but are attitudes, approaches, frames of reference in determining our positions. If by **liberalism** you mean a free, open approach to truth, realizing you don't know everything about anything and are willing to accept what is proven true and are prepared to adjust your position according to new light; then I am a **liberal**! However, if you mean a **conservative** is one who defends and stands upon what he believes, with conviction, until new light or evidence broadens understanding and signals change, then I am a **conservative**!" At the close of the session, that professor came to me saying, "I enjoyed this today! We should do it more often." Then he added, "I don't mind telling you, I learned something today!" I wished I could have known that man better. His liberal friends probably thought he had let them down; but he had proven to me that **he was a true liberal**! He had accepted new evidence and adjusted to it!

There are those who love the connotation of **liberal** as indicating noble intellectualism. It sounds good! It is a wonderful word with many gracious connotations. The tragedy is that it has been taken over by some of the most **illiberal** thinkers I know. Many of the most dogmatic, autocratic and bigoted people I know have called themselves, **liberal**. Some have been so **close-minded** that God Himself could not pry an idea into their minds! They cannot tolerate anyone who holds an opposing stance and heap scorn on those who disagree with them. They accuse those who will not accept their conclusions of trying to annul the twentieth century. Speaking of annulling the twentieth century: if they are referring to legalized murder of unborn babies, the so-called sexual revolution, the breakdown of the family, the crime waves, the drug epidemics, the spread of aids, **I would love to annul it**! Real old-fashioned am I not?

Transformed or Conformed

In Roman 12:2, Paul writes, "Be not conformed to this world: but be ye transformed by the renewing of your mind, that ye may prove what is that good, and acceptable, and perfect, will of God." We face many conflicting calls and pressures to conform to the ways of the world and the minds of men. We have many others making demands upon us. We have responsibility to our families, our employers, those to whom we have made commitments and the leaders of organizations of which we are a part. Jesus fully understands the beauty and blessings of loyalty, but He knew the dangers of conforming to the things of this world when there are conflicting loyalties. Our Lord dealt with these potential conflicts rather bluntly. In Luke 14:26, He said, "If any man come to me, and hate not his father, and his mother, and his wife, and his children, and brethren, and sisters, yea and his own life also, he cannot be my disciple." He made this very strong statement to underscore the vital necessity of total commitment to Himself above all else. He made direct references to the most precious things of our lives. Jesus knew that if we were not completely loyal to Him we would not be loyal to anyone else! I owe it to my wife, my children; and anyone else depending upon me to be transformed by the power of His presence. I can fulfill my responsibilities as priest, provider and protector of my home only when fulfilling my duties to Him. **To safely lead my family and others assigned to my care, I must follow Jesus my Lord!**

Unless I am transformed by the renewing of His Spirit within

I cannot be faithful to my commitments to doctrine or denomination. The true strength of any organization, especially a religious organization, depends upon the unity of its people which depends in turn upon their integrity before God! He said, "My sheep know My voice and come at My call." Each individual sheep hears the shepherd's call and responds. The sheep do not call a caucus or a committee meeting to get consensus. All of his sheep, responding together, move as a united flock; because they know His voice and respond to His call! **The greatest unity is not found in the pressures to conformity, but in commitment to Christ!** Like the spokes of a wheel, the closer they get to the hub, the closer they get to one another. Since that day in my home church in Lynn, Massachusetts: the will of God, as revealed by His Holy Spirit has remained the benchmark of my life. No one else can tell us the will of God for our lives. If we know, it will be because we have learned to detect His voice above the others demanding our response. This often brings us into conflict with others who do not understand His will for us. I have learned throughout a lifetime of experience that I can work in harmony with others and be loyal to them, as secondary benchmarks, providing we are all using the same major benchmark. Should the time come that I cannot fulfill my responsibility to some secondary benchmark and remain committed to the Benchmark of my life, I will break that association. I will not follow anyone who I believe is not following the Lord!

The spectre of institutionalism hangs over every human organization. There is great need of unity, commitment, loyalty and trust, but just how is this to be achieved? As organizations grow in size and complexity, primary contact and association is lost. There is a tendency for strong leaders to become rigid in their demands for conformity. These pressures to conform may become so intense as to make robots or clones of others. Such pressures from some dominating personality is one of the main forces that give birth to cults. God, Himself, refused to do this even though He could have saved Himself a lot of trouble had He done so. I have, personally, heard religious leaders ask candidates for service if they were willing to accept the will of the organization's leaders as the will of God for them! I have taken the position throughout my life of service that he who has the responsibility for an organization, has the authority to fulfill those responsibilities, and if I remain in that organization, I will be loyal to its leadership up to the point of conscience. There are many occasions in all associations when there are differences of opinion and we do not always think our orders are wise instructions. We can resolve many of these conflicts by refusing to take offense and doing our best to solve problems cooperatively. Too many times there is conflict simply because someone does not wish to bow to another's will or is rebellious by nature. We must make certain that our unwillingness to conform is born of conviction and not merely a personality conflict.

Authority and responsibility are like Siamese Twins, inseparable without severe consequences. Authority without responsibility is tyranny! And responsibility without authority is slavery. There must be a careful balance of both. In more than one situation, where I was given duties without the freedom to properly perform them, I have taken the position, "I will not accept the responsibility for that over which I have no control!" Only a great love for the cause and a genuine burden of responsibility can keep one of great authority from becoming dictatorial. Great authority is a dangerous commodity to handle. The human ego becomes a treacherous factor in its use.

It was the pressure to conformity that produced the Pharisees! It was said of their outlook, "The letter killeth; but the spirit giveth life." Theirs became the Law without Love. It was such pressure that brought about the crucifixion of Jesus! Even today, **God often loses control of organizations because the pressures to conform stifle the renewing of the mind that transforms**. Systems of theology have gone awry because they have developed a **consensus of human minds** rather than fasting and praying to know and **understand the mind of God**. We must preach from the convictions of a spiritually renewed heart rather than depending upon the eclectic compilation from human minds. This is not a plea for failing to study all possible sources of information; and becoming acquainted with the works of men who have proven themselves to be used of God. However, it is not so much what men say, but rather what the Spirit of God says to us when they say it. **Light comes when He speaks!** Remember, we are **His** witnesses.

Peace in the Family

The necessity for spiritual transformation, rather than the pressure for conformation, is just as real in the family as in the church and before the world! Our freedom to worship and serve God, personally and directly as led by His Spirit must be carefully treasured, even within our own home! Peace for our spouse and children must be based on their peace with God too. He alone gives that inner peace and tranquillity. That peace He alone gives and none can take it away. If you have peace, **He gave it**! If you lose it, **you gave it away**! Don't blame anyone else. The problem lies between you and the Lord. A spiritual burden often signals the need for self-examination lest you have come into conflict with the will of God, or lost that first love!

Peace is, essentially, the absence of conflict! During World War II, America and her Allies demanded **total surrender** of the enemy, not a cease-fire to permit maneuverability, not an armistice to negotiate, but total, unconditional **surrender**. Conflict with God, you will recall, began with rebellion in Heaven and that rejection of the will of God brought sin and spiritual death. The conflict became terrestrial and spread to man and he became contaminated with the spiritual virus of sin: when man rebelled. God, also, demands **total surrender**. "There is no peace for the wicked!" *Isaiah 48:2* How wonderful the assurance, "Therefore being justified by faith, we have **peace with God** through our Lord, Jesus Christ." *Romans 5:1*

Neither happiness nor peace are found in direct quest for such. They are by-products of a life adjusted to the person and will of God. "Godliness with contentment is great gain!" It is also happiness and peace! The world offers excitement and pleasure. God offers **peace** and **joy**! **Our peace is God's assurance to us that He has accepted our unconditional surrender**. When we have made peace between ourselves and God: we may then turn to ensuring peace within the family.

If the peace of God is to reign in the house, all in the home must, individually find their own peace with God. We men, in fundamentalism often err by demanding our wives and children bow to us; because we are head of the house. Unless our wives and children, also know the Lord we often have open warfare. Rebellion within our own little castle. God did not give me authority, as the leader in my home to browbeat my wife and children and to strut about asserting, "I am the boss around here!" When God assigns responsibility: He always assigns the authority to enable one to fulfill that responsibility. God charged man to be the **priest, provider** and **protector** of his own home. **That is what He gave him authority for**. A man who prayerfully fulfills his commission, under God, with love; and successfully leads his children to God, has every assurance of a family at peace.

The somber, even horrible truth is that many men demand recognition of their authority who have no interests in their corresponding responsibilities. They are often absent from the home, do not support it, and fail to be the spiritual leader in establishing their children in the faith. What about these men who **will not** use their authority for its God-given purpose? They become selfish, brutal and a totally destructive force in the home. Peace is not even a figment of the imagination, in such a home! These are the men making headlines as "deadbeat dads"; and "wife beaters"! **Are these men entitled to their authority?** I have come to know many Godly women who were forced to assume the responsibilities assigned by God to their husbands: while taking the brunt of his anger in the misuse of his authority!

It is my prime responsibility to **introduce my children to the Lord** and to teach them how to be led by the Spirit. **Only He can guide them unerringly** into the fullness of His will. He ordained that they should have the privilege of **walking with Him too**! He has given them conscience and intelligence and the capacity to love for just that purpose. Parents must not be so rigid in enforcing their personal beliefs that the children are more aware of what the parents expect than they are of God's will for their lives. If we truly raise up children in the way they should go we will be teaching them the first steps in walking with God! **If we fail to bring them to the time in life where God takes over the leading, we have failed in one of our most important duties.** When children, who have not been taught to follow the Lord personally, are suddenly isolated, they lack the depth of spiritual resources to meet the challenge by the tempter. Tragically, young people often betray themselves by breaking away too soon before they have learned to stand by faith. Parents who hold too tightly, too long, fail to prepare their children to face the world.

We who are believing husbands must realize that our wives, too, must be free to follow the leading of the Lord according to their own conscience. **I do not believe it was God's intent that man should upstage Him in matters of conscience.** The wife, too, must be free to follow God according to the conscience He gave her. The man is the "head" of the woman and the Lord is the "head" of the man. This is true regarding matters of administration and discipline, but we cannot replace Christ as the head of anything or anybody! Husband, wife and the children are all parts of that body of which Christ is the Head! Our wives and children must be permitted to function as they were created; and be directed by God through their own intelligence and conscience. **None of us should be placed in the position where our eternal destiny is controlled or sealed by some human mind or will!** We need not fear disunity, or family disorganization when we are all being led by the Spirit of God. The love of God is the strongest binding force that has ever existed, or ever will exist! Remember! Love to be genuine and real must be free! It is not a "command performance"! If husbands will love their wives, as God requires, Spirit-filled women will have no problem being inspired to reciprocate that love!

The responsibility, and the right of my wife to independent verification of the will of God for her life is no threat to my happiness, peace nor success. **It is a reinforcement**, a supplement, a second source of confirmation of the will of God for both of us. "One will chase a thousand and two will put ten thousand to flight!" Throughout our entire ministry, my wife, Joyce, has had independent confirmation, from God himself, concerning **every** major decision related to just where to serve! We are both strong minded, independent, creative people. The wonderful thing about our relationship is our love for God and each other. This should not be a surprise, for it was God who arranged our marriage. We prayed carefully for the will of God concerning our union. God would never guide into marriage, those He would lead in opposite directions. He has a task, a purpose, for all of us. Too many people marry without seeking the whole counsel of God, who knows what each should be and do. When people have different purposes and destinies, conflict is inevitable and peace is threatened.

Memory calls me back to a conversation, years after our marriage. We were discussing the matter of divine calls to service. Joyce remarked, "God called me to be a minister or a minister's wife; and I could never have married anyone not called to the ministry." Startled, I replied, "Hon, you didn't even know I was called to the ministry when we were married!" I can see the smile on her face now as she said, "You didn't!" God had confirmed my call to the ministry to Joyce; before He told me! It will help all born-again Christians in all of their relationships to remember they are all "cells" or members of one body, **His Church**! "For as the body is one, and hath many members, and all the members of that one body, being many, are one body: so also is Christ." *I Corinthians 12:12* May God help those who are members of that glorious Body to be carefully considerate of all others who make up that Body.

The church, denomination, doctrinal or family stance that most clearly expresses the will of God will be the most united, the strongest and the most peaceful. Having the Mind of the Spirit they will be most effective in building Christ's Kingdom, and the world will be a better place, simply because they were living for God in it! Let us not be afraid to do it His way! Christ, in us, is not only our hope, but the hope of the world! There are no limits to what God can do except those we impose through doubt or disobedience.

While still a Junior in college, we were asked to hold services for a Sunday at a small church in Providence, Rhode Island. A man called to candidate for the church, had taken ill and could not make the service. We had no thought, whatsoever, of taking that pastorate. As I laid my Bible on the pulpit to preach, a sudden, electric-like thrill shot through me from head to toe and I went goose pimples, all over. I became so conscious of God's presence and power as His Word was shared with those people! When at dinner, after the service, I told Joyce of that sense of divine electricity. She instantly replied, "That happened to me too when I placed my song book on the pulpit to sing!" I remember asking, "Do you think God is trying to tell us something? Are we supposed to pastor here?" He was indeed calling us there! While we were at dinner, spokesmen for the congregation were on the phone with the District Superintendent. He called the man who was to candidate to discuss the matter. That pastor asked the superintendent, "Who was the man who preached?" When the superintendent gave my name, that pastor immediately responded, "He's your man!"

There were less than thirty people in that congregation, including many small children. They were meeting in the renovated boiler room of the church building, which had been sold to a restaurant supply company. The parsonage consisted of some rooms compartmented off from storage space overhead. At an earlier time the church had sold adds in the hymnals for money to replace broken windows. Their total assets were a small lot in another neighborhood and eight thousand dollars. To survive they had to build, buy or lease both a church and a parsonage. **Someone had prayed through for that church** and God was on the move! The people did not know it yet, but my wife and I could sense the surging of God's Spirit within. We felt, as they would say on the coasts of Maine, "Happy, as clams on a mud-flat!" We were at home!

The city of Providence had a rather stiff building code for public buildings, but we immediately began planning the building and trying to raise funds. Those weary, discouraged folk couldn't understand why we were so exited about building. Our reasoning was simple. God called us to work for Him there and they had no church. Had we come to build the church or bury it? I told the folk that we did not believe God would have blest us the way He did on that first Sunday if we had but come for their church's funeral! Building was the only other alternative that we could see. Someone asked, can we do it? The answer to that was, "If it is the work of God, of course we cannot do it with our own strength and resources. However, if He wants it done, we not only can do it, we must!" The motto, "**If We Ought WE Can**" became the slogan on the bottom of our church bulletins until the building was dedicated.

We were convinced that God had sent us there to build and proceeded to have the blueprints drawn. The often expressed fears of the folk were: building materials were scarce because of the war; we had hardly any money and just a few people; and the people in the new community had indicated they did not think they needed, or wanted another church.

Attending Eastern Nazarene College in Quincy, Massachusetts required making the round trip of one hundred miles every day. I brought the nearly completed blueprints back from school on Wednesday. That evening in prayer meeting we, as a church, studied any changes we wished and approved the plans. Early the next morning at the usual hour of 5:30 a.m. I was having my devotions in the living room while Joyce prepared breakfast. Kneeling before an open Bible, I asked the Lord to talk to me and give me guidance for the day. No thought was given to the building plans, or project, I was just seeking strength and wisdom for the day. I do not make a practice of just opening the Bible and seizing the verse before me as any special message. I would pray over the opened Bible, and then turn to the passages chosen for the moment. However, that morning the Bible was open to First Chronicles, chapter twenty-two. As I moved my hand to turn to the devotional passage, verse eleven, the first verse at the top left-hand corner caught my eye: "Now, my son, the Lord be with thee; and prosper thou, and build the house of the Lord thy God as He hath said of thee!" It was David's charge to Solomon to build the temple. Of course I read the rest of the chapter. That chapter spoke to **every objection** that had been raised concerning the feasibility of building that church. Concerning building material, verse fourteen spoke of the building material; verse fifteen of the abundance of workers; verse sixteen of the gold; and verse eighteen, "The land is subdued before the Lord and His people!" Still on my knees, I read verse nineteen, "Now set your heart and your soul to seek the Lord your God; **arise therefore, and build** ye the sanctuary of the Lord God, to bring the ark of the covenant of the Lord, and the holy vessels of God, into **the house that is to be built to the name of the Lord**." I have never been more certain of anything! **God had commissioned me to build that church.** The glory of His presence filled the room and it felt as though my hair were standing on end. I rushed to the kitchen to share that revelation with my wife and we just praised the Lord. That little church in Providence, Rhode Island became a reality in my mind. It was as real to me that morning as it was the day we dedicated it! Had my people thrown me out of the church I would have gone around some corner and built it anyway.

      Revival broke out in the church and miracle followed miracle. God did, indeed provide the material, the money, the people and we were accepted in the new community. Just twenty months from the day we first arrived at the church, we dedicated a modified colonial church building complete from basement to steeple. The church was packed, upstairs, downstairs and in the balcony. There were many who could not even get in the doors. In addition to this small, but beautifully complete church we had purchased an eight room, brick parsonage with a two-car garage in the heart of the community! This was not an example of God **blessing our work**; but of God performing **His blessed work** through us. May God grant us the wisdom to pray, "Lord, what wilt Thou have me to do?" Then, just trust and obey!

True Riches

      One of our greatest assets throughout our ministry was our family. Our home was open to the people of our church and they knew they could find comfort, refuge or just fellowship, anytime they felt the need. Many have said they were refreshed, comforted and inspired, just by spending time in the parsonage. Our children so expected there would be guests invited home from church, they wondered what was wrong when nobody came. Thousands did come through the years. Students at nearby schools, servicemen stationed nearby or traveling through, traveling folk and business persons, old folk who seemed to be lonely, or just someone we wanted to encourage; all were invited to Sunday dinner. We have had as many as nine folk at dinner that we did not know were coming when we went to church! We tried to keep any visitor from going out to a restaurant and eating alone. We informed those who did not know the Lord, of His presence at the table; and sought to introduce them to Him. We would tell those who did know Him, "If you do not feel at home, it is your own fault; this is your Heavenly Father's house!" Can God direct those who are lonely; hungry, hurting in body and soul to your house, assured you will not fail to minister in His name?

We were not perfect, and my wife and children often did disagree with me. However, we loved God and each other and His peace did rest on the home. We prayed constantly that we might live so that our Lord need not be embarrassed to share our fellowship. We prayed He, too, might be comfortable in our home. Dr. Kenneth Rice, Executive Secretary for our Department of Church Sunday Schools and General Superintendent, Dr. Lewis shared our fellowship at different times: and both said, in identical words, "Carlton, you are rich!" The Book of Proverbs comments upon the home where the wife **has not found peace** and is in emotional turmoil, "It is better to dwell in the corner of the housetop, than with a brawling woman in a wide house." Proverbs thirty-one reports the assessed value of the strong minded, independent, creative woman who has totally surrendered to God, and her total being flooded with His joy, love and peace. "Her price is far above rubies! The heart of her husband doth safely trust in her!" I was rich indeed! I am rich! ✣

9. Playground or Battleground

The "Tent of Meeting" in the wilderness, the old New England meeting house, our churches today, are all **holy places** set apart where **people could meet God**. Consecrated places, holy ground, sanctified by His presence. The altar and pulpit are centers of focus for those coming to be reconciled with God in most evangelical churches. They are much as the mercy seat was in the temple. The altar in our churches is the closest way we may come, physically, to the foot of the cross. Now we have direct access to God, with only Christ as mediator. Here we may worship, wait, and be anointed with His love as He comes to own and bless. Since God made man for His fellowship: He has set aside places for us to rendezvous with Him again. In Matthew eighteen, Jesus said, "Where two or three are gathered together in My name **there am I** in the midst of them." Actually Jesus is everywhere, all the time. He makes Himself known in fellowship when we seek Him with all our hearts. Then, He is there "to own and bless".

Please don't brand me legalistic nor out-of-date: but to me, those places of rendezvous **are holy ground, if God is there**! I come to church believing **He is there**. If convinced I could not meet Him there, I would not come. My **only** purpose in going to church is to meet God, worship God, wait on God, be strengthened by God, that I might walk with and work for God!

I am deeply convinced that when people come to church they should expect to see God high and lifted up, and His train filling the temple. Remember what Jesus said to Martha just before raising Lazarus from the dead? "Said I not unto thee, that, if thou wouldest believe, **thou shouldest see the glory of God!**"

What could be more spectacular than God in His glory? So many tolerate sin in their lives: simply because they have not seen God in His glory! When we have a vision of God in His holiness: we like Isaiah, of old, will see the contrasting filth of our own sins. It is such a vision of God's holiness that brings conviction for sin and desire for cleansing.

At creation, God provided, abundantly, everything necessary for man's survival, well-being, happiness and ultimate destiny. When God denied access to the forbidden tree in the garden, He was not denying them pleasure but protecting them from evil! He was acting to ensure fellowship with Himself and the joy unspeakable that would bring. Satan knew perfectly well why God had forbidden that fruit. He beguiled Eve into believing she was being denied pleasure and status. Knowing man's susceptibility to self-indulgence, he successfully tempted Adam and Eve with prospects of personal wisdom, independence and sensual fulfillment. This exploitation of human weakness has worked well for the Devil ever since. Unfortunately, he has stepped up his campaigns of seduction as his time runs out. We are now in those days spoken of in II Timothy when men would be, "lovers of pleasure more than lovers of God." Luke warns of the riches and pleasures of this world choking out the truth planted within us by God, making it impossible for Him to produce the fruits of the Spirit in our lives.

This hedonistically-minded generation perceives this world, even the church, to be a **playground**! Here we are to find sensual fulfillment as the greatest good. "If it feels good, do it!" "Do your own thing!" These are the slogans of our world today. This is the gospel of the **humanist**, inspired by Satan. The key to happiness and total fulfillment cannot be found in **self-indulgence**; but **self-control**! Jesus said, "If any man will come after Me, let him **deny himself**, take up his cross and follow me!" Mark 8:34 Humanism marks the value systems of the world! That is horrible; **but it gets worse**! Countless thousands of churches, **professing fundamentalism**, have become hedonistic and **practice humanism**! For them too, the church has become **a playground**!

Humanism the Gospel of Satan

We are brainwashed with humanism from early grades in our public schools, by the news media, politicians, court decisions and sources of entertainment. All these presenting humanism as the way the real world truly is today. It is so easy to pick up the beat of their drumming. The humanists assure us there are no moral laws established by a Creator God, therefore there can be no true guilt for breaking them. There is no God to whom we are accountable. Guilt is an imposition from other human sources, or the consequence of our own frustrations and failures. Right and wrong are determined by the consensus of a given society. True fulfillment is found through self-indulgence, rather than through discipline and self-denial. The driving force of humanism is **lust**! Man becomes the center of his own existence: his main point of reference.

All the basic premises of humanism are totally contradictory to the teaching of the Gospel of Jesus Christ! How can it be, then, that so many churches have catered to the humanistic philosophies of our day? Humanism and the New Age people have stances contradictory to each other, but both are in direct antithesis to Christian faith.

I cannot describe how awful I feel when I go to church and find the pulpit removed and the platform turned into a stage: where sequined performers respond to thunderous rock music, accompanied by flashing lights, so intense, they have actually given me double vision, as my eyes went out of focus. Those programs differ from the world's rock concerts only in the lyrics and some physical gyrations. Why should the church turn to the very forces that, like the Pied Piper of Hamlin, had called a generation of youth from the church to be lost in a world of sex and drugs? Has Satan convinced the very church itself that it was being denied pleasure and status? Have we heeded the call of hedonism? **The church does not need what the world has! The world needs what God gave the church to share with the world**. Have we lost that first love? Do we still have anything worth sharing? It is obvious, we cannot share what we do not have!

We do not need new doctrines, witch hunts, or great earth shattering programs; we simply need to pray in total surrender to God until the Holy Spirit moves upon us with power and glory. He will distinguish the genuine from the counterfeit gospel. Many reacting to legalism and perfectionistic self-righteousness have found themselves in the ditch of humanism, on the opposite side of the road.

"He that hath the Son hath life. He that hath not the Son, hath not life." *I John 5:12* The whole Bible points out, He is the Way, the Truth and the Life, no man is reconciled with the Father, but by Him. It is not theories about Jesus that saves, but His presence within that means life.

There is a **subtle heresy** that seems to be sweeping much of Christendom! Many professed Christians, even very sincere folk, are caught up in it. Those promoting this heresy tell us, "Times have changed!" What used to be effective in promoting revival **does not work anymore**! People no longer come just to see Jesus! **The Bible is no longer relevant** enough! No longer sufficient for our needs! This new generation has needs that are not being met, for they feel empty inside. **We must have some "drawing card"** to bring in the people and maybe they will see Jesus and be saved. They **seek** some famous, **far-out character**, the more wicked the better, who **now professes** to be born-again. We bring them in to bring those people back who have lost their appreciation for the Immaculate, sin-less Son of God who died to redeem us! These men may well be redeemed from lives of shame, but why are they elevated above those who have walked with God and honored Him through the years? Could it be because of a subtle fascination with evil? Could it be we, subconsciously, identify with their past failures?

These **contemporary** days, are the ones prophetically spoken of in Paul's letter to Timothy. That time has come! Iniquity does abound and the love of many has run cold. What does Paul say we should do about that? **"Turn away!"** The message in Timothy **does not convey the thought** that to be **entertained and know pleasure is evil**, but the **evil lies** in that we **love pleasure more than we love God**! Such professed believers have **lost their first love**, if they ever had it. They will seek entertainment with greater interest than they do a closer walk with God. We follow that greater interest and hunger. We pay the highest price for that which we value most.

Times change? **The Devil hasn't!** What is happening in many churches today, happened in **Ephesus in the first century**. According to Revelations chapter 2:4, they **had lost their first love!** Oh yes! They still hated evil and loved holiness; but **Jesus was no longer first in their affections**. Somehow He was **no longer sufficient** for their needs. God's loving grace alone was not enough. They thought they needed something more! John tells us in his First Epistle, chapter two, "If we lose the love of the Father, **we will love the world**! We become like the "foolish virgins" whose **oil ran out**. Our Lord frankly told the Ephesians, it was they who were **deficient** in their love!

We used to come to church to have our **hearts set on fire with the love of God**! That we might survive, victoriously, in a **cold**, Christ-less **world**. Now that our **hearts are cold**, many want to **bring that cold world into the church** so they will feel at home. We will seek that for which we hunger most. Hungering and thirsting for righteousness, or, loving, and hungering for, the things of the world? We will search to **satisfy our greatest hunger**! We turn to exciting programs; new forms of religious, and even some not-so-religious, entertainment. We turn our Bible-centered chancel into a theater and it becomes a stage for **human performers**. Please do not misunderstand me. I am **not condemning special events, programs or people**. I am protesting their introduction to the church as, **drawing cards, for those who think, Christ alone, is no longer sufficient**.

There are **times** when **God speaks of His Presence and communicates His love through music**, vocal and instrumental, **more effectively** than through a preached **sermon**. I personally doubt He ever blesses music as a **substitute** for praying through. When Jesus came down from the Mt. of Transfiguration, He found the disciples had made a failed attempt to cast a demon out of a boy. Jesus rebuked the Devil and cast him out of the lad. Later, the disciples asked, "**Why couldn't we do that?**" We should never forget His reply. "Because of your unbelief! **This kind goeth not out but by prayer and fasting.**" *Matthew 17* It is those who **wait upon the Lord** whose **strength** is **renewed** and whose **spirits soar** on spiritual wings. It is well-said, "**People need the Lord!**"

Direct appeals to sensual emotions detract from the true worship and adoration of our Lord, Jesus Christ. I sense no spirit of true worship at such concerts and cannot attend them without becoming critical and negative. Neither the religious hootenanny nor religious whoopee bring down the glory of God. They but stir up human emotions. I believe, across Christendom, **we have worked a religious theme into the very music that brought out the worst in that generation we lost**! This could be a conviction to you, **only**, when you have prayed through and God has spoken to you affirming such to be so. Can you honestly believe that Our Lord needs such pied pipers that **He might share the stage with them**? The Light of the World stealing a little of the limelight from some earthly performer?

What has happened to the church that we will prefer entertainment above the glory of His presence? I fear it has been so long since God moved with the power of His glory on the church, many of our folk, especially the younger ones, have never seen His glory in the church! They have never witnessed true revival nor evidence of their Pentecost. In the absence of His glory they have sought to put on an earthly show of glitter and glamour to fill the void! We are not praying, waiting, trusting and obeying until the glory of God breaks upon us. In the absence of His glorious presence: we create our own substitutes. I hunger and thirst for what only God gives! He gives it when I pray through for it. I am fully aware that many **sincere folk** are **trying**, by innovative methods, **to reach the lost**, as did Paul who said, "I become all things to all men that I might by all means, save some." Yet, how terrible when **the Savior of the world is no longer a sufficient reason for coming to His church**! We imply such when we seek spiritual fulfillment through **entertainment** rather than **intercession**! Many do not feel the need to be born-again because they are having a **fun time** with earthly pleasures. Happy with the junk foods of the world, they have lost their appetite for the things of God.

Our hearts are filled with joy and happiness after we are born-again and filled with His Spirit! (All Heaven, too, responds with joy over every sinner that has repented, according to Jesus.) "These things have I spoken unto you, that **My joy might remain in you**, and that **your joy might be full**." *John 15* If we truly have tasted of the Bread of Spiritual Life, we should never again be satisfied with the Devil's junk foods.

Many have become lost to the world because **love for Christ had grown cold**, if it ever existed. Will they love Christ again **because the world they love is now in the church**? **Hunger for the world can never be satisfied in the church**! We can never successfully compete with the world in entertainment and sensual pleasure! However, the world cannot match our joy when **His Glory is revealed**. The church at Ephesus was called upon to **repent** "**before the lights go out**"!

How many of us truly believe our Lord will keep that promise, "Said I not unto thee, if thou wouldest believe, thou shouldest see the glory?" We recognize this was His assurance to Martha at the tomb of Lazarus, whom he was about to raise from the dead. How grateful I am that I can testify, "I have seen His glory!" In November of 1964, in Trenton, New Jersey, Church of the Nazarene: I spoke on the theme from Hebrews, "We have an altar whereof they have no right to eat who serve the sanctuary." Spiritual burden weighed heavily upon my heart and mind throughout the entire message; and there was no sense of effectively conveying the message God had given for the hour. There was a frustrating feeling of failure as we began to sing a Christ-exalting hymn in conclusion. About five minutes after twelve, as we began the second stanza: The Holy Spirit, in response to our invitation, **swept across that congregation like wind through a field of wheat**! We heard no rushing wind, saw not visible fire nor heard any tongues; but we had **Pentecost**! I alone saw the wave sweep across the congregation; but everyone in the building saw what followed. That visible wave broke in the back left-hand corner of the church, swept across the aisle and down to the front pews. The wave was marked by a sudden look of shock on the faces of the people, as though someone had struck them forcibly on the back. They dropped their heads, broke into weeping, then headed for the altar. It was not some contagion that broke out in the front and brought response. Those in front knew nothing of it until they were struck by that unseen force. By the end of that stanza, the wave had reached the front of the church; and all aisles were full of people rushing to the altar.

The organist and pianist were urged to keep on ministering through their music; and I knelt before seekers asking what it was they sought from the Lord. However, **it was the Holy Spirit who worked that altar that morning**! This continued for more than an hour. People would come to the altar then arise and go back to ask forgiveness, make restitution, or confess faults. Then both persons involved would come to the altar together. One mother and daughter were estranged, for nearly twenty years, even though they worshipped in the same church. I watched as they wept and hugged each other in the pews, then came to pray. People confessed and asked forgiveness from their pastor for problems they had created in the church. People were born-again, filled with the Spirit, healed in their bodies. Forty-five people were baptized shortly after that meeting.

There were no emotional demonstrations, no shouts: only praise, love and unspeakable joy. The evidence of the presence of the Holy Spirit was everywhere. **No one there that morning had the slightest doubt we were experiencing Pentecost!** Folk coming for the evening service, knowing nothing of what had happened in the morning, asked, "What is going on here?" The atmosphere still seemed to be a spiritually charged **force field**! Two years of almost continual revival followed that unforgettable morning. Hundreds of people still vividly remember that morning when we saw **God's glory**!

Such memories make it impossible for me to accept superficial substitutes for God's glory! The pitiful truth remains, we are not paying the price for such outpourings; nor are we expecting

God to so move. As we respond to His invitation to come to Him; let us tarry, giving Him time to respond to our invitation by coming to us! Many folk now attending church have never seen His glory! "Come Holy Spirit, we need Thee!"

Christ told the Laodicean Church, your **lukewarmness**, brought on through compromise, makes Me sick! People have left the church because it was not worldly enough; but many more have stopped coming because it was too worldly! They gave up on the church – not because the Lord was no longer sufficient, but because they did not see Him when they did come! Those who are hungering and thirsting for righteousness will not continue to return unless they are fed. They who **truly love the Lord** will not stay **where He is not lifted up** in praise and obedience! Such folk are **not rejecting the Lord**! They **are rejecting the church** because of its **failure to honor the Lord**!

Many churches have **lost their own relevance** and their very reason for existence because they have become so much like the world. Many polls and surveys, recently, find very little differences in the lifestyles of the world at large and those who profess to be born-again Christians. What a tragedy! Our Lord arranged for us to be new creatures through whom He could present Himself to the world. We are supposed to be His Body on the earth, lights on the hills of earth! Those watching us should know what we believe by the way we live. We mock God when we profess to love Him and carry on a flirtation with the world at the same time. So many professed Christians try to be as much like the sensual world around them as possible; and still get to Heaven. Their familiar identifying cliché, "What's so wrong with it?" Their question should be, "What is right with it?" How many times have you heard someone say, "I know I ought not to," or "I know I ought to, but!" Such people are alibiing their failure to walk in the light God has given. Those seeking to serve God are asking, like Paul, "Lord what wilt Thou have me to do?" – then doing it!

Paul said, "I am determined to **know nothing but Christ, and Him crucified**." That is where I stand too! **Let's lift up Jesus!** Let's fast, pray, trust and obey until the "**Beauty of Jesus is seen**" **all over the place ... wherever we meet in His Name**!

I was thrilled to hear Dr. Billy Graham, near the end of a ministry that has exalted Christ before more people, of more nations, for a longer time frame than any other man; say, "I have preached the **same message** of the **same Savior**, the **same way** throughout the years." He also said, in effect, "**He has not changed, man's spiritual needs have not changed, neither shall I change!**"

He is still the Way, the Truth and the Life.
The whole world still needs to see Jesus.
Let us exalt His name together! "The hour is come that the Son of Man should be glorified!" *John 12:23*

How to Walk with God

I am not speaking as a relic of the past, trying to turn back the clock. I am assured by memory of wonderful moments when the Lord stepped in and spoke His peace to us, and even now enjoy an awareness of His presence as I walk with Him every day! I believe he will visit us now and make the present a glorious experience of shared love. **Our future**, too, can be as **bright** and **beautiful as the promises of God**. The **best days** of the Christian are still up ahead. "Eye hath not seen, nor ear heard what God hath in store for His people **who walk uprightly**." "The path of the just is as a shining **light that shines more and more** until that perfect day in His visible presence!"

Jesus was relevant the day He was born of Mary, for He came in the "fullness of time". Untold millions of years from now: **Jesus will still be as relevant as He was the day He walked out of the tomb**! "Yesterday, today and forever, Jesus is the same." You may be with Him too, if you have maintained faith in the sufficiency of His grace. If we learn to walk with Him now: we can follow Him all the way home! Providing He is our first love!

He is all that I need! All that I want! For He has told me what He told Paul, "My grace is sufficient for thee." So many of our problems would be solved at the altar if we would but pray through and totally surrender: all that we are or ever will be, all that we have or ever will have, to God in total surrender. Too many fail to let God solve their problems; and turn to something, anything that will make them "feel better". So much of human counseling is simply an exercise in helping people deal with the symptoms and consequences of sin rather than curing the disease itself.

King Saul disobeyed God and was terribly distressed in spirit. Instead of repenting and seeking forgiveness: he sought musicians to play for him so he would "feel better" without getting right with God. "And it came to pass when the evil spirit from God was upon Saul, that David took an harp, and played with his hand: so Saul was refreshed, and was well, and the evil spirit departed from him." *I Samuel 16:23* Down through the centuries, ever since, when under conviction from God; many men have sought **entertainment** instead of **seeking God in penitential prayer**. Saul felt better for awhile but died in his sin, a suicide.

How completely Jesus heals: body, mind and spirit! So many of our personal, marital, social and spiritual problems would be solved, almost automatically, if all were totally left up to Him. What were not made to disappear, at our place of total surrender, could be solved by talking it out with Him. He is very wise, knows all the answers, and will share His secrets with us if we will only learn to listen! "All to Jesus I surrender." Was not Isaiah correct when he called our Lord, **Wonderful Counselor**, Mighty God, Prince of Peace? Do you truly love God with all your heart, mind and strength? Does He have first place in your heart and life? He will come into your heart and life upon your invitation and total surrender. However, He expects you to stop your **flirtation** with the world!

There is a place for religious entertainment in the life and activities of the church. We need to rest, rejoice and enjoy good, wholesome things in fellowship together. Music plays a huge role in our meditation, praise and worship. Our musicians and singers fulfill the role of the Levites in Temple worship. It is very important to realize that **entertainment addresses our physical, temporal, sensual body** through all five physical senses. It is through them we experience **pleasure**.

Many folk differ widely in their musical preferences. Some appreciate symphony, light symphony, pop, Southern Gospel, traditional church hymns and yet others. What is brought into the church should not be determined on the basis of whether or not we like it, but **can God use it** as a means of communicating His presence with love. I believe our pulpits and lecterns should be reserved for those who are ministering in and through the Spirit of God. Those in whom He may live, move and have His being.

Through true worship and intercession we address the hungers and needs of our spiritual, eternal nature. Through them we experience the joy of the Lord which is our spiritual strength and power. When we give entertainment priority over worship and intercession: we "Sow to the flesh and of the flesh reap corruption." When we "Seek first The Kingdom of God and His righteousness," we sow to the Spirit and "of the Spirit reap everlasting life." *Galations 6:8* Sensual pleasure fades quickly. However, there is a continuing afterglow when His joy remains in us. We must not forget, serving Christ, in fulfilling the Great Commission, is not a spectator sport.

Do we really want true revival and an outpouring of His Spirit? Do we want to sing from overflowing hearts, "My Jesus, I love Thee, I know Thou art mine?" "Friendship with Jesus, fellowship divine, O what blessed sweet communion, Jesus is a Friend of mine!" "If you truly know the Lord, you need nobody, nothing else! Do you know Him whom to know aright, is life eternal? He is reaching down to us! Let us reach up to Him! "All that I need He will always be." His presence is revival! "Revive us again, fill each heart with Your Love may each soul be rekindled with fire from above." Hallelujah, Thine the glory, revive us again. Let this be our heart's cry!

Let the voices from Heaven testify of **His sufficiency: "Thou art worthy, O lord**, to receive glory and honor and power: For Thou hast created all things, and for Thy pleasure they are and were created." *Revelations 4:11*

The Church a Conservatory

Many new believers, with hearts aflame in their "first love," seeking to be trained and used of God, go to some church or school seeking a conservatory of their faith. Pastors, teachers, professors and church workers play a tremendous role in preserving the faith and guiding the development of their parishioners and students. It is of vital importance to challenge those under their guidance and care to learn how to be taught and led by the Spirit of God. Only God truly knows His will for each life; all must establish a personal relationship that He might bless and direct.

Too often instructors, in their zeal, pressure the student into their own mold and mindset – not teaching them to use their own heart and mind in accessing the mind and heart of God. All of us must keep open minds and be teachable, for even those who teach should be constantly learning. Students turn to instructors seeking to learn what they know. However, we must make certain that nothing or no one interrupts the teaching of the Holy Spirit within.

Many professors, teachers, pastors and others: in an effort to open minds to new truth, try to empty those minds of the very dreams and aspirations that impelled them to seek more instruction. I have sat in classrooms and heard professors tell the students, "Forget what you have learned up until now and start over; free your minds from prejudice and prior conditioning." They have even gone so far as to reflect against guidance of counselors in the past, theoretically, to open the minds of the students. This can be a very subtle effort to **force conformity**; rather than to **stimulate creative objectivity**.

We must have open minds and hearts and be receptive to new data, even when we must adjust our thinking to make room for new facts in evidence. This is the truly free, liberal mind. It is very important that we conserve established ideals, truths, values and lessons learned by previous experience that characterize our "first love"! While keeping open minds we must build on the foundations already laid.

In my youth, I heard a man commenting, "If I could only live my life over again, knowing what I know now! How different things would be!" I recall thinking, "Oh Lord! Wouldn't it be wonderful if he only could!" The Lord seemed to say, "He cannot, but if you could learn the lessons he has learned, for you it would almost be like another chance!" That lesson was so vivid to me that I vowed to learn all I could from the lessons and experiences of others and apply those insights to my own living. Ever since that day when hearing folk express a similar sentiment, they had my attention and I wanted to know what it was they would do differently. This did not mean that everything about them, and their lessons, applied to me, but I was determined to learn all lessons that did apply. It has been said, "Experience is a great teacher, but the tuition is high!" Thank God! In learning from others, I have saved a lot of the costs of tuition!

Unfortunately, many insecure teachers or counselors consciously or subconsciously, simply attempt to discredit previous concepts of truth, emptying those minds that they may stock them with their own ideas, unopposed and unquestioned. This constitutes "brainwashing" under the guise of a release from the bondage of prior prejudices. In this manner, many sound ideas and values are destroyed and many precious relationships between parents, pastors and prior teachers have been canceled out.

There is a great deal of what has become known as parent bashing taking place by counselors. Not understanding just how to instruct clients to deal with their problems, attempts are made to fix the blame elsewhere. They encourage their clients to shift the burden of responsibility by finding someone else at fault. It is important to understand the genesis of a problem. Many are haunted by past experiences and abuse by others. Often hypnosis is resorted to, that problems buried deep in the subconscious be brought to light. So many times psychiatrists and others offering psychological counseling, convince their patient that the guilt with which they are struggling was imposed by over-zealous parents, pastors or other religious folk. While this may be possible to some extent, it is more likely their guilt lies within themselves because of their own failures.

The doctor heading the mental health institutions at Providence, Rhode Island and I were returning from an interview with what the doctor considered a classic case of schizophrenia. He spoke of the twenty-five percent increase in that mental disorder, within the population as a whole, over recent years. I asked what he attributed this increase to and what he believed were its underlying causes. His answer was concise and direct: "Guilt brought on by the increasing complexity of our society and the individual's inability to deal with that guilt. Unresolved guilt, buried in the subconscious, becomes a guilt complex that induces schizophrenia." He went on to say that the percentage of increase was lower among Catholics because of their frequent confessions. Apart from any theological aspects, facing the guilt and consciously dealing with it was a mental therapy. This tended to prevent the conscious mind from retreating and denying the reality of guilt and simply burying it in the subconscious. A consciousness of guilt provides the basis for the normal mind to deal with the problem. Guilt is, in fact, the **handle** by which we can take hold of the problem and know when the problem has been resolved. When we lose the handle and guilt is buried in the subconscious, we are still troubled by it, but, are no longer able to deal with it. We have learned by later research that chemical imbalance can cause schizophrenia. One may well ask, "Can a guilt complex be the psychogenic causative factor in schizophrenia?" Could unresolved, buried guilt, in itself, cause chemical imbalance? This we do know for certain, guilt is a terrible affliction of heart and mind and must be dealt with honestly, openly and factually. To ignore the problem, bury it, or try to blame someone else is to play with your mental health.

Guilt is the response to our mental and spiritual nature that calls us to accountability for offenses and wrongdoing. This is a God-given alert telling us something is wrong and needs to be dealt with and corrected. Although others may accuse us falsely and unsettle the insecure, creating troubled minds; true conviction of guilt is God's call to our soul that something is wrong that must be made right. Too many of us seek to resolve guilt by convincing ourselves there is nothing wrong about what seems to be troubling us.

God tells us exactly how to deal with guilt! We are told to face it honestly, confess it fully to Him, forsake that which causes guilt, surrender it to Him and ask forgiveness. Don't make the horrible mistake of just forgetting it and burying it in the subconscious: give it to Him in sincere confession; and **He will bury it** in the sea of **His forgetfulness**. It will then be gone forever so far as He is concerned. When He gives assurance of forgiveness and we have peace, then we should forget that guilt and its causes. We can do so safely with regard to both spiritual and mental health. It is no longer a problem because it has been correctly resolved.

There is so much more that we could write of guilt. My purpose is but to challenge us to face it for what it is; and resolve it as God instructs. Let us be reminded: guilt is more than the embarrassment of being caught! Guilt is born when God catches up with us and confronts us with wrongdoing. Too often people fail to find relief from guilt because in their time of confession they confess only what they think others know. **Our confession is to God and He knows it all.** Our confession should be a time of baring our soul as we understand it before God. How can someone be dishonest or insincere in confession to the God of truth and expect to find absolution of sin?

I owe a great debt to my old-fashioned mother who demanded accountability for my youthful transgressions. She never punished me until it was very clear to me that I had actually disobeyed her or my Lord. I was never chastised unless aware of my guilt. Long before I understood the psychology or theology of guilt, I found relief from it as mother called me to accountability. There was always a sense of peace following chastisement, for I cleared accounts with God and my mother. Rather than resenting mother's firm discipline, I fervently thank God that she never, knowingly, permitted me to openly transgress without confronting me. God, our wise and loving Heavenly Father, will not let us do so either!

During my college years, working as a tree specialist, I visited a greenhouse on an estate in Brookline, Massachusetts. It was midwinter and very cold. Stepping into the greenhouse, that plant conservatory was like stepping into another world. Coming in from frost and snow I entered a world of plants and flowers. There was a spectacular profusion of flowers of every color and the air was heavy with the scent of them. Especially beautiful was the tremendous variety of orchids. All this life and beauty in the midst of a New England winter! I thought, this is what the church ought to be! A conservatory of spiritual life and beauty in a cold, hostile, sin-cursed world. The church should be a place of protection, shelter, nurture. A place of refuge from the forces that would destroy everything beautiful about our hearts and lives. Jesus said, "I will build My Church and the gates of Hell shall not prevail against it." Is our church His church? It is **not truly His church, unless He is on the throne**, in it! Can we say from the depth of our hearts, "He is Lord?" Let me say with the psalmist, "My soul doth greatly magnify the Lord."

What a catastrophe it would have been, had the power to that greenhouse failed, cutting off heat and light and someone opened the doors to the frigid winter air! That is what happens to the church when we quench the Spirit and "the lights go out"! Then someone opens the door for the world to flood in, destroying everything of eternal beauty.

Hungry hearts still come to church, saying like the Greeks who came for Pentecost, "Sirs, we would see Jesus!" Let us dedicate our lives to doing everything possible that they may see Him! He is not only relevant today: He is still the only Way, Truth and Life!

Miracles

Our total walk with God is one great, unfolding miracle! That we even exist is an intervention by God. That we are spiritually reborn is a miracle. Whenever God interrupts a natural chain of events, it is a miracle. I have come to expect that intervention every day. I can personally testify to hundreds of miracles – times when He has intervened and witnessed to by others. In one seven-week period, during our pastorate in Philadelphia: there were seven miracles in eight Sundays when everyone knew God had manifested His miracle-working grace. Some of them verified by X-rays! In fact, if there is an extended period during which I do not see evidences of His miraculous intervention, I become concerned.

Let us recognize and remember certain facts about miracles. Miracles are not performed by God in our lives that we might say, "See what God has done for me or through me," but that we might see and know who He is and realize **He is directly involved in the lives of men, women and children who trust Him**, all the time. We should know when we pray: He does hear us! Does care! And does answer according to His promises, monitored by His wisdom and motivated by His love. Faith, hope, and responding love, clear the way for manifestations of His presence. **We do not believe because we see miracles!** We see miracles **because we believe**! I do not believe God works miracles to convince a skeptic, but to honor the faith of one who believes. There have been so many obvious miracles along the way in our lives, others have made reference to my gift of healing. I do not believe I have had gifts of healing, but God steps in, simply because I truly believe! I believe, if self is truly crucified, we are obediently walking in the light, standing on His promises and pray in the Spirit; **miracles will take place**!

God does not perform miracles that we may boast of our gifts or healing hands. No man may put God on a schedule of healing, timed perfectly with that man's agenda. Sensational claims concerning miracles on demand have discouraged sincere Christians who want and need God's intervention in their hours of crisis. We do well, at this point, to remember our Lord said Satan would perform miracles in the last days, almost persuading even God's own elect. When men are lifted up in their own hearts, they open the door for just such demonic demonstrations. **We must not permit the excesses of others to interfere with our own faith concerning miracles.** Don't hit the ditch on the other side of the road!

As we have already observed: Jesus did not have to die to perform miracles! The only miracle He had to die to perform was our new birth! However, **we have to die** to ourselves, **if He is to work miracles in answer to our prayer**! Many have prayed for and received a miracle but were not sure whether or not it was, indeed, a miracle. Such folk often fail to give Him the glory. If you would be certain that God has answered your prayer, **be so specific** when you pray: the answer could not be coincidental.

A simple story illustrates this truth. A few years ago, my woodsman friend, Eddie Stanley, knowing I hunted turkeys: asked if I would send him some wild turkey feathers to be used in tying trout flies. It took longer than expected, but the day came when a wild turkey was persuaded to part with his feathers. Some of these feathers were neatly packaged and sent on to Eddie without an accompanying note of reference. Eddie didn't need a note. He had asked me for wild turkey feathers and had no doubt who sent them! When I, specifically, ask God for something and get it: I have no doubt Who sent it! I do not hesitate to thank Him, giving Him praise! When I pray in detail for another's need, and that need is met precisely as requested: I know I have prayed through and God has involved Himself, once more, in my affairs. Remember the ten lepers? **Only one** returned to give God the glory. When I ask anyone for anything, and receive it, I say thank you **to them**. Want to be sure your prayer is answered? Don't hesitate to **tell God exactly** what you want. Don't worry. If your request is not in keeping with

His precise will, He will monitor it. How grateful I am that He did not give me **everything** I have asked for.

Permit me to praise Him for yet another, very specific, answer to prayer. It happened in Providence, Rhode Island in nineteen forty-nine. We were bringing the construction of our new church to completion but had no parsonage. We had just weeks left before we must vacate the old church property. With little or no money, we faced the need for obtaining a new home. We thought of using land, adjacent to the building under construction, as security in obtaining a construction loan to build the new parsonage. We believed we could carry such a loan for $13,500.00. You need to remember it would require at least seven times that amount to build the same house today. Short on both time and money, we sought to find a house to rent or one we could purchase for the maximum of $13,500.00. I scoured the community for weeks and checked out listings with real estate agents, yet came up empty. We almost panicked as our zero hour approached.

There was one house, in the very center of our new community, that we never even checked out. We were certain it would be about seven thousand more than we could pay. On one particular day, the problem reached the crisis stage in my mind. Driving down one street after another, I prayed, "Lord we must find a home, time has run out. You know, Lord, we have to live somewhere. You know just where that ought to be. Will you please help me now?" **At that very moment I was driving past that house we had considered untouchable.** Suddenly, the Lord's reply exploded in my mind: "**You can buy that one for $13,500.00.**" I jammed on the brakes, backed up, and took the name and phone number from the real estate sign. Driving up to a pay phone at the end of that street, I called the Realtor. I shall always remember that conversation verbatim. Introducing myself, I informed him, "We need to buy a house and are interested in that property at 25 Alexander Street. You know the minimum the owners will sell for, I know the maximum we can pay. If your minimum meets our maximum, you have a sale!" He responded, "Reverend, that house was listed at $19,900.00 but they came down to $17,500.00. Some time ago a man offered them **$13,500.00**; but they turned him down. They are getting worried now for it's coming fall and they do not want to carry it through another winter empty. Just this week they called to ask if the man who offered the $13,500.00 was still looking for a house. I had to tell them I had sold those folk another house. Reverend, I believe that tells me if you offer them **$13,500.00**, with a $500.00 binder, you will get the house." A meeting of our church board was called; the vote to purchase was unanimous. One of our gracious ladies, Carrie Grist, advanced the five hundred dollars, the purchase was made, and in less than thirty days we were living in that home! **Here a specific request was answered specifically.** Could anyone doubt it was the Lord who spoke and I heard Him correctly?

Can you carry on conversation with God like that? Perhaps you already do. You certainly can if you want to, for He created all of us with the ability to do so. God is trying to talk to you through so many ways! If you will learn to listen, and respond, **you may carry on a conversation with Him too**.

Only my spiritual rebirth is more precious than this privilege of walking and talking with God in daily fellowship. Talking with the Lord is as natural as breathing, and for our spiritual life, just as necessary. How horrible it would be if I could not get through to Him, or He to me! Please, God, "nothing between"!

"God is, and He is a rewarder of those who diligently seek Him." Be sure you pray **in Jesus' name**! God needs to prove nothing to us. God is trying to **prove and prepare us** to walk in His presence now, and through eternity. God will not be impressed by the prayers of those who seek miracles related to time and material things: if they are not interested spiritual things. Remember, "**Seek ye first** the kingdom of God and His righteousness; and all these things will be added unto you." *Matthew 6:33*   "Ask and ye **shall receive**, that your joy may be full." *John 16:24*

Asked in His Name

There is a very real sense of hesitation when approaching this subject of miracles. We have witnessed hundreds of them. Our intent is to list but a few of them as illustrative examples. There is a genuine fear of placing the focus on what God has **done for me, rather** than on **who He is**! We all want appreciation for our expressions of love, but we do not want to be valued in terms of what we give. I have never treasured a friend for his gifts, but for who he was as a person. Who wants the friendship of one whose attitude is, "What's in it for me?" It is so easy to focus on the gift rather than on the giver.

This was one of the few mistakes of Judah's great king, Hezekiah. He led Judah in an unprecedented revival, fought idolatry and trusted God in times of national crisis above all other alliances. Hezekiah spread his problems out before the Lord with fasting and prayer. He waited on God until God stepped in and sent an angel who cut off the leaders and captains of Sennacherib, King of Assyria, and they went home in defeat. Verse twenty-three of Second Chronicles, chapter thirty-two, reports the root cause of one of Hezekiah's mistakes. "And many brought presents to Hezekiah King of Judah: so that he was magnified in the sight of all nations from thenceforth." God's favor brought abundant riches to Hezekiah and he focused more on the gifts than on the giver. He depended upon what God had given him more than on God Himself. He boasted of these riches to the princes of Babylon and displayed all that he had. Isaiah rebuked him sharply, "Thou hast done foolishly. Those

Babylonians will return and take everything of which you have boasted."

Many religious leaders have become great in their generation, only to fall in their human weaknesses because they were lifted up in their own eyes. Biblical and current history record many such tragedies. It is far more difficult and dangerous to handle success than failure. Paul was keenly aware of such dangers: for God had given so many visions, revelations and worked so many miracles, in establishing the witness to salvation through grace. Paul believed his danger of being "lifted up and exalted above measure" was so great, God had given him a thorn in the flesh to keep him humble and dependent.

Billy Graham, speaking to this issue at a prayer breakfast, testified he lived in constant fear, lest consciously, or subconsciously, he take praise or glory belonging only to God. "He will not share His glory with another!" Dr. Billy Graham is, perhaps, loved and respected more than any other religious figure in modern history. That testimony may well signal the reason.

If we are greatly blest and focus on the gift, God comes to be viewed as a benevolent Santa Claus giving us whatever we ask for. We become more conscious of receiving than giving. We forget love demands we share. The very nature of love cries, "Let me give!" If we feel secure in the abundance God has given us we lose our sense of need and dependency. Sometimes God has to deal with us very sharply to bring us back to reality. God has been very good to Joyce and me. He has truly given "more than we could ask or think!" We have been given more than we need: not only to spare, but to share. I am constantly reminded, "To whom much is given, much shall be required." *Luke 12:48* This failure of one as righteous as Hezekiah stands as a constant warning to me. We pray every day for wisdom to use what He has given for the purpose He gave it.

It is my prayer that these reported miracles will not sound like a liturgy of what God has done for us, but, come as a reminder of His love, power and interest in all of us. He truly is no respecter of persons. There are no unimportant people among His created children.

One of those seven miracles referred to as happening in the Philadelphia church involved a gifted soloist who had lost his voice because of sin and the misuse of his talents in night clubs. It was early in our pastorate there and we were doing the preaching in our own revival services. We had The Eastmen Quartet as our special music. One day, as the quartet was practicing in the garage of one of them, they noticed a man lingering outside the door. They involved him in conversation. He told of his own heartbreak. He once had a lovely tenor voice God had given, formal voice training, his Gospel singing, his fall from grace and the loss of his voice. He had heard them singing; and everything within him cried for reconciliation and the restoration of his voice. Those quartet boys witnessed to the Savior's love and invited him to come to church with them the next Sunday morning. At the invitation, he came to the altar and I knelt to pray with him, asking what he wanted the Lord to do for him. He told me what he had told the quartet and we prayed earnestly for God's will to be done. I tried to keep an open mind, but was this just delusion of grandeur? Was this forlorn figure ever a great singer? After the altar service we stayed to praise God and hear the testimony of those who had found victory. Ron Landis stood up and told the whole congregation what he had confided to The Eastmen and me. He testified that God had forgiven him and that he had asked God to give him back his voice. Suddenly, he lifted his head and began to sing the hymn *He Lives*, without any accompaniment. I was so embarrassed I felt like hiding behind the pulpit. His voice seemed cracked and without melody. Then the strangest thing happened. His voice seemed almost as a caged bird, beating its wings against its confinement. Bits of melody came through and then as though escaping its prison, a beautiful tenor voice flowed from Ron Landis' throat and just seemed to take flight! Everyone in that church that morning knew they were witnessing a miracle. Untold thousands have since been thrilled and blest by the singing of Ron Landis. I shall never forget that morning when God, in answer to prayer, working a miracle, gave him back his voice!

Almost immediately upon our arrival at Philadelphia we attended a youth meeting at the church. One of the very faithful and dependable young adults could not be there because of illness. She had made the request that I call to pray with her. I need not hesitate to use Roberta's name for she has recently testified to this miracle on tape. Making my first call of the pastorate, I went to the VanDerveer home to learn that Roberta had been diagnosed as having a large tumor. In simple faith, we prayed in Jesus' Name and turned that tumor over to God. Roberta followed with a prayer of her own. It started as a prayer of commitment and trust. Suddenly, that prayer became a prayer of praise and thanksgiving for God's healing. Later, the doctors could find no trace of the tumor. It was gone!

It was there in Philadelphia we met Jim and Rossie Barnhill. They were the kind of folk who tried to convince everyone: that it was their privilege when helping others. Shortly after our arrival in the city, a snowstorm crippled transportation and I was away, out of the state. At the height of the crisis, one of our daughters was stricken with appendicitis. There was no transportation; and we had no medical insurance. Jim Barnhill came immediately, took Jan to the hospital and pledged payment for the operation. Just eighteen months ago God performed a miracle for Rossie. A group of us had met for reunion at the home of Carlton, Jr. and his wife,

Cheryl. Early in the evening Rossie confided she had a large cancerous lump on her upper thigh. That lump was clearly detectable through her clothing. She described her problem to both Carlton and me. Because of her illness: she felt it necessary to leave early. Carlton came and said, "Rossie wants us to pray for her before she goes home." Rossie sat in a chair and about eighteen of us stood by touching one another as we prayed. Rev. Richard Herring and I both prayed for the Lord's will to be done. That prayer session broke up and we became involved with visiting among ourselves. A commotion broke out near the fireplace, and Carlton said, "Rossie wants to say something." She was shouting, "It's gone! The lump is gone!" **It was gone!** Before recording this miracle, I called Jim last week to verify the facts. That very real cancerous lump just disappeared that night and had not returned! Would it not be negligent not to praise the Lord?

There was a young couple in our first pastorate in Providence, Rhode Island who had lost two or three children to miscarriage. One evening about midnight, Bill called to say Anita, in her third month of pregnancy, was having labor pains. That night, standing at the foot of her bed, I took the matter up with the Lord. I remember praying, "Lord, only you know what is ahead for this baby. Only you know whether or not it is your will this baby should live. Lord if it is consistent with what you know to be best, **will you please give me the life of this baby**?" The labor pains **instantly ceased**! That beautiful dark-haired baby girl was born just months later, perfectly whole! I truly didn't think much more about it, for God was doing so many wonderful things, answering so many of our prayers. Then came the day for that baby's dedication to God. The miracle of her birth was not in the forefront of my mind. It has been my custom, through the years, to lift the newly dedicated baby up that the choir members behind me could see the baby, too. That morning, as I turned to face the choir, holding that baby girl high, God spoke to me, as clearly as He had ever witnessed, saying, "You asked for her; I have given her to you as you requested." That baby was a living, breathing human being: alive because God honored my prayer on a moment's notice! A great surge of joyous praise swept through me and I came very close to shouting. We witnessed then, before the church, of the miracle that gave her life.

One of the very nice things the Lord has done for me was to bring David Johnson and I together in friendship. We both love God so much and are so thrilled with our walks with Him. Our times together are filled with His praise, and we are truly excited about our tomorrows as we rejoice over our yesterdays. David came to work with me in the development of Liberty University. He had come from Ontario, Canada to study for the ministry and ran into problems about being able to work here. God brought us together for our mutual benefit and joy, helping us to work out David's problems. One day David came into my office, obviously troubled. He confessed he was deeply troubled and burdened. He and his wife, Marilyn, were married nearly seven years before having children. They had feared they might be childless, but God gave them Daryl. Daryl, then a small boy, was suddenly taken very ill and was in the hospital that very morning. The doctors could not determine just what was wrong, but the boy was seriously ill. David was truly anguished and distraught. It seemed God spoke peace to me about it and moved me to ask David, "Were it in your power to heal Daryl, would you do it?" David was stunned! He told me later, the question shocked him into questioning why anyone would ask a concerned father such a question. He then assured me, "Of course I would!" Then I could relay God's assurance, "David, there is someone, here in this very room, right now, Who loves Daryl more than you do, and He can!" David and I prayed, hands clasped across the desk, for Daryl, asking that God with His great love and power would heal him. God gave both of us such a sense of peace and joy. **Daryl went home from the hospital that afternoon!**

Rev. David Johnson, Marilyn, and Daryl, now joined by Janet Mae, are pastoring Bethel Baptist Church in Orillia, Ontario. God is doing wonderful things for the Johnsons and the church because He is able to express His love through their hearts and lives. Preaching at that church, I shared my belief that God must have loved them very much to send David to be their pastor. Right at this moment, I am reminded to pray for them, for Satan hates those whom God loves so much.

Spiritual Gifts

Every normal human being is naturally endowed with tremendous potential for creativity. God created man in His own image and He was the Creator of everything! Only the creative person can be truly happy and fulfilled. There are no happy human parasites. A parasite is an organism that feeds off another without contributing anything to the life of the other. If we give way to self-driven seeking for our own indulgence, nothing will ever be enough. The more we get the more we want. There never was a period in human history when so many people had so much; yet people were never more discontent. Jesus warned, "Take heed and beware of covetousness: for a man's life consisteth not in the abundance of the things which he possesseth." *Luke 12:15* It is what we do and what we are that gives contentment and fullness of life and marks our identity as the children of God.

There are many ways we express this creativity. Our tendency to excel in any of these forms of creativity may be considered talents or gifts. These natural abilities or talents are not, in themselves, **spiritual gifts**. The talent to communicate effectively, often becomes the very essence of the con artist. The nicest way to refer to a very talkative person is to say they are loquacious. This is not, in itself, a call to preach. Our talent or ability to make money – the Midas touch – may signal a greedy, acquisitive nature. The ability to lead people may come from: a domineering ego with all the potential of a dictator, a con artist or a preacher, a miser or faithful steward, a Moses or a Hitler. That all depends upon the spirit that dominates our lives. Satan would exploit all human abilities and potentialities in his effort to thwart the purposes of God. God does have a purpose for every life, but **only He knows what it is until he tells us**.

    I take exception to the idea we should psychoanalyze ourselves to discover the will of God for our lives. I do not wish my destiny to be determined by my own self analysis, nor that of anyone else. God may well have given us the natural ability to communicate that we might be an effective sales person or teacher. Our ability to make money may be His way of raising up men to finance the work of building His kingdom. Our qualities for effective leadership may signal His need for a Christian businessman or administrator. There are many pitfalls in trying to figure this out for yourself by some psychological profile. **Don't try to second-guess God!** You can **ask Him** personally! Do you really want to know His precise will for your life? Ask Him!

    Many have failed to respond to God's call to the Gospel ministry because they did not feel they were talented for it. What about Moses? God appeared to him on Sinai and told him to go down to Egypt and lead His people out. What did Moses say? "That's not my gift! I have no talent for it! I just can't talk to people!" According to some counselors I have heard, God was unreasonable to place this burden on a man so lacking in gifts and talents. Apparently Moses thought so too. Isn't it wonderful God insisted, "You are My man! I will give you everything you need!"

    God granted me the great privilege of hearing Uncle Bud Robinson preach on several occasions. Known as "Uncle Bud" to a multitude of people he was converted in a tent meeting on the western prairie. He immediately believed that God had called him to preach. When he told others of his call, almost everyone tried to talk him out of it. Why? He had no talents, no gifts, no education and he stuttered so badly it was difficult to understand him! Nothing stopped Bud Robinson, for God had called him! Uncle Bud Robinson became known from coast to coast and was more in demand than any other preacher of his day. He won untold thousands to Christ and provided the education he was denied to hundreds of young people. God healed Uncle Bud of his stuttering; but he had a lisp that became an endearing trademark for the rest of his life. There is one vignette on Uncle Bud I shall never forget. Someone asked Uncle Bud if he believed in **election of grace**. To the consternation of his Arminian friends, he replied, "Thure I believe in the electhion of grathe!" He went on to add, "The Devil hath cathed a vote against me, the Lord Jethuth Chrith hath cast a vote for me, if I vote for mythelfth, I win the electhion!"

It is also unfortunate, to the point of tragedy, that many persons have gone into the ministry because some loved one or pastor convinced them that, with all their talents and gifts, they were called to preach. Only God confers a prophet's mantle! "How shall they preach, except they be sent?" *Romans 10:15* There have been so many heartbreaking experiences during our ministry when I have prayed, "I know you called me into this, please get me out of this trial." Had I not known for certain He was leading, I may well have panicked.

God's gift to the unsaved world is His Son! *John 3:16* His gift to His children is the Holy Spirit. It is the Holy Spirit that gives us those **spiritual gifts** so essential to fulfilling God's will for our lives. As I have written elsewhere in the book, **every** Spirit-filled child of God will have **fruits** of the Spirit. Gifts of the Spirit are severally and separately, enabling us to perform our assigned tasks and glorify God.

The Father's great gift to His children is the Holy Spirit. Hear again Jesus say, "I will pray the Father, and He shall give you another Comforter, that He may abide with you forever. He shall teach you all things, and bring all things to your remembrance, whatsoever I have said unto you." *John 14:* I do not believe God will permit any honest, obedient, Spirit-filled child of His to get out of His will. It is our total surrender to God that enables Him to lift us to the highest plateau of human creativity and the fullest development of human potentiality! Paul asked the right question, at his conversion on the Damascan Road, when he prayed, "Lord, what wilt Thou have me to do?" The Lord told him precisely what to do. He immediately arose and did just that! That question should dominate our hearts and minds today. Whatever God calls us to do: He will give us everything we need to do it!

God's Call to Service

One church that I pastored was dominated by a very strong-willed man who considered himself **the** voice of authority in the church. One day, asserting himself, he began speaking by saying, "We hired you to..." He was stopped right there as I asserted, "I am no hireling! I came because God called me, and I have assumed you had prayed through and had been instructed by Him to call me. I am not here to work for you, but with you, and have presumed you too were being led by God Himself." If any one man or clique rules the church, Christ is not enthroned in that church! No congregation could pay me enough money, nor give enough benefits for me to pastor a church where a man or men were enthroned.

When discussing an invitation to pastor: the board of that

church was informed, "If I come to pastor, the church will be without a human boss! I will not dictate to the church nor permit any individual or faction to do so either. We will prayerfully seek the will of God, that He might lead through His Holy Spirit. The church is not a democracy but a theocracy under the regency of The King of Kings. We function along democratic methodology in determining what is conceived to be His will. Let us remember, the **church does not belong to us**: it is Christ's body in the earth; and we are a part of that body. **We belong to Him and to His church!**"

I have been told, by respected friends, this is too idealistic. Nevertheless, when I pledged my life – all that I had, or ever would have, all that I was or ever would be – I did not make that commitment to men, but to Jesus Christ, my Lord! I am His servant. I promised God, when taking my first church: I would never serve in a church for a paycheck and a parsonage. When He calls and gives a burden, I serve! It is necessary for me to believe my Lord has said, "These are my sheep; I want you to look after them for Me until I change your orders!" When that burden lifts, I leave. When I lose the burden or sense of responsibility: I have lost my authority. I would not serve unless confident I was a "worker together with Him!"

God granted me a good degree of success in the business world. Upon assuming the new role of pastor, I went on record to friends, that I would ask God what He wanted, and have more confidence in His instructions than in any battery of business statistics. I promised to step out on faith so boldly, people would either say, "What a wonderful God we serve!" or "What a mess that preacher made!" **Unless we attempt more than is humanly possible we are not living by faith.**

This is not to stress my **independence from men**, but my **dependence upon God**. If I cannot truly be led by the Lord, in the very center of His will: who am I to attempt to lead others? The Lord calls that "the blind, leading the blind." **Follow no man, who is not following the Lord!**

It occurred to me, very early in life: if I were to make a proper introduction of two people, I needed to know both very well. Were one, attempting an introduction, to say, "Mr. Jones, I want you to meet my good friend ... er, er, now what was your name again?" That introduction would lose much of its effectiveness. I believed then, if I were to effectively introduce others to Jesus, my Savior, it was necessary to understand people and know my Lord intimately. The desire to do both became a driving force in my life.

During the later stages of World War II, I found myself leading the packing and assembly division of the United States Naval Base 167, in Brisbane, Australia, as a chief petty officer. A former commanding officer from an assignment in New Guinea, became my new commander in Australia. On the day he took command, I explained our responsibilities of knowing all naval bases – and the ships that were to be stationed in their area for the next few months – by their code names that we might deliver everything ordered by them on purchase order or invoice. He was shown our total operations in assembling, packaging and transhipment. His reply: "I will never be here long enough to learn all this; this is your baby, you rock it. If you need gold-braid, I've got it." That man was a wise administrator who found a man able and willing to follow orders and gave him everything needed to carry them out, including the necessary authority.

Naval Lieutenant Duncan Briggs, was a son of the owner of a chain of lumber yards and building supply stores across central New York state. When the war was over he asked me to be his executive assistant in New York as I had been in New Guinea. He was told of God's call to study at Eastern Nazarene College and my intention of returning there. He replied, "I am going to pay you so much you cannot refuse!"

Years later, after Joyce and I had accepted the pastorate in Providence, leaving behind the home we were buying near the college and the salaried position with F.A. Bartlett: college president, Dr. Samuel Young, told of earlier concerns. He said, "Carlton, I was worried about you. I have seen many students, blest by God with a good position in the business world, forget what they came to school for. God gave them a source of income that they might finance their education and they made it their career." He added, "It must have been a very difficult decision." The sincere response: "Dr. Young, I would like to be a hero and say in effect, it was a tough fight but we won. That wouldn't be true at all. That decision was made when, at seventeen, all that I ever had or would have became God's to command. My only question, "Lord, what wilt Thou have me to do?" Nothing else was really important. Until that time, I did not know what God had called me to E.N.C. for. However, that desire to introduce others to Him had remained the driving force of my life.

God gave many signals concerning my call to the ministry through the years. They were not clearly understood, for He was leading step by step. I could well believe God was answering mother's prayer, even though she died before I even went to college. Perhaps the Lord has told her! It is also possible that many of those, introduced to the Lord here and now in Heaven, may have already been introduced to my mother! I don't really know what goes on in Heaven. Jesus did tell us there is rejoicing in Heaven over every soul redeemed on earth. Why wouldn't all Heaven rejoice when they came home? It would be so nice if some of those new arrivals would say to mother, "I am here because that son you introduced to Jesus, introduced me to Him too!" Jesus is so compassionate! Isn't that like something He would do?

The first of those signals of His calling came in that revival at Lynn when the Lord told me to forget myself and help Him help others. The whistle of that train, echoing across the wilderness, was yet another. In my early twenties. When God spoke of no one standing in the gaps for Him and I volunteered, was yet another. At that time, I had but one year of high school, family responsibilities, no money, and too many debts. It did not occur to me that I was being called to the ministry. It seemed greater intensity of service, as a layman was indicated, and I responded accordingly. Even when brought to E.N.C., I only knew I had been called to prepare for more effective service.

When God called to that pastorate in Providence, Rhode Island, all the fog lifted: and the vision was crystal clear. Once again I had a Commander who gave clear orders and provided everything needed for a successful mission: including authority, if I would but faithfully accept and carry my burdens of responsibility. Naval experience taught me the vital necessity for obeying orders. The total strategy for our theatre of war came down from the Commander in Chief, through the chain of command. Anyone along that chain disobeying orders or failing to fulfill his mission, aborted his own mission and that of those for whom he was responsible.

Our calling does not come with clarity because we have correctly analyzed our perceived gifts, but because we have learned to listen for His response to our prayer, "Lord, what wilt Thou have me to do?" We also need clear orders: that are faithfully obeyed, lest we abort our mission too.

These personal references, though reluctantly shared, seem necessary, for I am being a witness to reality. Nothing in this book is just an illustrative story, unless clearly defined as such. It is my prayer that these steps, carefully delineated, may encourage others as they seek to walk with God. ❖

10 Secrets of the Lord

"The secret of the Lord is with them that fear Him; and He will shew them His covenant." *Psalms 25:14* I am told by Biblical scholars the word for secret in Hebrew is sod. This indicates a whispered intimacy among close friends. Secrets not to be shared with their casual and careless acquaintances. Such secrets measure a mutual confidence, trust and love. Abraham's servant, explaining his quick success in finding Rebecca to be Isaac's wife, said: "I being in the way, the Lord led me." He was walking in intimate fellowship with the Lord and the Lord confided His instructions.

Jesus instructed His disciples, in Luke twelve, "Take ye no thought how or what thing ye shall answer, or what ye shall say: for the Holy Ghost shall teach you in the same hour what ye ought to say." Some have taken this passage to excuse indifference, laziness and lack of preparation: saying, "All I have to do is open my mouth and the Lord will fill it!" Paul tells Timothy, "Study to show thyself approved unto God, a workman that needeth not to be ashamed, rightly dividing the Word of truth." Throughout Proverbs we are urged to get wisdom: "With all thy getting, get understanding. We are urged to have reasons for the hope that dwells in us. That passage in Luke is not a comfort for the indifferent, but assurance, in spite of our limitations, He will always supply the needed answer. The Lord assured his disciples, if they would be led by His Spirit, in the hour when they had reached the end of their human resources: He would whisper the answer to them. The Holy Spirit will tell us just what to say in the hour of crisis, if we are walking with Him in loving obedience.

There have been so many times during my lifetime when I knew something was just right. I did not know why it was right, but it was right: subsequent events proved it to be absolutely right! How could I know? Simply, He had whispered the answer! I do not have to know everything or have all the data to reach a logical conclusion if I have learned to listen to the One who does know! How careful we must be **not to take personal credit**, but give God the glory.

No Scientific Atheists

One day at Brown University, a discussion group had focused on environment as a social control. Their consensus seemed to be that environment was the prime, almost exclusive factor in determining human behavioral patterns and values. They concluded a man was the product of his environment. To change a man you must change his environment. This opened the door for their social engineering. My Bachelor of Arts major was in philosophy.

Graduate studies were in sociology and I was having some difficulty reconciling the related technologies. As I listened to their discussions, in keeping with their major premises and in light of their own experiences, they were being logical. I asserted as much: going on to say, "If I came to the same conclusions you did I would be totally illogical." Explaining, "I have seen men changed in a moment, who went out to change their environment. Their environment became the product of their character and creativity. A man knelt at an altar of prayer in our church, half drunk, and arose cold sober. That man went out to change his environment and is president of our youth fellowship today!"

As a Christian fundamentalist minister I was the recognized opposition in the prevailing liberal consensus. Their chief spokesman, a brilliant student who had graduated with high honors, immediately challenged by saying, "Something new was added to his environment, you!" This was cleverly facetious, for he did not believe such an encounter would suddenly change anyone. He was simply keeping the focus on the word environment. Their concept of environment was related to education, institutions, social programs and laws. **That is when the Lord started feeding me my lines!** I responded, "We need to define what we are talking about as being the environment. If by environment you are referring to everything outside of man's id, ego or essential personality, then I agree with you! For without the introduction of God into this man's environment, the change could not have taken place!" Their spokesman was stung into making the hasty statement, "There is no God!" They expected me to try to prove the existence of God from the Bible. The Bible is the truth, it does teach the reality of His existence, but they will not accept it as evidence. They simply throw such evidence out of the court of their minds. Instead of tempting me to prove **there was** a God, this young man had now placed himself in the position of having to be able to prove **there was no** God.

Making certain he did not escape on a technicality, I asked, "Do you stick to scientific procedures in reaching your conclusions? Would you accept mystic explanations about anything, mere beliefs, or do you insist on empirical data, scientific facts in evidence? He emphatically affirmed that he did so. The next question, "Is it scientific to deny what you cannot disprove?" Actually no scientist worthy of his salt, speaking scientifically, will deny what he cannot disprove, for many things thought not to exist, do indeed exist. A scientist may say, I do not believe, as a man of faith may say, I do. That young liberal champion had to admit it was not scientific to deny what you cannot scientifically demonstrate to be nonexistent. Then the conclusive question, "Just how then did you prove the nonexistence of God?" I was almost sorry for him as his young associates waited for him to say something clever. After a moment he affirmed, "I am not an atheist, I am and agnostic!" The obvious response, "You are saying then, you simply do not know!" That young man and I did become friends and we could positively discuss the reasons for my faith and confidence.

Please believe me, I am not staging false modesty. These thoughts had never occurred to me before that time. Somebody else was being quoted! To take credit would have been plagiarism. This I did come to understand, I can learn much of what others know, but they cannot learn what I know unless they know my Lord. The Spirit-filled Christian holds the advantage if he will but pray for an understanding heart,

Atheism cannot be considered as being the achievement of a very intelligent person. Profanity speaks of an impoverished mind, lacking an adequate vocabulary to express itself. Atheism speaks of a person's ignorance of spiritual reality. When a man denies the existence of God, he is saying but one thing! "If there is a God, I have never met Him!"

Descendants of Witch Doctors

On yet another occasion at Brown, the Lord came to my aid when a professor made the statement, "Of course we know that first religious practitioners or priests were witch doctors!" He said, in effect, "All religious practitioners or priests descended from witch doctors!" To the class he was saying, "There sits the descendent of a witch doctor!" His theory was the Gospel ministry evolved from witchcraft, mythology and superstition. That professor was really a good man who frankly discussed my faith with me later on. I knew he was having fun with me. He had been shooting down fundamentalist ministers for thirty years with the same gun. At first I thought, why bother to answer? On second thought, "Why let him get away with it?" Once again, the Lord put answers into my mind. As I raised my hand, that professor's face broke into a wide grin, he thought I had taken the bait and was going to attempt proving my roots from the Bible. When recognized, I said, "Professor, while it is true, according to some sociological studies made in certain primitive folk societies: the first religious practitioner or priest recorded in those studies was the witch doctor. He was also the first M.D.; and the first sociologist! We do not condemn the medical profession today because in a primitive society weird arts of healing were practiced. And I have been in these classes long enough to know we deal very gently with the sociologists!"

Those graduate students knew very well the witch doctor not only contended with the spirits – good and bad – and practiced his own brand of medicine; but, declared tribal mores telling what was taboo as well. They realized instantly, I had, in effect, invited my fellow descendent of witch doctors to take a seat beside me. That amphitheater erupted in pandemonium. The students pounded their desks and laughed, whooping it up. It was nearly two minutes before classroom decorum returned. We know everything about nothing. Yet we can know what God knows we need to know to effectively champion truth. We are ambassadors of the God of truth.

It is important I do not leave the impression that I received a degree from those studies. After that first year I came to the realization that I could not meet the demands of a church building program, a growing congregation and earning a degree at the same time. As the time for greater specialization – deeper study on a sharper focus – made its demands, I was already studying in areas not related to the needs of my parishioners. It became an issue: am I to preach or teach? I would like to have been able to teach and seek a doctorate, but, by now, I realized God had called me to the Pastoral Ministry. This necessitated my withdrawal from Brown.

Interim at Trenton

Twenty years of pastorate and four building programs later, I faced another period of decision crucial to my service for God. The problem had its roots in my concepts of the ministry itself. You could not pay me enough to take the responsibility for the souls of a congregation unless I was certain the Lord had called me to do so. Almost every time, when approaching the pulpit, in my heart I am saying, "If You go not with me, carry me not hence!" After the children of Israel had sinned at the foot of Sinai, God forgave them; but told Moses, "Go ahead, lead them into the land; but I am not going with you!" Moses pleaded with God, "If you go not with me, carry me not hence!" I know how he felt.

God lifted the burden for the pastorate in Trenton, New Jersey. We received an invitation to another church but God did not confirm the assignment. We were to wait six years for God to make His next clear assignment. I had no way of knowing it would take God six years to work out His will within me and prepare the way before me. At that time I would not have given up even the smallest pastorate for the largest administrative post. I had already turned down three such appointments. At middle age no one would hire me to a responsible position unless assured I would make a career of it. Who would hire me when I might receive a call from the Lord at any time, and respond. I could not make a binding commitment to any employer for my commitment to God's work was total. This necessitated going into business for myself that I might support my family and still be free to respond to His call.

An outreach ministry was established. We incorporated as The Upper Room Fellowship and worked through every open door. No services or activities were scheduled at traditional church time frames, for we were not trying to start another church. We worked with established churches whenever possible. We had the weekly fellowship of praise, prayer and Bible study. We had a robed choir that ministered on request and held services in small churches. We were committed to fill whatever **gap** God pointed out to us. A dedicated, Spirit-filled, self-perpetuating board of directors led this Fellowship, without membership.

Only God knows how many people we reached for the Lord that would not have been won through traditional church activities. There was one young man, however, who alone would have made that six-year interval worthwhile. Once again, God crossed my path with one to whom He wished to be introduced. Arborvale Nursery Incorporated, the business established to finance our family and outreach ministry, majored in estate care. We received a contract working on the grounds of Trenton State College. A handsome, athletic eighteen-year-old young man applied for work and was hired. He was the typical young man, without the Lord, who was adopting the ways of the world, then strongly influenced by the hippie generation. When hearing about the Lord and God's standards, he remarked, "Mr. Gleason, nobody ever told me such things before!" He was so open, honest, responsive and perceptive that it was startling. One day, after about two weeks, as we stood on campus, the Lord spoke to me about Rick and I passed it on. Right now, in my mind, I see that very place on the grounds where I made God's pronouncement. With the deepest of conviction, I stated, "Rick, you didn't just happen to drop by looking for work; God planted you here. You are special to God – a chosen vessel. I don't know what the Lord is up to nor what His will is for your life. Your parents don't know and no one else can tell you. You never will know unless you learn to listen and God tells you Himself! Whatever it is, it's more wonderful than anything you can imagine: just don't mess Him up!"

Rick worked for me for several days before the name, Herring, rang a bell. Upon inquiry, I discovered that he was the son of Dr. Todd Herring, vice president in charge of that phase of the building development. It was he who had awarded me the contract. Dr. Herring had not spoken of work for his son, however, he could have been the one who suggested it to Rick.

We had wonderful times talking about the Lord as we worked. Rick would say later, I cannot tell you how moved I was to hear you say, "Jesus is just as real to me as you are! I am no less aware of His presence than of yours!"

Upon my return from a fishing trip to Maine, Rick seemed rather moved about something as he sought advice. He told me of a recent crisis time when he had been invited to a pot and beer party in Florida and was planning to go. Late at night, alone in his room, he struggled with the issue. He said, "I thought, if Mr. Gleason is right, that would be wrong. Then, I'll do it this once and then quit it." Rick told me that day, "All of a sudden something seemed to sweep over me; and I said, 'If it is wrong then I won't do it at all!'

CREATED TO WALK WITH GOD

I was so moved I awakened my parents and told them all about it. They were shocked for they had known nothing of all this." He then asked, "What happened to me?" How thrilled and confident I was to assure him, "Rick, you were overshadowed by the Spirit of God!" Richard Herring went forward in a youth meeting to publicly confirm his commitment to the Lord. What an honor to be selected by God to introduce Rick to Him! Richard Herring responded wholeheartedly and began learning to walk with God.

Richard went on finishing his studies and earning his degree from the New York University System in Oswego. He became involved with Christian youth groups on and off campus and received the Holy Spirit in His fullness. After graduation, he taught school for one year and then felt called to the ministry. After two years at the Seminary at NYACK, he spent two years working in a cross-cultural church in Brooklyn, New York. Rick felt he was being called as a missionary to the orient. By the time his two years were up, he was pastor of that church in Brooklyn; and it was there he was ordained.

Rick told the leadership of The Christian Missionary Alliance of "the man who was to him what Paul had been to Timothy," and requested I have a part in his ordination. The officiating elders graciously invited me to take part. I was to pronounce the benediction. During those solemn moments of the laying on of hands, God spoke to me again. I am goose pimples all over again as I recall that moment. God's communication came with clarity, "I have kept My promise made when I told you Rick was a chosen vessel." The glory of God was sweeping through my total being as I stood to pray. "Lord, I want to thank you for keeping the promise you made to me when you told me Rick was a chosen vessel months before he was even saved!" I do not believe that total prayer was more than three minutes long. When I opened my eyes almost everyone in that congregation was visibly weeping! In my heart, right now, I am confident **God pronounced the benediction** at that ordination service and placed His seal on Rick.

There was one mystery about Rick that was not cleared up for years. Why did God single out this particular young man for such special anointings? Somebody prayed! But who prayed such prevailing prayer for such an extraordinary call? This question lingered in the back of my mind for years! Rick and his wife, Wendy, were appointed missionaries to Thailand and were on the west coast preparing to fly to their assignment. One day he called to say goodbye and tell of meeting his maternal grandmother, Genevieve Townsend. She brought out a treasured broach and gave it to Wendy with the explanation: the broach had been passed to her from her mother who had received it, in turn, from Rick's great, great grandmother, Alice Clarke Jackson. She had worn that broach for years as a missionary in South America. Rick's great, great grandfather,

Rev. Henry Godden Jackson, Methodist missionary, had been called the "John Wesley" of South America. He had won souls to Christ, built churches and established works throughout that country. **Suddenly I knew who had prayed!** God had honored a man who had honored Him to the fifth generation! That man had prayed for his children, his grandchildren and all progeny, until Christ should come.

Dr. Henry Godden Jackson died on November 10, 1914. A baby boy, then six months old, born in Lynn, Massachusetts: had been appointed by God to be the person to introduce Dr. Jackson's, as-yet-to-be-born, great, great grandson to his Lord and Savior! How absolutely wonderful are the ways of God! How careful we must be to walk each step of the way with Him!

I believe God honored those prayers by stepping into the life of his great, great grandson, Richard Herring. Doesn't this remind you of Paul's statement to Timothy, "I call to remembrance the unfeined faith that is in thee, which dwelt first in thy grandmother Lois, and in thy mother Eunice; and I am persuaded that in thee also." *II Timothy 1:5* How diligent we should be in praying for our own progeny; and for others. "The effectual, fervent prayer of a righteous man availeth much!" *James 5:16*

By special arrangement of the Lord, I stopped by to visit Dr. Todd Herring and Norma Townshend Herring, when Rick's grandmother, Genevieve Townshend, was visiting them. It was such a delight to talk of our rich heritages in Christ Jesus and hear her tell of the memories of her grandfather.

Rick and Wendy, with their daughters Natalie and Tammara, have recently returned to Thailand for their third term. He is now director of a Bible college there and is studying for his doctorate.

God arranged that Rick could meet two of his brother "Timothys" at Columbia when home on furlough this last time. George Cannon, while a student at Liberty University, came to our home regularly over a period of six years. It was obvious from the beginning the hand of the Lord was upon his life. I believe God sent him to us too. George referred to our fellowship as discipleship. To me it was sharing, for he was a blessing to us too. George wanted me to participate in his ordination also, which was scheduled in Columbia, South Carolina. Rev. David Johnson came down from Canada to participate in the ordination. It was David who directed George to our home in the first place. Tentative dates for the ordination were shifted because of circumstances. Rick, meanwhile, was trying to select a place for his doctoral studies. He had gone through two false starts and now felt led to do those studies at Columbia Bible College. He arrived in town **the day of the ordination**! Joyce was standing in the hall outside our door at the motel while I brought something from the car. Someone down the hall was waving energetically to her, and she thought, "He thinks he knows me." He surely did, for it was Rick! There was another religious group in town which had taken up most all the available motel and hotel rooms in town. Joyce and I had taken the last double room. Rick had the last single room in that motel! What a glorious reunion. Jesus was there, too!

God was so nice, bringing back three of the more outstanding young men I have known for a reunion in His love. Three of us would lay hands on George and his wife, Lori, at the ordination. Four of us would stand with hands on one another's shoulders and pray for one another and the works to which He had called us. That age had come, He had shown, "The exceeding riches of His grace in His kindness toward us through Christ Jesus!" *Ephesians 2:7*

George and Lori have just accepted the pastorate of a Baptist Church in Angus, Ontario, Canada. I pray, almost every day, for these and many others, who are our progeny in the Gospel. There is a touch of guilt in all this, for I cannot identify, by name, the scores of folk that God has used to enrich our lives. To attempt to do so would be beyond the scope and purpose of this book. Those named are but illustrative of how God works in and through those totally surrendered to Him.

There is one more of that number I should reveal. Rev. Richard Waugh, now pastoring a Baptist Church in Rhode Island. His parents, Richard and Margaret Waugh, were the first couple I married after ordination. Stopping in to visit them on an impulse, I arrived just in time for the celebration of Richard's graduation from Bible Baptist Seminary of Springfield, Missouri. At the festivities, his proud dad, Richard Sr., held up a plaque honoring his son as the graduate most exemplifying the ideals and spiritual character the seminary sought to promote. As Richard lifted that plaque up for me to see, God gave me a "flashback" to the Sunday morning I dedicated Richard to the Lord with the prayer that God would place a love for Himself deep within that little heart that would be stronger than all other affections or desires. I asked God to build within him a homing device – the call of Heaven to guide him home. Just as his father had lifted up that plaque for me to see: I had lifted Richard, as a baby, for the choir and God to see. Once again, I was thrilled to the depth of my being for answered prayer. We pray for Richard and Nancy almost every day, by name! Richard's parents have been, "Dick and Margie," to our children through the years; and deeply loved by all of us.

Please permit me to introduce one more of those precious young men of God He sent our way. Stephen Nelson came to Liberty University to prepare for a life in God's service. He joined our team working to begin construction on Liberty Mountain and again the Lord witnessed He had sent someone special. His hunger for the truth, his open mind and his love for God led quickly to a strong bonding between us. When Stephen met Jesus Christ as Savior and Lord: he certainly did become a new creation. God gave me many precious memories involving Stephen. Stephen went to assist a vibrant church in Manhattan, New York. It was people like Olga Soukiouroglou that made that church vibrant. Once again, God turned matchmaker and Stephen and Olga married. They now have four beautiful children who reflect the influence of a Christ-centered home. Stephen is now assisting the pastor in a Baptist Church in Lake Mary, Florida. I know of no man more gentle, yet firm, nor humble, yet poised. How wonderful if this man's Christ-like spirit and quiet strength could spread like a contagion throughout his church and ministry. Stephen faithfully walks with God and I find joy in our fellowship, sensing we are truly kindred spirits.

God Calls to Jury Duty

There was one assignment, one gap, God had me fill while going through that trying seven-year period in Trenton, that I still do not understand! I know He ordained it, but, do not know just why! God intervened in one of New Jersey's most sensational murder trials by planting me on the jury. There is full confidence God arranged the acquittal of a man accused of murdering his wife and used my presence on the jury to do just that. His guiding hand was evident in my selection to the jury. My name appeared on the list of prospective jurors as a clergyman who was also an independent contractor. The reference to clergyman did not appear on the list to which the prosecution made reference. After the trial the prosecuting attorney told the press my name would have been stricken had he known I were also of the clergy. God used my background in business to refute two of the prosecutions main thrusts in the first ten minutes of deliberations. He also gave me the gift of **total recall** for the entire trial. God's Holy Spirit witnessed within my heart and mind as to the verdict!

At the onset of the trial I was determined to make judgment based on facts in evidence, not how I felt, nor upon my personal opinions. When the prosecution rested its case, and before the defense had begun: the prosecution had all but convinced me **the man was innocent**! They used the fact that a check, supposedly dropped in the mail slot before the mail was delivered, ended up on top of the pile. This in refutation of the defendant's assertion he was at the house at an early hour. I had sat at my office desk and watched mail come through the slot in the door. Very often the first letter through would fall free and end up leaning against the door. When the door was opened, that leaning letter would be folded over on top of other mail. The defense also testified later, a teen-age daughter had filed through the mail after its arrival.

The prosecution had sought to cast a cloud over the man's

character by alluding to the man's possession of unregistered, illiquid, nonnegotiable stock. That sounded terrible to the uninformed. However, I sat there in the jury box having ninety shares of unregistered, illiquid, nonnegotiable Arborvale Nursery Incorporated stock in a safety deposit box at the bank! What no one seemed to catch is, **all stock, at the founding of a company**, is unregistered, illiquid and nonnegotiable! That stock becomes liquid and negotiable later, when evaluated and registered. The defendant was a stock broker who specialized in the organization and incorporation of new enterprises.

Particularly offensive to any father with a pure genuine love for his children: was the prosecution's references to the obvious, mutual love and respect of this man and his children as being abnormal. There were other accusations that did not stand the test of fact or logic. It was also offensive that the prosection should attempt to play upon the jury's emotions with inflammatory rhetoric.

The defense attorney and the presiding judge did much to restore my respect for a somewhat tattered and tarnished judicial system. Both were quietly objective, incisive and decisive in the performance of their duties. There were no theatrical attempts by the defense attorney to appeal to emotion above reason.

Jury deliberations began rather tentatively, for the foreman seemed to have had little experience as a chairperson. I offered a suggestion to initiate the proceedings and he invited me to open the proceedings with my point of view. By simply stating those items already referred to and speaking to other charges: about six of the prosecutions charges were laid to rest, never to come up again in the deliberations.

There was a small group of jurors, who, believing the man guilty, stated they were going to prove him guilty. A mild version of their stated purpose might be listed as saying, "We are going to nail him!" They were offended with me when I reminded them, "I am not the defense attorney, nor are you the judge or the prosecution. We are the jury. We are charged with determining, beyond reasonable doubt, that the State had **proved this man guilty**! If we cannot function as a jury we should admit it and abort the trial!"

One of the jurors called for an opinion poll as to whether or not we thought the man guilty. I said, "No, there will be no opinion poll; we are not here to give our personal opinions! We are here to determine whether or not the prosecution proved its case!" The juror who had raised the issue shot back, "Who is going to stop us? You? I can swing from the chandelier if I want to!" They were told, "Swing from the chandelier if you want to but there will be no personal opinion poll!" Then the question, "How could you stop us?" They were informed, "If you attempt an opinion poll, I will go to the marshal outside the door and abort these proceedings." In response to their questioning, "Would you really do that?" They were told to try and see.

The prosecution had relied heavily on their **smoking gun** theory to bolster the weak case. This was based on the testimony of a secretary who asserted the defendant had called, indicating his wife had not picked up the children before he could have legitimately known they were not. The assumption was: he knew why they were not going to be picked up. This secretary gave precise testimony concerning the white memo pad and what was done with it. The defense team recalled a memo in a file that had been turned over to them and checked it out. That memo was a sheet from a yellow legal pad noting the calls referred to by the secretary. It was her **actual recording of calls** for that time frame. Other calls referred to were checked with those calling in. This established her testimony as falsifying the time of the defendant's call and supporting his testimony of the sequence of events. This legal pad notation, in her handwriting, totally refuted her **smoking gun** testimony. Following her questioning by the defense: the prosecution sought, in cross-examination, to reinstate her earlier, disproved testimony through suggested suppositions.

This secretary's testimony was the issue that kept the jury deliberating into the second day. That night, in my hotel room, I took it up with the Lord. I recall telling the Lord, "I don't know if this man is really guilty or not, but the prosecution certainly has not proven it. I shall have to vote for acquittal, but, I do not want to set a guilty man free. Please help me to know whether or not this man should be free. Let the decision be made in such a manner, I will know you did it!"

During the deliberations that next day, I sought to point out the ploy of the prosecution in seeking to reinstate the original smoking gun testimony through supposition in recross questioning. One of the jurors, rather belligerently said, "Are you trying to tell us what we heard?" They were assured they did not have to take my word for it, just have the transcript read. This was done several times that day. That transcript supported what I had said verbatim! There had been total recall of every testimony during the trial.

A fellow juror, an executive from *The Wall Street Journal*, whispered to me and said, "No use arguing with them, they are only fighting you!" Taking his advise, I rested my case. Shortly after that my friend from *The Journal* said, "Something is going on, they are just talking quietly among themselves." **I believe God had stepped in!** They called for one more reading of a portion of the transcript and admitted the lack of facts in evidence. One of the more vocal of that group told the press later, "That case should never have come to trial; it was based on supposition: we had no real evidence!" When our foreman announced in court, "We find the defendant not guilty," a thrilling surge went through me from the soles of my feet to the roots of my hair! God did confirm to me **He had voted acquittal**. I still do not know the facts concerning it all as He knows it. I know He brought about this acquittal, but do not know why He did so. This hangs in my mind as an unanswered question to this day.

Wilderness Wandering?

There are many times, during that transitional period, I seemed to be wandering along, feeling my way one day at a time. There was not that sense of destiny unfolding that usually marked my walk with the Lord. Sometimes I felt more like Elijah under his juniper tree. At what I considered the peak of preparation for service, I did not know just where to serve. It seemed at times that God had placed me upon a shelf and had forgotten where He had put me. Looking back upon that period I see many vital lessons being taught. I learned the lesson of Satan's influence through reaction, to be offset by taking things directly to God in prayer. I learned to praise Him **for** hardship and suffering rather than **in spite of** them. He taught the way to overcome resentment over the wrongdoing of others was to put them on top of a very special prayer list. Apparently I needed an extended time of waiting before God.

One day, walking the floor of my living room, I prayed, "Lord, whatever you are trying to do, will you please do it. Give me what I need to make me **something** You can use!" Now, you may question the vocabulary, but God spoke to me in good old, down-Maine terminology: "You nogginhead, you are walking the floor asking Me to make something out of you that I might use you: I am trying to make **nothing** out of you that I might use you!" Had you been in the room at that moment, you would have heard me say out loud, "Lord, I'm lower than a snake's ankles right now! How low do I have to get?" It seems there had been too much Gleason in what I had been doing. This came at my lowest point and God was preparing a new calling. It was only weeks later God called me to work with Dr. Jerry Falwell in the building of Liberty University.

The timing was perfect! Dr. Jerry was not ready to begin construction on the mountain until just that time. During those nearly seven years of preparation, among other things, I updated expertise in estate care and construction, learned new lessons in management and learned to listen to the Lord more clearly. Equity had been built up in the house and business and a new era had dawned for us financially. During my entire ministry, up until that time, we had lived from week to week, never building any financial security or reserve. The Old Time Gospel Hour purchased my entire inventory of equipment, we sold our home for nearly $25,000 more than we paid for it and both Joyce and I became employed by the ministry of Dr. Jerry. We purchased land and had a custom-built home constructed upon it. Today we have a home free of debt and owe nothing on anything. Our income exceeds our needs; and, we have been given enough to share with the needy around us and with others laboring for the Lord as He directs. **Neither our security nor our joy rests on these things, but upon our wonderful God who has given them!** How I thank God for those seven years of preparation. That really wasn't wandering at all. God was just staging for future campaigns! ✢

11 *In the Presence of the Enemy*

Understanding the Opposition

Success in warfare demands we have good intelligence concerning our enemy. We need to identify our enemy, know his strengths, weaknesses, and his battle stratagems. Many who deny God are very much aware of the Devil. As God's Holy Spirit is quenched and God is grieved, there has been a great revival of the demonic and the occult. In my youth, people joked about the Devil and his impact on our society as a whole. It is no longer a laughing matter to those who are alert to the revival of satanic powers. The activity of satanic cults and societies are shocking even the seasoned law enforcement officers who have to deal with them. They see much greater evidence of Satan than of the power of God because more people are giving way to Satan, than are being led by the Spirit of God! As people reject God, Satan moves in to fill the spiritual vacuum. All nature abhors a vacuum! We were designed at creation to be a habitation for God's Holy Spirit. If we reject His right to reign, we "give place unto Satan"!

Satan is not a bad god, he is a bad archangel! He is not God's opposite, he is God's opposition. He is the enemy of God, and of everything good. He never could stand in direct confrontation with God. He, himself, was created by God as the most beautiful of archangels. Satan can successfully strike at God only through others less powerful than he. He led rebellion in Heaven, and a third of those subordinate angels joined his rebellion. Cast down to earth he incited rebellion in Adam and Eve, bringing the horrible disfiguring, destructive power of sin onto the human race. He is God's opposition and ours as we seek to serve God and win lost mankind back to Himself.

There are ditches on both sides of nearly all of life's pathways. Our tendency to extremes, on one side or the other, is often referred to as **the swing of the pendulum**. We often hit the opposite ditch in reflex action. Finding the **golden mean** or traveling the middle of the road is often difficult. There are two ditches we must avoid when dealing with the occult or the satanic.

Those on one extreme consider the Devil to be the figment of another's overactive imagination: that he, too, is just a myth. He is no joke! It was he that brought degeneration to mankind, broke the heart of God and necessitated the death of His only Son! He will cause eternal, spiritual death to all who follow him. It is imperative we take him seriously and seek to oppose him under the whole counsel of God. He can be just as real to those who submit to him: as God can be to those who submit to Him! As master, he will promote his agenda through his servants, even as God works out His will through those who surrender to Him!

The ditch on the other side of the road is also very dangerous. Many, aware of who and what he is, are obsessed with a fear of him. **To have an obsession with the satanic is almost as bad as being indifferent to him.** Many sensitive Christians live in fearful fascination concerning Satan and his forces of evil. We never need fear Satan if we truly fear God and serve Him faithfully. Neither God nor Satan can posses us without our consent. God has given us the power of choice. We make the choice of masters. A born-again Christian may be oppressed by Satan, but cannot be possessed, if he is "walking in the light" of the known will of God!

We must neither be indifferent nor obsessed. We will serve Satan or serve God. We must reject Satan to serve God, for we are born in servitude to Satan. Satan will not give up, however, until Heaven's gates close behind us. We need not fear Satan, if the Spirit of God indwells us. "Ye are of God, little children, and have overcome them; because greater is He that is in you, than he that is in the world!" *I John 4:4* Are you familiar with the word **osmosis**? Osmosis is a positive flow from the greater to the lesser density. We see this illustrated when a soaking wet sponge is forced up against a dry sponge. After a period of time they will both have the approximate density of water. Unless the Spirit of God indwells us: there will be a "backflow" from the world. Satan is so much more powerful than we. However, if the Spirit of the Living God does dwell in us, there will be a positive flow through our spirits to bless a sin-darkened world.

Visiting on the coast of Maine, I saw rack after rack of salting codfish. Those cod were so saturated with salt, they could rest in piles on a grocery store shelf without spoilage. What was amazing to consider: those same cod had been swimming in an ocean of saltwater all their lives without absorbing any salt. How come they now absorb it so completely? It was simply the principle of osmosis and the power of life. As long as those cod were alive, the life principle within them prevented the salt from seeping into them. When that life principle died, the salt could penetrate without resistance. We who are spiritually alive cannot become saturated with the world because we are alive! God have mercy on those trying to fight off the invasions of Satan without that indwelling power that is the greater force. The love of God, personified in the Spirit of God, is the only force capable of overcoming the forces of hate in the world!

There have been several times when Satan was as real to me as any object in the room. I knew just where he was. Only once did anyone I know claim a visible sighting. I have only the testimony of the man involved, but let me tell it to you as he reported what he saw. A medical doctor, to whom I had been witnessing, was in the hospital awaiting surgery for a condition verified by X-ray. I visited him the evening before the scheduled surgery, just after regular visiting hours. He was suffering from a high fever and the surgery was in doubt. As I recall, I was not aware of demonic presence at the time – just a deep concern, a burden, I thought, because of his physical needs. However, I prayed God to dismiss all malevolent power, guide the doctors and nurses, and pray that the Great Physician would oversee the operation. I prayed for his spiritual welfare, too, for a clear witness to salvation was lacking. After Bible reading and that prayer, I left. The next morning, I returned, hoping to find him doing well in the recovery room. He was still in his private room. He opened conversation with the apology, "You may not believe what I am going to say, but it is true! I am a doctor and know I was not hallucinating nor had I taken any hallucinogens!" He continued, "Almost immediately after you had prayed last night and left, the fever broke and evil little faces leered at me from that water glass. They mocked me saying, 'We are coming back, we are coming back!' I lay here in terror nearly all night calling on the name of Jesus, and pleading the Blood. About two o'clock this morning the faces disappeared and I went to sleep. This morning, when the operating surgeon came to prepare me for the operation, there was no sign of what they were going to operate for! I am going home later today!"

That afternoon I talked with his wife and asserted, "Satan cannot invade without consent, when was your husband involved with the occult?" She explained they had once opened their home to a spiritualist medium who encouraged her husband to play with spinning orbs and other items for divination. That was when my doctor friend was invaded by demonic powers! I hesitated to record this as being too sensational, but it was a clear testimony from an eyewitness in whom I have confidence. Then too, there are the medical records concerning his case.

There is another instance of attempted invasion by satanic forces, witnessed to by perhaps ten or more persons. Our granddaughter, Courtney, accepted the Lord as her Savior at about three years of age and her life testified to this with fruits of the Spirit. In her mid-teens she changed to public schools and established a new circle of friends. She invited a group of them to a pajama party at our daughter's rather spacious country home. Some of the girls were not from devout Christian homes, and one of them brought a Ouija board. The young people played with it for a little while and it responded to all questions. Courtney became troubled and went down to ask her mother, "Do we believe in Ouija boards?" Our daughter, Lynne, replied, "No, we never permitted them in the home for they are associated with the Devil!" Courtney went back upstairs and Lynne followed to stand and listen just outside the door. The young people were shocked at the thought the board was associated with the Devil. After a brief moment, our grandson, Jerry, spoke up and suggested they ask the Ouija board if it was associated with the Devil. The question was asked, and for the first time the board did not move. Someone suggested they ask it why it did not answer. The question was put to the board and the board spelled out, "God in the house". They then asked the board, "Where is God?" The board spelled out, "In Courtney"! Why Courtney? Her mother is one of the most spiritually-minded women I know. All others in the home knew the Lord, too. We came to the conclusion, after considering the matter, God had chosen Courtney to be His spokesperson, as she had been the one to first challenge the Ouija board.

Just a few years ago, a demonically possessed person infiltrated a youth group in a church in Canada, through a professed contemporary Christian singer. His influence was immediately felt. George Cannon told me of the suspicion this was true as he and a group from Liberty University were planning to hold youth services there. They met at our home, and the young people sought counsel on how to confront the demonic influence. Judging from past encounters, the following preparations were suggested. Take no one with you that is not truly filled with the Spirit. Fast and pray for power and grace and stay prayed up. It was suggested that God would probably single out one of them to lead the confrontation. This is what happened with Courtney. The group did go and were successful on their mission. It was very evident God had singled out the one to confront the demonic influence. Satan has no fear nor respect for us. He despises us for our vulnerability and weakness. He is impressed only when he is confronted by the Spirit of God within us. When he attempts to stare us down, and sees Jesus within looking back at him, he knows he has lost unless he can frighten us into unwise reactions.

George Cannon ran into another occultist when on maneuvers with the National Guard. This man had been boasting of tormenting professed Christians and baiting them into wrong doing. Someone asked him if he had tried that on one man known to be very devout. He is reported as replying, "I can't touch him. He is a real Christian!"

Do not play with anything related to the occult! The Devil won't be playing games with you! Remember, you are on a **battleground**, not a playground, and **Satan is the enemy**! When you play with spinning orbs, tarot cards, Ouija boards or any other fetish used in divinations, you are playing with the occult. You are also giving a measure of consent and opening the door, "giving place to Satan". Spiritual mediums and fortunetellers are also used to permit satanic powers to access our hearts and minds. He is no joke! He is the enemy that would cause your spiritual death if he could but get by God's Holy Spirit. I have heard folk jest of "kicking the Devil around"! Only God has the power to kick him around. Do not submit, through hypnosis, by anyone! When you surrender your mind to any other mind or spirit, **be very sure it is the Mind**

and Spirit of God! The rarest of exceptions occur when trained psychiatrists are probing for hidden guilt in a troubled mind. **Don't ever attend a religious gathering to laugh, mock, or watch what you think to be somewhat of a circus.** If it is satanic, and you are not there on official business for the Lord, you are quenching the Spirit of God within you, and have dropped much of your protective immunity and are endangered. If those people are truly worshipping God, in a manner strange to you, you are mocking God! I have gone, only once, to a service where I did not go to worship. That was in an attempt to free a young man who had become bound to that which distorted God's truth. At that session, when coming under attack, I followed the example of Jesus with, "It is written!" God has given the answer to everything vital to victory in this warfare in His Word! Michael, the archangel, faced the Devil's challenge correctly, according to Jude, verse nine. "Michael, the archangel, when contending with the Devil disputing about the body of Moses, "durst not bring against him a railing accusation, but said, the Lord rebuke thee!" It is not our resolve or authority that gives us the victory. "**Submit yourselves therefore to God.** Resist the Devil, and he will flee from you!" *James 4:7* **I now bear witness to the love and power of God**: there have been several occasions in my life when Satan was assuredly present. I have rebuked him in the name of Jesus, **commanded him to leave**, and knew precisely when he left. Again, if you fear God, you need fear no one else! When **Jesus sent out His disciples** to go before Him and preach the kingdom: He gave them **power and authority over all devils!** *Luke 9:1* Not just some of the disciples, **all of them!**

God taught me a great deal about dealing with the demonic when an afflicted woman in New Jersey called, seeking God's help. She was counseled a number of times on the phone and sent me a detailed warning for Christians on yellow writing paper, later. She would not identify herself in any manner. She began her phone conversation by describing her condition, mentally, physically and spiritually. I acknowledged the symptoms described could be physical, mental or spiritual but the evidence of a malevolent intelligence suggested demonic possession. Her reply, "I thought you would detect it. I am demonically possessed!" She went on to describe how she submitted to hypnosis at an office party and the person who hypnotized her was under demonic control. That demonic power took over her mind and had such control that he could read her thoughts and knew everything she was doing. I responded, "If that is true then he knows you are talking to me now." She affirmed that he did, but added, "I knew I was exposing you and your family to great danger for he is very jealous. I have prayed for you and **I know your Jesus will look after you**." She was asked, "If he has such power over you, how were you able to call me?" She said, "I prayed for **three hours calling on the name of**

Jesus before I had strength enough to pick up the phone!" I inquired as to why she had called me. She told me, "I knew you were of the Holy Spirit!" God's Spirit had witnessed to my spirit that I was a child of God, but here I had confirmation from the opposition. Remember, that happened to Courtney, too? In Acts nineteen, the demonic said, "Jesus I know and Paul I know; but who are you?" Satanic powers know your spiritual condition also. If the Holy Spirit abides in His fullness, Satan cannot possibly touch you unless you give place to him. Remember that admonition, "Be ye angry, and sin not: let not the sun go down upon your wrath: neither give place to the Devil." *Ephesians 4:26-27* **"Blessed assurance, Jesus is mine!"**

One of the very special young men God sent to us, that we might share His love with them, came to us during the first year of our ministry in Providence, Rhode Island. He was among the most deeply spiritual men we have ever known. Converted while serving in the United States Navy, and filled with the Spirit, he studied the Bible, almost exclusively, hours and days on end. He had asked that the indwelling Author of the Bible explain the Book to him. He would fast days on end, and memorized scriptures by the hundreds of verses. This man was **walking with God** in intimate fellowship the day I met him. He was, however, in spiritual turmoil. Satan must have known what God would do in and through that young man's life, for he set a very subtle snare in his pathway. The coldhearted, indifferent, materialistically-minded are seldom in danger of fanaticism. It is the fervent, all-out, seeking and totally surrendered Christian who is in danger of surrendering to the wrong spirit. In his zeal for everything God had for him, this young man had become ensnared by a demonic cult. He earnestly sought for everything they insisted he must have, and took part in all their expressions of worship. **Satan could not invade his heart for the Holy Spirit was already in residence!** It was **his mind** that satanic forces had invaded! He did not know for sure if he were sane or insane, saved or unsaved. This group presented so much truth he could not doubt it, and so much error he could not believe. Mentally, he tended to believe them to be of the Lord. Spiritually, the Lord restrained and protected him. I am certain it was the Lord who brought him to us. Satan had almost persuaded him to walk a path he could not walk or share with God. He was at a fateful crossroad!

We were not wise enough to supply the necessary answers in solving his dilemma, but God was: when this young man could relax in God's love and take time to wait for His assurance. Long months of sharing God's truth and love brought comfort, healing and the clear witness of the Spirit. The path to walk with God became clear again, and this very special young man was set free! One of the most wonderful things about all these crises lay in the fact this young man did not permit his disillusionment to steal his fervor nor his love for God! So many who have been caught up in the frenzy of fanaticism, lose their zeal and fervor when they lose faith in the deception. Simple faith is often crushed in the crisis.

We were delighted to share our home with this anointed man of God as we shared our love in Christ. He became, and has remained, a vital part of our family. Joyce would tease him by saying, "Give some nice girl a break and take her out on a date!" His response, "That is all up to the Lord. He will choose the girl I am to marry and I am not interested in just dating." He was true to his word. God led him to Bob Jones University, where he was still waiting during his senior year for God to tell him just whom he would select. A young lady, called to the mission field and also in her senior year, had made the same commitment: "Lord, you pick him out!" She would testify that she prayed, "Lord, I am almost ready to leave for the field, and I don't want to go alone!" One day God arranged their meeting on campus, and each of them heard Him say, "This is my choice!" They became engaged, but she went on to Japan before they were married. He stayed behind for another year of study. His main reason for remaining behind, however, was to train leadership to carry on the child evangelism and youth rally work he had organized. They were married in Japan one year later and have been working for God for more than forty years!

To report properly on their ministries alone, would require more than one book. Someday someone may write such a book. Only God knows how many thousands have found peace, directly and indirectly, through their expressed love for the Lord. Multiple scores of churches have been established. Their goal is to establish 100 churches by the year two thousand.

We who believe in being led by God's Holy Spirit: must guard against Satan's counterfeits. I could have a pocketful of counterfeit bills and not know it. If suspicious, I would take them to the bank and have them examined by an expert. It is very much like that in spiritual things. Satan's counterfeits are so cleverly done as to deceive even the elect of God. We need to take our problems of discernment up with an expert. In I John, four: "Beloved, believe not every spirit; but try the spirits whether they are of God; because many false prophets are gone out into the world." God does give discernment when His Holy Spirit leads and instructs.

Spiritual Fifth Column

During The Spanish Civil War the forces of General Franco were approaching Madrid, attacking in four columns from four different directions. As Franco and his staff studied the battle plans, one asked him, "Which of the columns do you think will reach the city first?" The general replied, " The fifth column; it is already there!" Rebel forces had already infiltrated the city and were organized, ready to strike at the moment of battle. We, too, have been infiltrated by a spiritual fifth column, waiting to undermine our defenses at the height of combat.

Much doctrinal controversy arises over our concepts concerning man's dual nature. This is about as close as I expect to get regarding negative positions. I have no desire to prove others wrong, but believe there must be a positive assertion of that which I most certainly do believe. **Man was created with a dual nature!** He was given a physical body for his walk through time. This body was just a temporary habitation for an eternal spirit. One day it was to return to dust. He was given many of the body functions of the animals God also made. We were given hunger and thirst that we might know when to respond to the body's needs. We were given sexual urges that we might perpetuate our species.

The evolutionists have used these similar, basic functions and instincts to prove Homo sapiens descended from other forms of animal life. There have been similarities through the years as we compare Cadillac, Oldsmobile, Pontiac and Chevrolet cars. Many of the popular features of the Cadillac end up in the Chevrolet, years later. Do Chevrolets descend from Cadillacs? Of course not! They all had the same designers and manufacturers in General Motors. Why should not all of God's creations reflect the creativity of their common designer?

We were also created in God's own image and given an eternal spirit that should live forever, somewhere. Our greater reality is in the realm of the spiritual. God created us to be indwelt by His Holy Spirit, that we might become temples of God. Through us, He intended to produce the fruits of His Spirit. Man, however, opened the door for invasion by a malevolent spirit we call carnal. This carnal spirit becomes the fifth column of Satan. This carnal spirit invaded mankind when Adam gave Satan access to his mind and heart through rejecting the commandment of God. Our carnal nature thus became **a third element**, effecting our inmost being. It is this **carnal nature, or spirit that must be crucified!** Paul said, "I am crucified with Christ, yet I live, yet not I but Christ liveth in me!" *Galations 2:20* What died when Paul was crucified? Certainly not his human nature. He said of his human nature, "I die daily." Or, "I die out to self, everyday. I keep my body under control. I discipline myself, permitting Christ to reign in me." **It was the carnal spirit, that fifth column of the soul, that was crucified.**

When we die out to self, in total surrender that we might be filled with His Spirit, **self is crucified**. When James speaks of the double-minded man, unstable in all his ways, he is speaking of the **un-crucified life**. This man still has that root of bitterness that springing up defiles. *Hebrews 12:15* He is fighting a war on two fronts. There are those who say there is no way to end this war in this life. They contend we must wrestle constantly with that fifth column agent throughout our lifetime. **That simply is not true!** We not only can die out to self, we must! When we are crucified with Christ, **the carnal spirit dies**! However, our natural, sensuous, demanding, human nature is very much alive. One might think of being in the flesh as being carnal. We must distinguish between natural human, sensuous nature, and the perverted **carnal spirit** that marks our spiritual fall. It is this carnal spirit that must be crucified. The natural human nature must be disciplined under the guidance of the Holy Spirit. Satan will seek to entice us through the perversion or misuse of our natural body. God's word says, we sin when, "drawn by our own lusts and enticed." *James 1:4*

How could this struggle between human nature and our spiritual nature be stated more clearly than in Romans, eight? Permit me to highlight portions of this chapter, four through fourteen: "The righteousness of the law is fulfilled in us who walk, not after the flesh, but after the Spirit. To be carnally minded is death; but to be spiritually minded is life and peace. The carnal mind is enmity against God: for it is not subject to the law of God, neither indeed can be. **But ye are not in the flesh, but in the Spirit**, if so be the Spirit of God dwell in you. Therefore, brethren, we are debtors, **not to live after the flesh**. For if ye live after the flesh, ye shall die: but if ye through the Spirit do mortify the deeds of the body, ye shall live. For as many as are led by the Spirit of God, they are the sons of God."

Many are thrown into confusion at this point because of the misconception that Romans, chapter seven, is a Christian's testimony. Strangely enough this chapter is wedged in between two chapters that **totally contradict it as a Christian witness**. We must remember this doctrinal book is written to contrast Law and Grace. Take a few highlights from chapter six, "**How shall we, that are dead to sin, live any longer therein?**" Knowing this, that our **old man is crucified** with him, that the **body of sin might be destroyed, that henceforth we should not serve sin**. Let not sin therefore reign in your mortal body (human flesh), that ye should obey it in the lusts thereof. Neither yield ye your members as instruments of unrighteousness unto sin: but yield yourselves unto God as instruments of righteousness unto God. Sin shall not have dominion over you!"

Please prayerfully compare these passages in chapter seven with those stated from six and eight. "For we know that The Law is spiritual: but I am carnal <u>sold</u> under sin. For that which I do I allow not: for what I would, that do I not; but that which I hate, that do I. For the good that I would, I do not; but the evil which I would not, that I do. I find then a <u>law</u>, that when I would do good, evil is present with me. O wretched man, that I am! who shall deliver me from the body of this death?"

How could one sold unto sin be redeemed? Could one say, "I am crucified with Christ" and still be carnal in spirit? Could one serving the flesh be led by the Spirit of God as instructed in chapter eight? **Could one quenching the Spirit be walking in the Spirit?** Could this be the testimony of the man who asked on the Damascan Road, "Lord what wilt thou have me to do?", **and got up and did it!** Is this the man that told the people of the churches how to live holy, victorious lives, actually doing the will of God? Is he the one who said, "**I can do all things through Christ who strengtheneth me**"? Could this possibly be the testimony of the same man who said, "I have fought a good fight, I have finished the course, I have kept the faith"? **Of course not!** Chapter seven is Paul's testimony as the zealous Pharisee who wanted to serve God, but found himself persecuting Christians instead. He is the man who **loved the law, but couldn't live it** because of the law of sin in his members. He had not yet become a new creature in Christ Jesus. Old things had not passed away, all things had not yet become new! Were that a Christian testimony in chapter seven, what died when Paul was crucified, what changed when he became a new creation in Christ?

Paul's Christian testimony begins in chapter eight, "There is now no condemnation to them in Christ Jesus who walk not after the flesh, but after the Spirit. For the law of the Spirit of life in Christ Jesus hath made me free from the law of sin and death."

This may well be upsetting to some; yet, I can see absolutely nothing in the Word that would mark Romans chapter seven as a Christian's testimony. I fear Satan has used this passage not only to confuse, but to provide an alibi for failure. Perhaps, even a rationale to sin! I have heard folk remark, "If Paul could not live the standards of the Gospel he preached, how could I hope to do so?" I have even had folk ask, "Do you think you are a better man than Paul?" As I had testified, God is able to keep and there is victory in Jesus! **To declare Romans seven, Paul's testimony as a Christian is a terrible put down of the great apostle!** Just study that testimony, comparing it with what he told the churches, in his letters, concerning how they should be living. Please do not tarnish the witness of Paul to, consciously or subconsciously, provide alibis for our own failures!

All of us find it offensive when someone boasts of their own holiness and perfection. We react negatively toward those who seem to say, "Believe what I say, be like me and you will be alright, too." Personally, I also react negatively to those who boast of their filthy, sinful state. They seem to say, "Poor, rotten, sinful, dirty old me, I am such a mess, but God loves me, a saint on the way to Heaven." How does the world distinguish between a sinning sinner and a sinning saint? What happens to the verse, "By their fruits shall ye know them"? Should it not be possible to tell what people believe by the way they live? What kind of witnesses should we be? What are we witnessing to? Did Jesus really die just to "fix our tickets at headquarters"? Does not God really see us as we are? Is He not trying to clean us up and fit us for Heaven? Does He really want us to be like Jesus? Is He like a sloppy housekeeper who sweeps things under the rug where He cannot see them? Can the blood of Jesus Christ, God's Son cleanse **from** all sin? Does the cleansing blood go deeper than the stains have gone? Is God able to cleanse and keep? **If He is able, why are we not delivered? We should not excuse in our lives, that which caused His death.** If I am not cleansed by the blood and made holy by His Presence, it certainly is not His fault! To reaffirm a previously stated belief, I see absolute, eternal security in the love of Christ. I see no security, whatsoever, in sin! Let us consider, again, what God said to Peter at Joppa when he let down the sheet from Heaven, "**What God has cleansed, call thou not unclean!**" He was referring to people in the persons of Cornelius and his friends. *Acts 10:14* Jesus when addressing the Father in His high priestly prayer, reveals something of what eternal life truly is. "**This is life eternal**, that they might know Thee the only true God, and Jesus Christ, whom thou hast sent." *John 17:3* Differing definitions of sin may be a problem. What constitutes sin? If by sin you mean all deviation from the perfect will of God: then of course you will sin in thought, word and deed every day. We finite creatures have no way of knowing the perfect, absolute will of our infinite God; let alone doing it. I do not consider my children disobedient unless they disobey my known will. I do not hold them accountable for what they do not know. I discipline them on the basis of what they do know, and what they would know if they were obedient. Only abusive parents punish their children on the basis of what they themselves know. I do not believe my God is such a Father.

No one can say they have not sinned and therefore do not need a Savior! There are, indeed, none righteous, no not one, before they meet the Savior. When He casts my sins into the sea of His forgetfulness, I become a former sinner, saved by grace. Old things passed away and I became a new spiritual creation. There have been so many times I have failed in my trying! But every time, I have asked forgiveness when convicted by His Spirit. I find myself frequently saying, "I am sorry, please forgive me!" to My Lord, my wife and very often to others. He still forgets, when He forgives! **Disobedience, born in a rebellious spirit, is still the root cause of sin.**

There will always be a struggle between our earthy, temporal bodies and our eternal spirit. When our bodies need food or water we hunger and thirst and seek out what is needed to sustain life. We may even be moved to indulgence. When physically tired out, we find rest in sleep. We have frequent medical checkups to be sure we remain healthy. Neglect the body, abuse it with bad habits, and you may cut years off your natural life span. Sometimes we indulge the body at the expense of our souls, and endanger our eternal relationship with God. Should we not take even better care of the soul than the body?

Fasting may take many forms. It may be: a denial of food or drink for the body, an extended period dedicated to prayer and meditation, or a period devoted almost exclusively to spiritual objectives. Whatever the form taken, it is basically our serving notice on the body; we are giving priority to spiritual things and the needs of our own souls and others. This is often necessary to keep our values and priorities focused on the eternal. This is what is referred to as mortifying the deeds of the body. Paul called it, "keeping the body under". How awful when our destiny is determined by sensual desire! Early in life, I became determined my body should be the servant of my soul. It is still my desire to be a servant of God who's body serves both God and myself at His command.

Playing The Fool or Keeping The Faith

There is a clear picture in my mind right now of an extraordinary young man. He is very tall, athletically built and handsome. People turn to watch him as he goes by. You just can't miss him in a crowd for he stands out so clearly. What is not so immediately noticeable: he is humble and self-effacing. He seems totally unaware that there is anything special about himself. He has great respect for his proud father who can trust him with responsibilities. What a promising young man!

There is yet another young man in sharp focus. What a contrast! This man is short and not very good looking. He is very opinionated, insisting he is right in just about everything: becoming very quarrelsome when disagreed with. Wherever he goes, trouble seems to follow him. He is often escorted out of public places because of disturbing the peace. He has been known to even physically assault those he disagreed with. No one would list him as one likely to succeed in anything.

By an unusual coincidence I happen to have conclusive evidence just how both of them did turn out. One shouted in triumph, "I have fought a good fight, I finished the course, I have kept the faith!" The other cried, "I have played the fool and erred exceedingly!" Had you not already identified these men: you would have thought, "I knew that young man of promise would make it big!" You would also have identified that troubled young man as having played the fool. How mistaken you would have been!

The Bible gives an accurate case history of both men. Strangely enough, both were named Saul! Saul, son of Kish, God's own choice for Israel's first king, and Saul of Tarsus, God's own choice as His first missionary to the Gentiles. What in the world happened to bring about such unexpected results? Why these surprise endings?

The Bible records, "And when Samuel saw Saul, the Lord said unto him, behold the man I spake to thee of! The same shall reign over My people." Again, "And Samuel said unto all the people, see ye him whom the Lord hath chosen, that there is none like him among all the people." *I Samuel 9:17, 10:24* **What turned all that around?** Saul's first great error, **He presumed to worship God in his own way, rather than as instructed**. In modern vernacular, "he did his own thing"! In his haste, and under external pressures: he presumed upon the priest's office and offered a sacrifice of expediency! Samuel rebuked him, "Thou hast done foolishly: thou hast not kept the commandment of the Lord thy God." *I Samuel 13:13* He was warned that such disobedience would cost him the kingdom. However, Saul, rebellious and being corrupted by his sense of power, went on to even more direct disobedience. This is recorded in chapter fifteen. Saul had been commanded by God to destroy the Amelekites to the last man and to take no spoil of the enemy. He greedily kept vast numbers of cattle and sheep and spared the life of their king, bringing him in as a trophy. Saul assured Samuel he had obeyed orders, seeking to talk his way out of the consequences for disobedience. Neither Samuel nor the Lord were impressed! Samuel's rebuke: "To obey is better than sacrifice. For rebellion is as the sin of witchcraft, and stubbornness is as iniquity and idolatry. Because thou hast rejected the word of the Lord, He also hath rejected thee." We have this recorded: God's Holy Spirit, grieved and quenched, withdrew from Saul and an evil presence invaded him. The rest of his life was one of disobedience to God and tyranny upon those under his authority. Finally, as life and his enemies closed in, at his **moment of truth**, when nothing else mattered, he cried, "I have **played the fool** and erred exceedingly." *I Samuel 26:21*

Saul of Tarsus, on the other hand, as a self-righteous Pharisee persecuted the Church, even to the point of slaughter. Blinded by his own prejudices, he thought he was **serving God** and defending the Law of God by **persecuting and destroying the followers of the Son of God**. One day, on the road to Damascus with warrants for the arrest of Christians there, the Lord Jesus Christ confronted him! Jesus asked him, "Saul why are you persecuting Me?" Startled and blinded by the light from Heaven, Saul asked, "Just who are you?" Our Lord replied, "I Am Jesus!" Saul was to say later, "I became an apostle, born out of due season." Saul of Tarsus, became Paul, the apostle! The newly called apostle asked, "Lord, what wilt Thou have me to do?" God told him, and **in obedience he went out and did it**! God confirmed Paul's commission to His servant, Ananias of Damascus, saying, "Go thy way for he is a chosen vessel unto Me, to bear My Name before the Gentiles, and kings, and the children of Israel." *Acts 9:15*

Paul, in his moment of truth, awaiting execution in prison, when nothing else really mattered: raised a triumphant battle cry above the carnage of his battlefields, "I have fought a good fight, I have finished the course, I have kept the faith." *Second Timothy 4:7*

Both Sauls were commissioned by God to great tasks in His causes among men. Both were told exactly what was expected of them. Each was anointed by God's Holy Spirit that they be enabled to fulfill their appointed destinies. **One obeyed, the other did not!**

Each and every one of us is either playing the fool or keeping the faith, right now! We may seek to evade the issue, postpone it, or even reject the concept. However, **our moment of truth will come, when nothing else matters**! It will then be too late to alter the verdict! Have you met Jesus on life's highway? Ask Him what he wants you to do, then obediently walk in the light He surely will give! **Jesus spoke to us of such a walk with Him**, "Observe all things whatsoever I have commanded you: and lo, **I am with you always**, even unto the end of the world! Amen." *Matthew 28:20*

God Developing Character

When Jesus reported the incident of the nobleman, leaving to build a kingdom, who called his servants and delivered them sums of money to be responsible for, he was not teaching them how to raise money, but how to raise men. When that nobleman left the money in stewardship, he was not after more money. He wanted to develop men of character to help him rule in the kingdom he went to establish. Upon his return, he left the original grant and the money raised with the faithful stewards and gave them their appointments of authority in his kingdom. He took the smaller grant given to the unfaithful steward, and gave it to the one proving most responsible. The size of the grant was not the important factor. It was the character developed in caring for his trust, the nobleman was seeking. He needed men to rule and be responsible in his kingdom. His grants were but exercises in building character.

Raising money is very important, to us, in the building of Christ's Kingdom on earth; yet, it is not that important to God. While we are trying to **raise cash** He is trying to **develop character!** Our attitude in stewardship, our diligence, commitment, sacrifice and devotion are what God is seeking. The faithful stewards both received the same commendations and qualified to rule with their master. The unfaithful steward had a bad attitude to his lord, thinking him too demanding. He thought what was required of him to be unreasonable and unfair, and decided to return his grant, intact, thinking that would be sufficient. His indifference, lack of vision and loyalty, cost him everything. He had **flunked out as a**

steward and was unworthy of honor.

The material **shortages** in our building of Christ's kingdom never have their roots in the lack of money. It is always caused by a **deficiency in character**! God knows no shortage of anything! The cattle on a thousand hills are His! He holds the whole wide world in His hands! **It is the way we hold what is in our hands, that tie His!** Thank God! He taught me this at the inception of my service for Him. We have always believed if we gave Him **all we had**: He would supply **all our need**! He has never failed, neither in personal nor church finances! Please believe me sincere. I have no desire to rule or have power – I am happy to serve the Lord. I ask no greater joy and peace than He now gives. However, we are told, "If we suffer, we shall also reign with Him: if we deny Him, He also will deny us." *II Timothy 2:12* So many have said, "If there were no Heaven to gain, the joy and the blessing of walking with God here is worth all it has cost!" To which I say, Amen! Praise God for those "riches in God by Christ Jesus", not only in glory but right here, right now!

We have a right to believe when we sow the seeds of faith, we will reap in due season if we faint not. God has the right to believe what He sows in our hearts, will also produce an abundant harvest, too. God invested so heavily when He gave His own Son for our redemption! He has invested in us that he might commission us to help Him win others. God recognizes just two classes of stewards, faithful and unfaithful. Our true call is not to raise money and build churches, but to save the lost, helping to build His kingdom!

Why did the Lord make so many references to money? Because it was so important to Him? Not at all. It was simply because money is so important to men! His pointed lesson to the rich young ruler was, "If you do not love Me more than you love your money, you cannot be my disciple." Our present well-being and future destiny is determined by where we "lay up our treasures". Right now we are determining just where those treasures are! Are we faithful or unfaithful stewards? Only God can determine what constitutes **faithfulness** for each of us.

The very wealthy have great difficulty bringing up their children to have a proper evaluation of money and to take personal responsibility. How should they share their love and wealth without spoiling their children? Jesus knew what He was talking about when He said, "How hardly shall a rich man enter into the kingdom of Heaven?" It is the **love of money** that is the root of evil, not **how much money**. You do not have to have any money to love it! Just what do we treasure? Wealthy parents are torn by their desire to share their abundance with their children, and their concern about failing to develop character. The newspapers are filled, almost daily, with horrible records of failure to decide correctly. They want to do their best, but do not know just where to draw the line. God, however, knows just where that line is to be drawn and He will not spoil His children! **If we depend upon riches, we will never have enough.** If we are truly trusting God, **we will always have enough**. "But my God shall supply all your need according to His riches in glory by Christ Jesus." *Phillipians 4:19* God is not limited by what He has, but how much we can receive and still remain dependent upon Him, and not depend on what He has given. He knows just how much we can handle while building character.

God's demand of the tithe is a measure of discipline in drawing the line. He is teaching discipline and responsibility. He informs us in Malachi, "The tithe is Mine, you are a thief if you do not return it to Me." We cannot truly make an offering until we have paid the tithe. Joyce and I have never pledged our tithe: we just pay it. God has already declared, "It is Mine". God continued instruction to His People, in Malachi, "Be faithful to Me and I will open the windows of Heaven and pour out blessings upon you." This reminds one of an old cereal commercial, "Try it, you'll like it!" Which would you really rather have, nine dollars plus God's blessing, or ten dollars without it? Would you not stand at a street corner all day if you could pass out ten dollar bills and have folk give you one hundred dollar bills in return? Just a word of warning here: **our motive** in giving determines God's response. He is too wise to give to those seeking more money. He knows who is just trying to **prime the pump**! We simply cannot afford **not** to tithe! I have never known a faithful tither who was not better off financially because he had been faithful. I cannot understand God's mathematics, nor explain how a person who does not have enough money to go around has money left over when he starts tithing, but it is so. As a young pastor, I had been tempted to tell folk without money enough to go around, to just do the best they could, but God told me to mind my own business! Remember, this is not about raising cash but developing character!

The message of not being able to make an offering until the tithe had been paid struck home to one of our devout and generous ladies in a pastorate. She approached me after the service and asked, "Can I not make offerings out of my tithe?" Calling her by name, I asked, "If I owed you a hundred dollars and did not pay it: yet tried to show off before friends by announcing a gift of ten dollars, what would you be tempted to say?" She responded, "I'd want to know where the hundred was you owed me!" She was assured I thought the Lord would feel that way, too. The very next Sunday morning there was a five hundred dollar check in the offering plate, accompanied by a note, "tithe adjustment". (That would be like about four thousand dollars today.)

Tithing did not begin nor end with the Law given to Moses. It began with Abraham as part of his covenant of faith. It is still the basic test of faithful stewardship! At Bethel, after Jacob's vision, he promised God he would pay his tithe if God would give him a successful journey and see him safely home. Tithing was incorporated into the Law given to Moses, as an already established truth. Jesus told the Pharisees, who tithed to the smallest detail, "These things **ought ye to have done**," and not left these other important things undone. Almost without exception, those who tithe give far more than their tithe and are the most faithful in all other matters of stewardship. Can you be trusted with what God has given you in trust? Are you permitting God to build Christ-like character within you? When we pay our tithe, **we measure our honesty**! When we give an offering beyond our tithe, **we measure our love and gratitude**. How wonderful it would be to hear Him say, "Well done, good and faithful servant, enter thou into the joy of the Lord."

It has been a policy never to check on what parishioners gave through the years. It is important that I preach the Word as I understand it, without anyone thinking they may be singled out. At the close of one pastorate, I jokingly informed the congregation I had an apology to make. This surely got their attention. They were reminded of my policy of not checking who gave what; then they got nervous! They were assured no one had been checked up on. The apology was due for fear that I had misled them into thinking I **did not know** who tithed and who did not. The truth was I could have told them, within a five percent accuracy, who did tithe and who did not! Tithing brings obvious blessings. The side effects of not tithing are visible, too. Those who do not tithe lack confidence in God's providence. They also suffer financial reverses. No matter how much they had they still felt poor! They thought poor! They always feared they would not have enough! As God said in Malachi, they were like people pouring money into pockets full of holes. You cannot prosper on what you steal from God! Non-tithers were the first to complain about how much it costs to run the church. Their typical cry, "Always asking for money!" They were almost always negative about new challenges proposed for the church.

This reminds me of the story about the small boy on a farm in Maine who had a bantam hen. He was so proud of that beautiful little hen that followed him about the farm. He was devoted to her, too. There was only one thing about her that bothered him, **those tiny eggs**! Those big, old Rhode Island Reds laid such large, brown eggs! He tried just about everything to get her to lay larger eggs. He fed her a special laying mash and shells, and provided a nest of her own. Nothing seemed to work. One day, at a neighbor's farm, he saw a china egg in a nest, and asked the farmer what it was. The farmer informed him that was a china egg placed in the nest to give the hens an idea what was expected of them, and where they should do it. That boy thought to himself, "Maybe that's what I need!" He went home, took a big goose egg, placed his little hen gently into her nest, held that big old goose egg in front of her, and said, "Baby, take a good look at this thing and do the best you can."

Throughout the history of four building programs, including three complete churches, we have never hired a fund raiser, nor had "who-will-give-what offerings"! Like that little boy, I have asked them to take a good look, ask God for guidance and do the best they could. Some of those projects were very large goose eggs! We had much better results than the little farm boy had!

There are times when we need to call for sacrifice in raising cash. Remember, God is trying to raise character by the way we respond. That is why the poor widow casting her two mites gave more than the rich! If we do not develop character through response to the love of God, we will be unable to reach others through the churches we build. You cannot share what you do not have. It is so easy to get caught up in the mechanics of serving God and forget what God had commissioned us to do!

I have been told the story of a piccolo player in the orchestra of the great Toscanini. One day in practice session, the piccolo player, a bit depressed and feeling unimportant, failed to play his part. The orchestra flooded the hall with a tremendous crescendo of music. Suddenly, the great maestro tapped the podium and demanded, "Where is that piccolo?" His ear was tuned to every instrument and all were vital to the harmony of the symphony. **Our Master's ear is tuned to our heart's response. Each and every one of us is vital to the harmony in His symphony of love!**

We have learned this above question – the only thing more impossible than out-giving God is to out-love Him. Sure is fun to try, however! We must not limit our vision to what we think we can do. We must ask the Lord what He wants us to give and do! He knows what we have and what He will give if we trust and obey. I have never told anyone what they should give for I do not know. I might ask too much and be unfair. I might not ask enough, robbing them of blessing. Until we commit ourselves to more than we can do by ourselves, we are not living by faith. A professor at college, probably was trying to be nice when he said of the building program in Providence, "Carlton, if this turn of events takes place, you will have built better than you knew." I was truly upset and replied, "Professor, when we live by faith, we always build better than we know!" If we are not into God's work over our heads and beyond human resources, we are not living by faith! May our Lord give us understanding hearts to know exactly what is required of us as stewards that we may be faithful. **Let us live faithfully for what He died for!** If we want to **walk with Him**, let us truly **work for Him**!

Humility and Self-Image

Three of our daughters had unusual interest and talent for

the dramatic. Judith and Jyl played leading roles in their high school's dramatic productions. One day, during the presentation of one such play, Joyce and I had our own ego problems. We heard other parents about us, applauding those characters playing first and second female leads.

At the height of interest in one production, seven boys came to the house, under one pretext or another, during one of our family dinner hours. The following Sunday, two of the more popular boys in the church presented the girls with favorite long-playing record albums. On the way home, Judy, who was playing *The Unsinkable Molly Brown*, betrayed her keyed up emotions by her highly pitched voice and giggles. As a word of caution, I commented, "I hope the unsinkable Molly Brown has an 'uninflatable' head!" Some time later, Judy was taken from Douglas College campus in New Brunswick to New Jersey's Trenton State College campus to be introduced as the newly elected Governor of Girl's State. There were about a thousand young men attending Boy's State Convention. Judy confided later: "When that crowd of young guys stood up, hooted, whistled, stomped and cheered my introduction, it was quite an ego trip!"

Just how can we be popular, respected and successful and not become egocentric? I visited one of the most precious, humble, Christ-centered, consistent, diligent, devoted people that I had ever known. You could easily think of Rev. Roy Sturdevant, of Milo, Maine, as a beautiful person. I had always thought of him as exemplifying perfect humility. During one visit, I confided how I wished to spend more time with him. His response was instantaneous and characteristic, "Why would a man like you want to spend time with a man like me?" My sincere response: "I want to be more like you!" An incredulous look came across his face and he said, "You want to be like me?" My reply was a confessional: "Roy, I believe God is telling me that He wants a little less Gleason in what I am doing. If you were to hear Him speak, I believe you would hear him say, 'I want a little more Sturdevant in what you are doing!' " I write this to honor the memory of him! That man never did realize how much he was admired, nor of his worth as a very special human being!

On the way home from that visit, the question persisted: "When is extreme **humility** a **poor self-image**?" Conversely, "When is a **good self-image** just an **ego trip**?" Humility is such an illusive characteristic. Most often, if you think you have it, you don't! This reminds me of the humorous reference to the man, who was reported to have said, "Humility is the family trait of which we are most proud!" How can we have a good self-image and not become egotistical? How can we be honestly humble, yet confident, poised and assured?

Humility is as elusive as happiness. They cannot be found when we search for them per se! If you search for humility, per se, what happens when you think you have found it? What happens when you despair of finding it?

Humility has it's roots in knowing **Who God is and what we are**! Isaiah saw the holiness of God, high and lifted up when His train filled the temple, and he saw himself in contrasting human weakness and sinfulness. He never forgot the holiness of God, nor his own human frailty. His whole life and writings reflected humility born of those realizations. **In his quest for the perfect will of God, for himself and the nation, Isaiah found humility!**

Isaiah had discovered the secret of humility Jesus referred to in Matthew. "He that loseth his life for My sake shall find it." *Matthew 10:39* Jesus was saying, if you die out to yourself, I will stamp **my own good image** upon your heart and life.

"Oh! to be like Thee Blessed Redeemer, pure as Thou art!
Come in Thy sweetness, come in Thy fullness;
stamp Thine own image deep on my heart!"
William J. Kirkpatrick

Humility is the absence of pride as light is the absence of darkness! Pride and humility cannot coexist. The roots of pride are dealt with when our carnal spirit is crucified. Does this mean pride is no longer a problem? Not at all! Our human nature remains to be denied and disciplined. It is very easy to be lifted up within ourselves, when greatly blest of God, unless we are very careful to give Him all the praise and glory. Paul makes reference to his "thorn in the flesh, lest he be exalted above measure!" He, too, saw the danger of being lifted up within himself by great blessing. The best assurance of not being lifted up within ourselves, is to **lift Him up!** Samuel said to Saul, "When thou wast little in thine own eyes," referring to the days of Saul's humble walk with God until his pride and ego took over. Biblical and current history have recorded so many tragedies when men could not handle success. Far more men and women are destroyed by success than by failure!

How much success can we handle? Only God truly knows! He will not let His trusting, obedient children get in over their heads. He can detect the signs, as was the case with Judy, when success is getting to us and our ego is becoming a threat to humility. Meekness is one of the essential ingredients of humility. Jesus said, in the beatitudes, it was the meek who would inherit the earth. The Army has a catchy recruiting slogan, "Be all that you can be in the Army!" God says, "If you will be meek and walk with humility, **I will make you all that you can be!**"

Did you ever want to be a **superstar** in something? The world's greatest football quarterback, a super basketball or baseball star? Muhammad Ali used to say, "I am the greatest!" How would you like to be declared **the greatest** by the most respected, the wisest, and the most knowledgeable of pollsters? I have a secret, **you can be just that!** The God of Heaven has said, "He that is slow to anger **is better than the mighty**; and he that **ruleth his spirit** than he that taketh a city." *Proverbs 16:32* Conquering self, sin, Satan and circumstances, while working together with God, is the most exciting of adventures, and makes possible the **greatest of conquests**, being a **superstar in His sight**. "He that **humbleth himself, shall be exalted**!" *Luke 14:11* A false humility, or lack of character, cannot be construed as meekness. Humility and meekness are born in the strength of Christian character, not in weakness nor in the presence of a negative, indecisive spirit!

The severity of Moses' punishment for his outburst at the waters of strife, once troubled me greatly. Moses, the friend of God, who walked and talked with God face to face, was denied entry to the promised land because of that one sin! Certainly God was just and had His reasons, but I needed to know what they were. I asked God to help me understand why that sin carried so great a penalty. I believe the truth concerning the control over our own spirits and our reactions to evil about us provided an insight. Moses, reacting to the provocative misconduct of the people, lost the battle for control over his own spirit! He failed to pray through in taking the problem to God, and waiting for instruction and anointing to act in the Spirit.

God told Moses to **speak** to the rock and He would bring water from that rock. Moved to anger by the evil-spirited mob, Moses **reacted** to their stimuli, **smote** the rock in anger, and said, "Must **I** bring water from this rock?" After many years of provocative behavior, this carnally-minded people finally got to him. His angry response failed to glorify God. God rebuked Moses later, "They failed me: then in human frailty, you failed Me too!"

The severity of punishment for this failure underscores the necessity of our refusing to react to negative stimuli, and permitting God to act through us. If we react to evil, we are controlled by that evil and God loses control of our immediate behavior. Truly, he that ruleth his own spirit is greater than he that taketh a city! When we react to evil, the world with its undercurrents of hate is in control. God wants us to do nothing not motivated by His love. Only God's love can conquer hate. One day, according to His Word, "The whole earth will be filled with His glory." Until that day He depends upon us to reveal his glory, love and holiness to a skeptical world.

May we recognize our native human weakness, and realize that we hold heavenly treasures in earthen vessels. However, we must also realize we are called to be **"more than conquerors"**! Let us make total surrender to God, do the best we can, by His grace and permit Him to assess the results.

The Dynamics of Faith

It is so important that we not only understand the nature of faith, but that we have faith! "Without faith **it is impossible to please Him**: for he that cometh to God must believe that He is, and that He is a rewarder of them that diligently seek Him." *Hebrews 11:6* We often refer to our religious system of beliefs as our faith. Faith is much more than simply believing. There is an element of doubt in mere belief. One man is recorded in the Bible as crying to Jesus, "Lord I believe, help thou my unbelief!" You might ask me to change a twenty dollar bill, and I would confidently say, "certainly", for there is no doubt that I have it. You might have asked, "Can you change a hundred dollar bill?"; and I would hesitate, saying, I **believe** I can because, though I believe, I am not absolutely certain! Many **believe** things to be factual that are later proven untrue.

To be confidently secure, and obtain the promises of God, belief must lead to **faith**. Many have said, "I have faith that such or such is going to happen", but it did not! They said they had faith, but they were really meaning, "I believe it will happen". When does belief become faith? Faith is born when God speaks through His Holy Spirit. When energized by the witness of His Spirit we are brought into direct communication with God, confirming our beliefs and giving us faith. We, natural men, who cannot discern the things of the Spirit, may now be taught all things through the dynamism of God's Holy Spirit. When God so speaks we have been given dynamic faith. Why dynamic? Because it is real and really works. So many times we know facts of truth that only God could reveal. Faith is born in the hearts and minds of those who have learned to wait on God and listen to the "still small voice" of the Spirit within.

God has often worked miracles in answer to prayer, that were merely expressions of my desire and belief in His grace. There had been no clear-cut stand of faith. Yet every time I was certain God had spoken and I stood on that promise, He answered prayer. When God gives faith, there is victory! Count on it! Stand on it! It will happen. Only those who fast, pray and wait can have this confidence. Do you want faith like that? Kneel before an open Bible, and pray, "God I believe; help Thou my belief." Ask God to talk to you from the Book He has written that you might know what He has on His mind and heart. When He answers, and He will: you will be in communion with Him! This is essential if we are **to walk with Him**!

Faith might be described as a spiritual **radar system**: by which man reaches God, and by which he commits to God, in trust, all that which is beyond the reach of his reason alone. With a physical radar system, signals are sent out as probes into space. If there is nothing out in space, there is no responding "ping". However, if there is an object in space, responding signals, bounced back, are picked up on the radar screen verifying its existence. These systems are now so highly developed that shapes, sizes, speeds and so much more are confirmed as real. God equipped man with a beautifully functioning system for confirmation of His presence and His will. We may call it faith. Faith is **not irrational**, nor is it **confined to reason**. It is more than just the reach of the human mind alone. It is **supra-rational**! It cannot be condemned as non-rational or irrational because it begins upon a foundation laid by reason, but reaches out beyond reason. The resulting spiritual harmony, coherence and confirmed tangible evidence attest to its validity, and faith is vindicated by rational processes. There is faith that works! Man does not reach God through institutions, programs, nor religious doctrinal beliefs, but by faith! We have an example of this at Ceaseria Philippi, when Jesus told Peter, "Flesh and blood did not reveal this unto thee, but My Father which is in Heaven." *Matthew 16:17*

God's Radar

God is also tracking us on His systems of spiritual radar! He knows just where we are and where we are going. He is aware of everything about us. It is a comfortable feeling, for those who love God and seek to walk with Him, to realize we are locked into His radar systems, too. It has been wonderful, through the years, to have him send in course signals, adjusting our flight paths through time and space. There have been times when I could almost hear Him say, "Uh, uh! Not that way" as His Holy Spirit has prevented me from doing some intended thing. There have been times His Spirit has whispered, "This is the way, walk ye in it!" Thank God for this wonderful version of mission control. Modern aviation has become very dependent upon the flight control systems about our airports. They give guidance, assist landings and avert disasters because they have the entire picture of flight patterns before them. I find great peace in the assurance of a Flight Controller who never makes a mistake or misses a call. I am determined that when He signals, He shall have my full cooperation.

King David was aware of God's radar locking in on him. "O Lord, Thou hast searched me and known me. Thou knowest my downsitting and mine uprising, Thou understandest my thoughts afar off. Thou compassest my path and my lying down, and art acquainted with all my ways." *Psalms 139:1-3* I often wondered: how could God keep track of everybody, all the time? How could He keep in touch? I knew that He did for I was aware of His scrutiny.

God's Internet

Just recently our daughter Janice's husband, John Ruggieri, and I were discussing the expanding sources of information accessible through the Internet. As John explained the amazing geometrically progressive explosion of knowledge made available through the Internet: God suddenly brought the whole issue of His guidance through the years into sharp, clear focus. **I had been**

accessing God's Spiritual Internet since childhood, and with it much of the data on His physical Internet, as I sought wisdom, understanding and spiritual discernment. Why should the God of Heaven confide such to me? It must have been becuse I loved Him, others, and truth so much that He had answered my prayer for an understanding heart. He dropped the barriers that locked out my access to His Internet. Not because of my intelligence, but because of my hunger and thirst for righteousness, regardless of the cost to me. However, this is God's **common response to all people** who hunger and thirst for righteousness, and have established primary contact in a personal relationship with God, by His Holy Spirit, **through faith**!

The significance of **learning to listen** became so clear that evening with John, as we discussed the sudden development of the Internet via the computer. God had been giving me access through the Bible as taught by His Holy Spirit. No wonder I felt as though I had found a **benchmark** for my life, a point of certain, abiding reference. So that was how He was sharing His secrets through the years! Let me remind you, "Knowing this first, that no prophecy of the Scripture is of any private interpretation." *II Peter 1:20* What God does for one, He will do for everyone, if they ask, trust and obey. God's Spiritual Internet has been in operation since the dawn of creation. Men have been led by God's Holy Spirit wherever and whenever they have exercised faith with obedience. Men have been able to access the mind and heart of God, and to know what they needed to know to do the will of God. It is my conviction: God will give all the knowledge and wisdom we can be trusted with. As a wise parent, He will not give us that which would lead to degradation and self-destruction.

When Can Man Be Trusted with Knowledge?

God planted the tree of knowledge in the garden, but forbad man to eat of it. "And out of the ground made the Lord God to grow every tree that is pleasant to sight, and good for food. The **tree of life** also in the midst of the garden, and the **tree of knowledge of good and evil**." Genesis 2:9 "And the Lord God commanded the man, saying, of **every tree** of the garden thou mayest eat freely: but of the tree of the knowledge of good and evil, **thou shalt not eat of it**, for in the day that thou eatest thereof thou shalt surely die!" *verses 16-17* God did not deny Adam access to the **tree of life until after he had sinned**. Satan approached Eve with the temptation to disobey God's clear commandment, "Yea hath God said?": questioning God's right and judgment. Eve replied, "We may eat all of the fruits, but the tree in the midst of the garden, we shall not eat, or touch it, lest we die." Satan continued, "Ye shall not surely die! For God doth know that in the day ye eat thereof, then your eyes shall be opened, and **ye shall be as gods**, knowing good and evil." "The woman saw the tree was good for food, and that it was **pleasant to their eyes**, and a tree **desired to make one wise**. She took of the fruit thereof." *Genesis 3:1-6* God had made it possible for mankind to access His heart and mind; that He might freely share His love and blessings, but Eve gave that access to Satan, through her disobedience. Satan's access impregnated mankind with an evil mind of unbelief: the carnal spirit. Man became sinful by nature and fellowship with God was broken. Satan had induced man to rebel and disobey: bringing evil, degradation and death! Mankind was then denied access to the **Tree of Life**, lest he obtain immortality through other than the will of God. Jesus gave instruction on just how to obtain eternal life. "He that believeth on the Son hath everlasting life; and he that believeth not the Son shall not see life; but the wrath of God abideth in him." *John 3:36* "For as in Adam all die, even so in Christ shall all men be made alive." *I Corinthians 15:23*

Does not God want man to be wise and have knowledge? Of course He does, but He knows just when we can be trusted to handle it without our self-destructing. God knew Adam and Eve needed to learn how to access His heart, through His **Spiritual Internet, before** entrusting him with the knowledge of the empirical and the physical. **Adam and Eve sought to access the wisdom of God without reciprocating the love of God!** God had given man the power of choice and that forbidden tree was a test to see what man would do with this potential. Man failed that examination! Satan, knowing they could not handle it either, successfully exploited their pride and sensual desires. **He is still successfully exploiting people today by the same methodology!** The humanists not only question God's word, they even deny His existence. They come up with fairy tales of "father time" and "mother earth" as conceiving all this complexity of creation through time and chance. There is no greater misnomer than that of "The New Age Movement". Their movement is as old as the rebellion in Heaven; when Lucifer, the archangel, said, "I will be as God." This is the bill of goods he sold Eve in the garden: "You will be wise; you will be as gods!"

God purposed to grant man access to His mind when man had learned to access His heart, identifying with Himself. God's own Son asserted this! "Nevertheless I tell you the truth; it is expedient for you that I go away; for if I go not away, The Comforter will not come unto you; but if I depart I will send Him unto you. And when He is come, **He will reprove the world of sin, and of righteousness, and of judgment**." *John 16:7-8* In the same discourse, Jesus said, "When He is come He will teach you all things, whatsoever I have said!" Satan **introduced evil**. God's Holy Spirit came **to provide truth and holiness**! This was to come in the fullness of time when man was ready to handle the responsibilities for such privileges.

Men Denied Access to God's Internet

After the flood and approximately four thousand years ago: the people of the earth began to use their access to intelligence data to escape responsibility to God. In Babylon, they sought to build a tower to reach Heaven. The Bible records in Genesis eleven: "And they said, go to, let us build us a city and a tower, whose top may reach Heaven; and **let us make us a name**... And the Lord came down to see the city and the tower... And the Lord said... and this they begin to do: and now **nothing shall be restrained from them which they have imagined to do**." He confounded their language so that they could not understand each other and scattered them upon the face of the earth. God was not the least bit concerned man could build a physical tower to reach Heaven. If the entire earth were "pyramided" into one tower it would be as nothing in space. That tower they were building was a ziggurat for the worship of the earth, the moon and the stars. It was an attempt to achieve immortality by means other than God had provided. In their pride, they had, in terms familiar in my childhood, "become too big for their britches"! God knew full access to His physical Internet would lead them to self-destruct and He cut off that access. Once again man had proven himself not ready to be trusted with too much knowledge.

Promise to Restore Access

Our Pre-Incarnate Lord appeared to Daniel in a dream to foretell events in the near future, centuries later, and in the end times. Most of these events have taken place exactly as the Lord told Daniel they would. However, God told Daniel to seal up the vision of events that would mark those last days, except for these facts: "Many shall run to and fro and knowledge shall increase." *Daniel 12:4* God also added, "Many shall be purified, and made white, and tried: but the wicked shall do wickedly and none of the wicked shall understand; **but the wise shall understand**." *Daniel 12:10* Atheism has its roots in ignorance, not wisdom! We see many will stand approved in their use of knowledge; others will accelerate their own degradation. Our knowledge of atomic energy can bless or burn. There are those who speculate God is too good to bring judgment upon the earth. I do not believe He will have to, for men will self-destruct. Peter, that uneducated fisherman of two thousand years ago, tapping God's Spiritual Internet said, "But the day of the Lord will come as a thief in the night; in which the heavens shall pass away with a great noise, and the elements shall melt with the fervent heat, the earth also and the works that are therein shall be burned up. Seeing then that all these things shall be dissolved, what manner of persons ought ye to be in all holy conversation and godliness." *II Peter 3:10-11* The Greek philosophers in their great wisdom could not envision atomic fission. Here an unlettered fisherman described it perfectly. In an atomic explosion the elements of the atom are dissolved – releasing their energy with a tremendous noise – melting other elements about them in the tremendous heat. I honestly fear that man in his rebellion and refusal to seek the Godly wisdom of faith, will trigger atomic fission that will wipe out much of the earth as we know it.

Now, approximately twenty-five hundred years after Daniel's prophecy, God has lifted the restraints and granted access again to His physical Internet. We are eyewitnesses to that explosion of knowledge. Until the last one hundred and fifty years there was no mass transportation. The best mode of travel on land was by horses. I can remember when horses were the chief method of locomotion in our community. Radio was invented just one hundred years ago in 1895. I can remember when the first tiny crystal radio sets first came to our town. One hundred and nineteen years ago man's audible voice was carried over a wire between two rooms. Alexander Graham Bell is reported to have said, "What hath God wrought!" Powered flight is not yet one hundred years old. Today we fly on a Concord jet at about three times the speed of sound. Men have been propelled to the moon and back. We talk to a space probe billions of miles in space, and see what is actually then taking place on distant planets. The field of electronics is changing so rapidly that the latest of inventions is made almost obsolete in six months. Where do we go from here? I wonder: is there any danger we will again get too big for our britches? Can we be trusted with all this knowledge and power?

The Greek philosophers sought to probe ultimate truth through the reach of their own minds. They came quite close in some things. Some of them concluded that ultimate substance was in the nature of fire. Democratus posited that all matter was composed of tiny, submicroscopic building blocks, he called atoms. None of them knew how to release the latent energy of the atom or reduce matter to fire, let alone control that fire. The practical release of this energy was brought about by Albert Einstein in the early thirties. We must remember man invented none of this! **He had but discovered** laws, principles, powers and physical **facts built in by design in God's universe**. Man can but use and manipulate what God has already wrought.

It is unfortunate that there are misconceptions arising from Einstein's theory of relativity seeming to deny absolutes. There are absolutes! He would be correct in saying there are no **static** absolutes because absolutes are **in flux**. There is a **constant flow of both physical and spiritual energies**, force fields that effect consequences and changes. The science of chemistry is a studied art on how to effect the flow or introduce changes in the flow of chemical absolutes creating predicted consequences. These potentials have further accelerated man's expressions of knowledge. Man can still only discover or rearrange absolute properties and potentials by his own engineering.

It is tragic that the denial of absolutes has carried over into the theory of **moral relativity** with horrible social consequences. Man, denying the restraints of moral law, finds himself **adrift in a world of his own creation**. Having abandoned God-given restraints, he is out of control: self-destructing like an engine that has been stripped of a governor. We need to remember, God is still monitoring the behavior of men. When He comes down again, He will say, "That is enough!" Please do not let your **doubts** and unbelief, **raised by incomplete knowledge** of God's physical Internet, deny you access to God's Spiritual Internet.

Jim Caldwell, a fellow student in college, and a brilliant student, was having problems because of an imbalance of knowledge through his philosophical and theological studies and simple dynamic faith. Having earned degrees in theology and philosophy, he stood head and shoulders above me as a scholar. He was handicapped because he was not brought up in the Christian faith and had but a limited spiritual background. We were close friends and he recognized that my faith was strong, having found peace and personal stability through God's Spiritual Internet. During studies for his master's degree at Boston University, Jim frequently spent weekends with us in Providence. Joyce used to almost dread his coming for we would talk far into the nights. So many of Jim's doubts arose from knowledge beyond my reach, but I understood enough to apply the principles of my faith. My faith, building since childhood, was broad and firmly established. The burden of knowledge was very light by comparison, giving the stability of a pyramid. Jim Caldwell, on the other hand, had very narrow bases for his faith and a tremendous weight of doubt-producing knowledge. He was having great difficulty handling the liberal, humanistic pressures that challenged him. Philosophically and spiritually he was as an inverted pyramid. Jim was accepted into a doctorate program and sought my counsel on the matter. I urged him to take studies in theology before taking on a greater burden of unresolved doubts. Jim did just that! He went to seminary, obtained a master's in theology, and then went on to obtain his doctorate.

Dr. James Caldwell became chairman of his department at college and married Dr. Shirley Caldwell, professor at Vanderbilt. We still treasure our friendship and thank God for adequate understanding to maintain a philosophy of life, with abiding faith-giving purpose, meaning, hope and peace to our lives. I believe when we have such stabilizing faith, God will entrust us with greater knowledge and insight. Now that God is permitting deeper penetration into His secrets of the universe: have you developed faith through God's Spiritual Internet that you may be safely trusted with greater vistas of knowledge? Can you handle the weight of this present explosion of knowledge without becoming self-centered and egotistical? Will your newly acquired knowledge help you in your walk and in your work with Him?

Seeing the Invisible

Have you ever heard anyone say, "I believe what I see"? Surely they cannot really believe nothing exists unless they had seen it! We all accept so much by faith! Were it possible to find a man who had never heard a radio or seen television: can you imagine how he would react if you told him the room was flooded with scenes and sounds from all over the world? He would probably head for the door thinking you were crazy. Nothing could be seen or heard, for human eyes and ears cannot pick up the sound waves and transcribe them into audible and visual reality. However, the TV has been constructed to pick up those electronic impulses and bring them into visible and audible reality. Just turn it on, see and hear.

"Moses forsook Egypt; for he had endured as **seeing Him Who is invisible**." *Hebrews 11:27* Jesus, speaking of the Spirit, said, He shall glorify Me for He shall receive of mine, and show it unto you." Again, in Luke, Jesus said, "For everyone that seeketh, findeth, and to him that knocketh it shall be opened." Do not think any one is special just because he has accessed the mind and heart of God! It is God who is special and especially loves every one of us.

Through God's Spiritual Internet we not only access His mind, and He ours, but we can contact others and they may contact us. Sometimes God responds to us, through others. There are many cases cited in this book where God has used me to answer the prayer of someone else, and he has used others to communicate with me. This is the very essence of Christian fellowship. When meeting someone who is deeply in love with the Lord: we sense a common bond, almost without exception.

You may question the reality of my access to God's Spiritual Internet. I challenge you to take an open Bible, open your heart and mind, and pray, "Lord, if you are real and know about me, and this is your Book; please talk to me and give me faith!" I have known so many who have prayed like that and He has responded, giving them access, too. In fact, I have never known anyone who sincerely prayed like that and He did not respond! If we but learn wisdom, with an understanding heart; nothing will be impossible for us either. We may then be lifted to the highest possible plane of our potential creativity. We may do so safely for our good, God's glory, and the benefit of mankind. God will put all our facts into focus if we but permit Him to do so. Remember, if you knew every fact available on the computer's Internet, you would have but partial knowledge. God deals in the absolutes and He will tell us what is vital for us to know! They are all available on His Spiritual Internet!

A Confluence of Internets

It is clearly evident that God has dropped much of His veil of secrecy: permitting man to access His **physical Internet**, unlocking the secrets regarding the composition of the earth and all matter, and even of life itself. God is at the same time granting men ever clearer insights into the secrets of His **spiritual Internet**. It is my firm belief that this confluence of data flow from both Internets marks a final period of testing and examination for mankind. "There is a God in Heaven that revealeth secrets, and He that revealeth secrets maketh known to thee what shall come to pass." *Daniel 2:28-29* How anxious He must be as He studies the effect of such an explosion of knowledge. God said the wise would use it to reconcile others to their Heavenly Father. "And they that be wise shall shine as the brightness of the firmament, and they that turn many to righteousness as the stars forever and ever!" *Daniel 12:3*

Daniel spoke to these issues so beautifully, when sharing God's secrets with Nebuchadnezzar. "But as for me, this secret is not revealed to me for any wisdom that I have more than any living; but for their sakes that shall make known the interpretation to the King. He giveth wisdom to the wise, and knowledge to them that know understanding. He revealeth the deep secret things: He knoweth what was in the darkness, and the light dwelleth with Him." *Daniel 2:30, 2:21-22*

When God comes for final inspection, may He find us using what He has given us to help prepare ourselves, and others for an eternity of fellowship with Him.

"Now faith is the substance of things hoped for, the evidence of things not seen." *Hebrews 11:1* When God speaks, spiritual things become just as real as the things we can taste, touch, or smell. In fact they become more real. Everything we can verify with our physical senses will pass away. It is those unseen things revealed through faith that are eternal. Some folk may say, "**Show me and I will believe.**" God says, "**Believe and I will show you!**" God created man in **His own** image. Too many of those whom He created are trying to **create a god in their own image**. The essential ingredient of Christianity, is not its outward forms, nor in its ethical codes, but in the tremendous force of divine love released within the individual by dynamic faith! You can know the truth; that sets you free!

The agnostic says, "God is not knowable. I don't know, neither do you!" He would accuse us of living in a mystical, fantasy world of our own creation. The atheist says, "There is no God for anyone to know!" The men and women of faith, say with Paul, "I **know Whom** I have believed, and am persuaded that He is able to keep that which I have committed unto Him against that day." II Timothy 1:12

We cannot know the specific will of God for given moments or needs until He reveals it to us. The deeper, specific truth needed to make faith a vital factor in our daily situations of life, comes by **revelation** as His Holy Spirit communicates with us. Again that truth in Romans eight, "As many as are led by the Spirit of God, they are the sons of God." "For with the heart man believeth unto righteousness; and with the mouth confession is made unto salvation. So that Faith cometh by hearing, and hearing by the Word God." Romans 10:10, 17 How can we walk in fellowship with God if we have not learned to communicate with God? "How can two walk together except they be agreed?" Amos 3:37

Faith or Fantasy?

Faith and hope are vitally essential to keeping life in positive focus during the crises and tragedies of life. When **life kicks back**, the future looks dark and foreboding; we need assurance that there are better and more beautiful things up ahead. "And now abideth faith, hope, love, these three, but the greatest of these is love." I Corinthians 13:13 It is God's love that gives us faith and hope! We know that love to be real because of His Holy Spirit's energizing presence within!

It is imperative, therefore, that our **faith** be a God-given assurance. Too often our human minds conger up **fantasies** born of our human desires, and we mislabel them faith. Failure to properly distinguish between God-given faith, and human fantasies or personal dreams and desires, can have heartbreaking consequences. This creates barriers between ourselves and God, and effects our fellowship with those who share our lives. We doom ourselves to isolation in our own little dream world. Others cannot share with us for they are not governed by our fantasies, and God will not be swayed by our notions or assumptions. So many tragedies have been caused by those who have confused **fantasy** with **faith**. This is one of the basic elements in the formation of cults. When an outstanding leader identifies his particular belief, fantasy or expression of worship as being the will of God: obedience to his concepts are seen as essential to salvation. A human leader thus imposes himself between his followers and their God! God loses control of yet another man and his works. This man, though often sincere, has misguidedly "given place to Satan", and yet another cult has been born.

We must be very honest and very careful to seek the truth as God would reveal it. We must not seek to impose our will upon Him, but let Him reveal His will to us. We need to pray like Jesus,

"Not my will but Thy will be done!" Please God! Let this be the cry from our hearts. Remember, through faith, under the anointing of His Spirit: we are given **the access code**, to the heart and mind of God! We can know anything and everything vital to our redemption and our faithful stewardship before him right here, right now! When we testify, thus saith the Lord: let us make certain God has spoken. Remember: you don't have to take my word for it. Ask Him yourself! That is not only your privilege; it is your duty!

Mastery Through the Spirit

We have observed earlier in the book: how our eternal spirit was housed, at creation, in a temporal, animalistic body of flesh. Satan was given access to man's heart and life through disobedience, and a third element, the carnal nature, was born within man's very nature. It is this nature that must be crucified as we die out to it. When God's Holy Spirit, once again, takes up residence in our hearts and lives, we become temples of God. "If any man defile the temple of God, him shall God destroy; for the temple of God is holy, which temple ye are." *I Corinthians 3:17* "For ye are bought with a price: therefore glorify God in your body, and in your spirit, which are God's." *I Corinthians 6:20*

Even though our carnal spirit is crucified, we still must live in a natural, human, animalistic body. These bodies, though now temples of God, were created for our convenience in the journey through time. It is subject to all sensuous desires related to our survival and the perpetuation of our species. Romans chapter eight, tells of the conflict between our spiritual and fleshly natures. "Therefore, brethren, we are debtors, not to the flesh, to live after the flesh. For if ye live after the flesh ye shall die: but if ye through the Spirit mortify the deeds of the body, ye shall live." *Romans 8:12-13*

We are living in a day when the masses of earth's people know little, or nothing, of an indwelling Holy Spirit, and are dominated by preoccupation with the demands of their physical bodies. They call it, "doing what comes naturally." They know only the pressures and demands of a hunger-driven body. Our sexual urges are the most compelling forces in our natural body, and they dominate the life not directed by God's Holy Spirit. Our sexual nature is not in itself, evil: for it was created by God as part of our natural endowment. It is dirty or evil, only when we dirty it by expression outside the guidelines of God. It is the instinctive drive to be a father or a mother, and as such constitutes the highest form of human creativity. It was meant to become the most beautiful and blessed of physical sharing between humans, within a context of love. It was given to us as a sacred trust and must be held as such! Indulgence outside of marriage was strictly forbidden. Sexual relations between unmarried people is fornication and adultery when one or more are married to others. Such aberrations to God's holy purpose are so repulsive to Him that He uses such behavior to illustrate idolatry as the ultimate sin. "Flee fornication. Every sin that man doeth is without the body; but he that committeth fornication sinneth against his own body. Know ye not that your body is the temple of the Holy Ghost which is in you, which ye have of God, and ye are not your own? For ye are bought with a price: therefore glorify God in your body, and in your spirit, which are God's." *Romans 6:18-20* If God's Holy Spirit does indwell you, you have a power greater than the natural demands of the body! He provides the power for mastery over self, sin and Satan!

To Bless or Burn

The sexual drives of our human nature are very much like the power of atomic energy. Both can be tremendously beneficial forces: both, released out of control, have horrible and deadly consequences. Their potential for blessing or destruction is so great they should be carefully regarded. God has laid down careful ground rules for their control. Scientists live in fear that men may trigger an explosion that will set off a chain reaction of explosions that could wipe out the earth as we know it. This could be possible for, as we know, all matter is a composition of atoms. We are seeing about us now, the horrible consequences of uncontrolled sexual behavior among the peoples of earth. The outbreak of deadly, uncontrollable sexual diseases are among the consequences of failure to follow God's guidelines. We should not be surprised: for God has said He would not be mocked and that men would reap what they sowed. Men are mocking God in their so-called sexual **revolution**. God knows perfectly well that it is sexual **rebellion** against His declared standards. The "New Morality" is nothing but the "Old Immorality", renamed. We have hardly begun to see the price mankind must pay for this folly.

People without the guidance and the power of God's indwelling Spirit are quite helpless before Satan's subtle attacks. He seeks to instigate illegitimate use of natural, God-given powers. He would have God-given powers of procreating life turned to the destruction of body, mind and spirit. If you want a liturgy of the horrible side effects, read your daily newspaper.

I am particularly concerned for the youth of our day. They are brainwashed by every avenue to their minds. Our public schools do not believe in teaching moral absolutes, but do not hesitate to treat our youth as sexual animals that need to be taught how to degrade themselves and avoid the consequences. Our youth are often "blindsided" because we have failed to set this matter of their sexual nature in proper perspective from God's point of view.

As pastor, I have often sat for hours talking frankly to our youth about their sexual natures, and answering any questions they might ask. They were told what this natural force truly is and how God said they should control this sacred trust, without dirtying it. They were warned not to play with their emotions for they might well trigger emotional explosions beyond their control that would wipe out their hopes and dreams. They were urged to keep their bodies pure, not only for the husband or wife they would one day marry, but keep their body an undefiled temple of the Holy Spirit. They were assured, if they would purpose to do that, God's Holy Spirit would see them through the hours of temptation. We cannot win this battle alone, but His grace is sufficient for us.

Our society is so brainwashed with the ooze from filthy minds: through the press, avenues of entertainment, advertising and almost every means of social communication. Even the professed Christians in our churches have been effected. I have been shocked at the pornographic videos, films, magazines and the soap operas that professing Christians permit to pollute their minds. **You cannot have a dirty mind and a clean heart at the same time!** How can one filled with the Holy Spirit enjoy a dirty joke? Would you eat garbage from a can in the alley? Would you drink water from a sewer pipe? Then why feed the world's filth into your heart and mind? "As a man thinketh in his heart: so is he." *Proverbs 23:7* "Keep thy heart with all diligence, for out of it are the issues of life." *Proverbs 4:3* **"Who shall ascend into the hill of the Lord? Or who shall stand in His holy place? He that hath clean hands, and a pure heart!"** *Psalms 24:3-4*

The humanistic consider themselves to be animals of spontaneous origin, and they are to eat when they are hungry and drink when they are dry. They follow their instincts, even sexually, much as an animal submits to his drives and hungers. Man, in so doing, sinks far lower than the animals: for animals have more refined senses of instinct. Man who does not live by conscience and intelligence is far worse than an animal, and much less predictable. It is so disturbing to hear professed fundamentalist believers expressing the same philosophies of self-indulgence espoused by the humanists.

When a very small boy, I was challenged by Daniel, who refused to defile himself. I have prayed through the years that God would help me live that my body would be servant to my soul and mind, and that I might be a servant of the Lord. I found victory came easier when I was saying yes to something positive and good, rather than just saying no to evil. When too obsessed with saying no, the temptation seemed to stay fixed in my mind. Phillipians four, provided good advice in this struggle. "Be careful for nothing (don't worry about anything); but in everything by prayer and supplication with thanksgiving let your requests be made known unto God. And the peace of God, which passeth all understanding, shall keep your hearts and minds through Christ Jesus. Finally brethren, whatsoever things are true, whatsoever things are honest, whatsoever things are just, whatsoever things are pure, whatsoever things are lovely, whatsoever things are of good report; if there be any virtue, if there be any praise, think on these things." Just remember, whatever you treasure tells where your heart is. If you love filth, you do not truly love God. ✣

12 *When God Steps In*

Mankind is now facing the most crucial days in the history of the human race! Humanity has always been bombarded by forces beyond effective control. We can control, directly, but few of the forces that determine our destiny. In our crisis-ridden world today, few things seem predictable anymore. We find difficulty understanding the facts of history, as critic and historian alike, attempt to restructure, or reinterpret events of the past. We seem to have lost our guidelines; as humanism seeks to rob us of values, principles and a purpose for living. The masses today, are critical about life and feel estranged and unloved. Few of us feel any measure of confidence concerning our ability to predict the future. Thinking men and women, young and old, are trying to find the answers and the guidelines that will bring stability and direction. **There are a-priori values, principles, and laws** that underlie, and influence the realms of both the material and the spiritual. Though they are **absolute**, we cannot absolutely understand them. We are blest if we even have **adequate** knowledge of them. How are we finite creatures to comprehend the wisdom and absolute truth related to our infinite God? We could dip up the Mississippi River with a bucket easier than we may fully fathom truth as God sees it. **We need help!**

It is doubtful that the masses of human society are concerned with the fine points of our theology. It is unimportant to them as to just how churches differ from one another in their beliefs. There are, however, questions to which they would like very much to have answers! Such things as: Is there a personal God out there somewhere? Does He know about me? What I am, who I am, what I need? Can He, will He, do something to meet my needs? Does He really love me? What can I expect from God? What does God expect of me? **These questions speak to our sense of helplessness** in the face of life's challenges as we meet them, day by day. How can I know Him? How can I establish communication with Him? **In the hour of my crisis, will He really step into the affairs of my life and become involved with me?** The most accurate book on human history, tells of countless times when God did involve Himself in the affairs of men. The Bible is filled with promises, from Genesis to Revelation, assuring us: He surely will meet our needs and give meaning, purpose and a sense of destiny to our lives.

There is the historical record of three Hebrew men, captives in Babylon, who, though greatly honored in the land, had displeased their king for failing to worship an image he had created. The penalty for such disobedience was cremation in a furnace of one of the brick kilns of Babylon. This history is recorded in Daniel, chapter three. Given a second chance, those men said, "We do not have to think this over. Our God is able to deliver us; but even if He doesn't, we will not bow down to any graven image!" Furious, King Nebuchadnezzar had the ovens heated seven times hotter and the men thrown in with all their clothes on. **Then God stepped in!** Nebuchadnezzar, staring vindictively at the scene, suddenly leaped to his feet with the startled cry, "Did we not cast three men bound into the furnace? I see four walking; and the fourth is like the Son of God!" It was, indeed, the Son of God! The pre-incarnate Jesus had come to deliver those men who were faithful to the death. They were unharmed even though those who threw them into the furnace were overcome by the heat.

Remember Hezekiah, King of Judah, who had received word from the Lord, he was about to die? His faith was strong for God had answered prayer, miraculously, before, and God extended his life by fifteen years. Hezekiah requested the shadow on the sun dial move backwards ten degrees, assuring the promise. **Then God stepped in**; and contrary to all physical laws, the shadow did move backwards ten degrees and Hezekiah did live fifteen more years.

After the crucifixion of Jesus, the disciples, shattered by what they saw as a catastrophic death, not only of their Lord but of all their hopes and dreams. Frightened, and believing they were next to be slain; they huddled in a locked room expecting to hear the sound of marching feet. They were helpless, without hope, and thoroughly terrified. Suddenly, Jesus, Himself, **stepped into the room**; and said, "Peace be unto you!" *Luke 24:36* Jesus had conquered Satan, sin, death, Hell and the grave; and would make them more than conquerors. Those fearful, confused, inept, uneducated men went out to "turn their world upside down," and reach their world and generation with the Gospel!

What about today? Does He still come to us in our hours of need? Does He still care? Will He still step into your life's situation, and say, "peace be unto you?" Can we honestly, actually walk with God throughout the journey of life? What wonderful assurance in Hebrews, thirteen, "Jesus Christ, the same yesterday, today, and forever." "Every good and perfect gift is from above, and cometh down from the Father of lights, with whom is no variableness, neither shadow of turning." *James 1:17* Jesus said in Revelation, three, "I **stand at the door** and knock, if **any man** hear my voice and open the door, **I will come in**!" There is nothing consistent with His will for our lives that he cannot and will not do, if we trust and obey!

We object to the humanistic and liberal theologians, who strip miracles from the Bible; yet we often criticize those who express full confidence in their expectation of miracles. They call us **mystics, super saints, fanatics**, or just plain boastful!

God graciously gave me a mother who believed in miracles

and with good reason. She **expected them**, and **God worked them**! Perhaps someday I may tell of them too. This may be the right time to tell you of just one of them as illustrative of others. As children we lived in a family that was, certainly, financially handicapped. At one time we lived in the country, without transportation. With three younger children at home, mother would send the three older boys to Sunday school at a church in toward town. One day, standing by the kitchen window, she saw the three boys come over the crest of a distant hill. The Lord spoke to mother and said, "The boys have been swimming!" Mother stood by the door as they filed past her – not a spot of mud, no blades of grass, hair neatly combed and they had Sunday school papers. They even told what the lesson had been about. I would have dropped it right there. Not mother! Addressing my oldest brother, she challenged, "Joel, why would you go swimming on Sunday?" He was shocked almost out of his wits! He did not deny it; he simply asked, "How did you know?" Mother told him the Lord had told her and that he had better come clean in a hurry, assuring him the longer it took to get the facts, the worse it would be for him. He confessed that for about three weeks they had been going down a creek halfway to town. Just out of sight from the road, they would take off their clothes, neatly fold them on limbs of trees and go swimming. Before others returned from Sunday school, they would dry off, dress, comb their hair and inspect each other for telltale evidence. Meeting the returning Sunday school children, they would either get papers others had brought for them, or take them away from the less cooperative. With a mother like that we had no problem believing God could communicate accurately with folk who had learned to listen.

Through the years of ministry, I have seen the Lord step into life's situations, solve problems, and witness to His presence in a fellowship of mutually shared love. He has turned tides, broken fetters, given supernatural strength to bear burdens, endure trials and overcome seemingly insurmountable obstacles. There were many occasions when He responded instantaneously to our invitation. I would be dishonest to tell it differently because of pretended false modesty. The secret lay not in what I had done but what He did, and He is worthy of praise!

God has walked into our lives in the shoes of many precious people through the years. The problem lies, not in those named, but the many that cannot be named within the scope of this book. Betty Ide was used of God in so many ways to minister to our needs. She became my chauffeur when my leg was in a cast because of a shattered knee cap. Betty taught my wife how to drive, and encouraged her to become a school teacher. As a result, Joyce completed her work for her degree at Trenton State College. Betty served as an unpaid secretary in three churches and secretary of the board of directors for The Upper Room Fellowship. Throughout the years she has been God's faithful servant and our beloved friend.

Dr. William Downey, a dentist in Pennsylvania, was and is, even now, one of God's chosen servants helping wherever God indicates a cause or person in need. He regularly provided dental care for many who could not afford it, visited foreign missions fields to care for the teeth of missionaries, held services in his home and worked in the local churches. It was in one of those small churches where I first met him. This occurred during that interim period when our finances were being provided through my estate care business. I had purchased timber rights and was running a logging operation near Middlebury, Pennsylvania. This became a venture bordering on the disastrous. So many things went wrong! I was standing on a huge oak tree with a power saw at full throttle, preparing that oak for a stringer on a bridge, when it rolled down the mountain. That was a close brush with death. Heavier than usual snows finally made it impossible to continue logging. One night, as I lay in bed, the Lord made it very clear: I was out of step. I can remember praying, "Lord, if I am out of place here, I will return to Trenton, but I must have work to support my family. If you will give me work in Trenton by **five o'clock Monday**, I'll know that I should stay in Trenton, and suspend work here." All available assets were tied up in the logging, and I did not have enough money to even get home. God walked in again, wearing Dr. Downey's shoes. Bill Downey loaned me one thousand dollars to help see me through that present crisis. Dr. Downey and his wife Betty, serving their Lord, had been used of God to see us through yet another crisis.

That following Monday, at **exactly five o'clock**, the telephone rang. It was Theresa "Pat" Sylvester, a precious friend and former parishioner in the Trenton church. She worked as a housemaid for three or four wealthy families. The Kesslers, for whom she worked, said they needed someone to care for their trees. Pat told them of my work and arranged an interview. I began the care of their trees on Wednesday and was never without work again until Jerry called to the work in Lynchburg, Virginia. Through Pat Sylvester, I took over the care of all the estates where she had been employed. This quiet, unassuming lady, considering herself quite unimportant, had been used of God to answer my prayer for guidance at a vital crossroads of our lives. This lady is precious in the memory of our whole family because of her many expressions of thoughtfulness and love.

God worked through George Rogers, Dr. Jerry Falwell's chief executive officer, to work out the details of our responding to God's call to work as project director in the early construction at Liberty University. George and his wife, Barbara, have been precious friends ever since. I have the strong belief our Lord ordained we were to be "workers together with Him!" When George called me in Trenton asking how soon I could be on the job, God clearly witnessed to the fact George was calling for Him!

While pastoring in Toronto, Ontario, one of our ladies requested prayer for her niece, whose condition had been declared terminal. This girl had a ruptured appendix for two weeks before her doctor consulted a specialist and a correct diagnosis was made. She had been kept alive with massive doses of penicillin. The startled specialist had her rushed to the operating room. When the incision was made, gangrenous puss oozed out of the wound. They closed the incision and announced she could not possibly survive. I went to St. Joseph's Hospital where a special nurse kept vigil at the door. She cautioned, "Just a few moments, Reverend." Entering the room, I found the girl wearing an oxygen mask, and in what seemed to be a coma. Her jaw had dropped and her eyes rolled back up in her head. That scene is so vivid to me right now! I held my New Testament in both hands, resting them on the bed, and quietly prayed, "Lord, she has gone beyond the reach of human personality. She doesn't even know I am here. Lord, she hasn't gone beyond your reach. You could speak to the life impulses in her body and call her back to health." Then after a moment, "Please God, call her back, for Jesus' sake! **Then God stepped in!** The split second, when I asked, "for Jesus' sake," that bed jumped under my hands. I looked up to see that girl looking at me with eyes as clear as a bell! I said, "Audrey, we are praying for you!" She smiled, said, "That's good!" and dropped off to restful **sleep**. Her complete recovery began at that moment. I neither touched, nor anointed her, just simply asked the Father for help in Jesus' name! The only **healing hands** there were **His**!

The doctors said, "It was a miracle!" Short weeks later, just before she left the hospital, I confided what happened that first day of my visit, from my point of view, saying, "Audrey, I don't want to take credit for what only God can do. There were hundreds of people praying for you; and I did not have to tell God you were a good girl for He knew the testimony of your life. But I shall always be grateful He permitted me to be the one here when He turned the tide." Then, for the first time, she told me of the situation from her point of view. She said, "I will never forget it either. That day, I was dropping, dropping, dropping and was about to let go when a voice called me, 'Audrey, come back!' I opened my eyes to see a tall man standing beside my bed!" I bear true witness: her name was not mentioned in the prayer, nor the words, "come back"! No power on earth could convince me that Audrey Vickery did not hear the voice of Almighty God calling her back from the brink of eternity! To fail to bear witness would be to dishonor God. I would be like the ungrateful lepers the Lord spoke of who failed to give Him the glory!

While still in Toronto, we became acquainted with a couple who had a boy ill with leukemia. There was much prayer for Wayne and he seemed to be getting better. He died rather suddenly and his mother, Flo, was emotionally shattered. She questioned why God had not healed her son. Was it because she was so long accepting Jesus as Savior and Lord? Was the Lord punishing her for something she had done? Had we prayed earnestly enough? She said, "Pastor, if I could only know it was God's will for Wayne to be taken, I could bear it." I remember saying, "Flo, just trust God and ask Him to give you that assurance. I don't know just how or when he will do that: but He will!" The funeral took place on a day of steady, heavy rain. As we came out of the funeral parlor on Dundas Street, in conversation with the funeral director, I commented, "It is difficult for a mother to lay a child to rest on a sunny day, yet it is so much more so in a sea of mud." After a moment, I added, "I wish the Lord would hold up the rain!" He was not a man who shared my faith, and skepticism was written all over his countenance. You could almost hear him say, "Kook!" With no intent to contend the issue, I asked him if he believed such were possible. I told him of Billy Graham asking God to stop the rain that was interfering with his invitation at a meeting on Boston Commons – the Lord did cut off that rain. Calling the man by name, I said, "You would say that was only coincidence, wouldn't you? He tried to be courteous through it all. Looking back, there was no intent to pursue the matter. However, just as we were turning into the cemetery gate, with rain coming down in sheets, on sudden impulse I turned to the man and announced, "I might just as well tell you, **I have asked the Lord to stop the rain at the grave side**!" That cortege pulled up along the cemetery plot and stopped. **Then God stepped in!** The rain stopped as abruptly as though one had shut off a faucet. During the internment service I caught myself hurrying the service, lest the rain begin again. God rebuked me so clearly, "If I am holding the rain it will not rain until the service is over!" As an expression of faith, I deliberately took even more time then usual. There was no break in the clouds – it was raining all around – but, not one drop fell on my Bible or on that service. When I went over to Flo, to comfort her, she looked up with a beautiful smile, and said: "Wasn't God good to hold up the rain as I asked Him to: now I know it is all right. It was His will to take Wayne!" That is when I knew why the discussion of rain had come up in the first place! That funeral director was so shaken up he would not drive me back to the parlor, but got me another ride. His exact words, "I have never seen anything like this in my whole life!" I wish I could have heard what he said moments later; for the very minute the people were in the cars again, the rain came down in torrents!

      The most dramatic intervention, for me personally, happened in New Guinea. I went from the moment of greatest despair ever experienced to that of greatest ecstacy, in seconds. We had been in the coastal jungles of New Guinea for several months. Most of our men were later hospitalized out because of the impact of that environment on our health. Temperatures reached as high as one hundred and twenty degrees, Fahrenheit. Ankle-deep mud would be turned to dust in one work day, as steam would spiral up to float across the Owen Stanley Mountains. In the intense heat and humidity, fungus grew on our bodies like mold on old bread. Japanese bombers often flew overhead for we were a secondary target after Port Moresby. The occasional Japanese sniper would interrupt our daily routines. What bothered me most, however, was the spiritual climate: everything seemed to reek of evil. I had no radio and, of course, there were no tape decks in those days. I had not heard a real gospel sermon or song during all those months. Lying on my bunk, I could reach out and touch a tier of three bunks on either side of me. Nine men slept within a ten-foot square area. All of them smoked, drank and cursed. It was a full year after coming home before I could hear an innocent remark without cringing – waiting for the inevitable double take. I came to feel as though I were in the very vestibule of Hell.

Satan was giving me a lot of personal attention, too. He was saying, "This is life, get used to it! Your mother raised you in a cloister; this is the way things really are. Virtue, honor, holy character are all figments of your imagination. They are all in your head!" Nothing I had ever learned of spiritual truth seemed to apply anymore. Had my destiny hinged on my philosophy of life or theological theory, I never would have made it through! One night, it came to the point where I was in such despair, I could take no more. Arising from my bunk, I walked down a jungle path along the bay. The air was filled with bats – having three-foot wing spreads – visible against the stars. Lizards made the kunai grass seem alive as they rustled their way through it. Deadly, poisonous snakes slithered across the trail, and clouds of malaria-carrying mosquitoes swarmed about me. Sounds of ribald laughter and voices spoke of a jungle juice party in progress not far away. Making my way across a small stream, I walked out on a coral reef jutting up from the bay. A large fleet of ships lay at anchor, silhouetted in the starlight. No lights were seen anywhere: blackouts were necessary because of the bombers.

Turning from the bay, I looked up through waving palm fronds, to the stars above, and in despair, cried out loud, "God are you up there? Do you see me down here? Do you care?" Then, I prayed out loud, "Lord, I don't know anything anymore!" No one ever spoke more clearly to my mind, "But you know Jesus!" You could have heard me say, were you there, "Yes, I know Jesus! I remember when He gave me peace and revealed His presence to me!" Almost without thinking, I began to sing: "My Jesus, I love Thee, I know Thou art mine. For Thee all the follies of sin I resign. I'll love Thee in life, I'll love Thee in death, I'll love Thee as long as

Thou lendeth me breath!" **Suddenly Jesus stepped in!** How can I describe the glory of His presence? That jungle glade became a cathedral. I have never sensed His presence more real in any church or cathedral. Wave after wave of exhilarating joy, peace and love swept over me. No human being's presence was ever more real than was Jesus' that day. I forgot all about the snakes, mosquitoes, bats, lizards, and that jungle juice party. Later, on my way back to the barracks, I felt as though I were floating along that path. That scene is still vivid in my mind. Never again, have I experienced the despair that brought about that blessed hour.

Thinking about it later, this realization struck home: but **what if I had not known Jesus**? Where would I be today? What would have happened to my life? This would be a good time to ask, "Do you know Jesus so real that no despair can blot out the knowledge of His presence?" I would love to introduce you to Him, too!

This reminds me again of that time when praying at the Garden Tomb in Jerusalem. Throughout that pilgrimage we had sought to identify with places where Jesus had walked. I did not know if we had actually walked in the footsteps of Jesus at any time during our tour of the city. I could not know for sure where **He had been**, but I knew **where He was** that morning, at the tomb. I know the **tomb was empty** that first Easter morning; because my **heart was full**! Please do not think all this as being too good to be true. There is no greater reality than that of His presence! **Surely the Creator has to be more real than His creation!** How wonderful His companionship; when we learn to walk with Him! If you want Him to step into your life: **open the door**! Don't forget He is either living **inside** your heart **reigning**, or on the **outside knocking**.

Miracles of healing or other visible manifestations of God's loving presence have tremendous impact upon our faith. However, they are but temporary and passing. Lazarus, raised from the dead, died again! Most of the sick healed in yesteryear, have since died. The greatest of miracles – the only one Christ had to die to perform – is for eternity! The miracle of the new birth, when we become new creations in Christ, and the dedicated temples of the Holy Spirit, is the miracle of miracles! Thank God for having witnessed many occasions when **He stepped in** to transform a life, and reconcile another of His estranged children!

Christianity is more than doctrine or belief. It is a way of life! It is a walk with God in the most precious of fellowships. "If we say we have fellowship with Him; and walk in darkness, we lie, and do not the truth: but if we walk in the light, as He is in the light we have fellowship one with another!" *I John 1:6-7* You may fully expect God will supply all of your needs, according to His riches in glory, by Christ Jesus. Just open the door and see for yourself! Jesus said, "I have called you friends!" *John 15:10-17* True friendship speaks of a bonding of mind and spirit that is empowered by self-forgetting love! Those of a lustful nature say, "What's in it for me?" Those moved by His love want to know how they can make the world a better place because they have lived in it. We were created to be friends of God, and permit Him to befriend others through our living. In the words of a familiar hymn:

"Lord, I am pleading; hear Thou my prayer.
Let me thy blessed fellowship share.
From day to day Thy servant I'd be.
Grant me a closer walk with Thee.
Oh for a closer walk with Thee!
Near to Thy side I ever would be.
Shield me and hide me,
constantly guide me into a closer walk with Thee!"

National Survival

What is true of individuals, is true of a nation comprised of individuals, with regards to both rewards and punishment. What we sow, we reap and God will not be mocked nor outwitted. "Righteousness exalteth a nation: but sin is a reproach to any people. *Proverbs 14:34* "The wicked shall be turned into Hell, and all the nations that forget God." *Psalms 9:17* Vital, dynamic faith in God is essential for our national survival! **Our freedom without faith becomes the power to self-destruct!** We cannot form a moral society made up of immoral men and women. It is well to be reminded that without freedom there can be no morality. Without morality, there will soon be no freedom!

Democracy without faith in God is like the mythical **Zombie** – a resurrected body, without a soul. Unless man uses his God-given intelligence, reason, conscience and moral sensitivity for his walk with God, he will self-destruct! When God loses control of a man, self takes over and Satan is invited in. Freedom is the very essence of democracy. The freedom of choice given by God was not that we might do as we please; but rather we could do, of our own free will, **what pleased Him**! We were created for a purpose – **His purpose**! Who knows better or cares more than He? When man fails to use his privilege for its designated purpose: he surrenders those gifts that distinguish him from other animal creations: and sinks to a level lower than an animal. This is the essential reason I am strongly opposed to alcoholic drinks and drugs. They immediately effect a person's mental and emotional control over behavior: the extent measured by intake. When people speak of release from inhibitions and highs, they are recognizing the effect of drugs on the very elements in their essential being that differentiates them from the animals. These restraints being neutralized, control is surrendered to the drugs. A man once told me he hated liquor. He was asked, "Why then, do you drink it?" He explained that his conscience gave him no peace when he was cheating on his wife. He went on to say, "After a few drinks, the world is my oyster!" When Satan is permitted to program the mind and spirit to oppose God's will and purpose: we have surrendered control to him. Righteousness does, indeed, exalt a nation, and sin surely is a reproach to individuals or nations.

Freedom to worship God and do right before God and man: is now seen to be a license to do what we please. It has become an exaltation of self-will above the will of God and the welfare of others. With every privilege comes a corresponding responsibility. Refusal to accept our responsibility, should disqualify us and deny us that privilege. We hear the battle cry of the selfish and the sensuous, "I want my rights! Give me what I want!" You do not hear them ask, "What are my responsibilities? What is my duty? What is right? How does this effect others?" This demand for individual rights, with neither restraints nor responsibilities, is fragmenting our nation! We are being divided into little "power cells" with ever increasing tension and strife. We are like an engine that has neutralized its governor and is racing out of control, vibrating itself to the point of self-destruction! When God loses control of a person, he is lost and out of control! The societal, moral and spiritual elements of control have been neutralized, and we are self-destructing! What ever happened to truth, honor, duty, responsibility, self-discipline and unselfish concern for others?

Self-discipline is the purest and best of disciplines. We were designed by God to monitor our own conduct through a mind, conscience and will, totally surrendered to His own will. This places us in harmony and at peace with God and all other forces under His control. Only those redeemed by Jesus, the Christ of God, know what freedom truly is! "If the Son therefore shall make you free, ye shall be free indeed." *John 8:36*

If we are not guided by God's built-in controls, we will be like unguided missiles: out of control, unless external restraints are forced upon us. I do not believe anyone enjoys being forced to do anything by anyone else or by some external force. If our professed love of freedom is simply the reaction of a rebellious spirit; there can be no peace with God or man. Our purest joy is not discovered by self-indulgence but self-control.

When men no longer are governed by honor and integrity, you cannot trust: your children to the teachers, your affairs to your lawyers, your money to investors, your body to the doctors, your security to the police, nor your soul to the clergy! Is it any wonder there are so many cynics around?

Just look around you and see for yourself! Unprecedented waves of crime: we are not safe on the streets, in our cars, places of business, or our own homes. Babies are being torn to pieces in their own mother's wombs, parents are murdered by their own children for an early grasp on their inheritance. People are indulging their lust for power over others through domestic violence and assault of the innocent. Drug addiction, and its related crimes, ravage our society from ghettoes to mansions. Uncontrollable social diseases pronounce death sentences upon millions. Children are born HIV positive, an inheritance from their mother. **These horrible things are not just happening, they are designed, initiated and promoted: through the abuse of our freedoms!** Why? Because we have lost our faith in God! We have become so degenerate our own government is doing much to cancel out God's message of hope and deliverance. Many in government are trying to stamp out the sparks of faith that remain. Those **for whom God has stepped in** and said, "Peace be unto you," are our nation's only **unprotected minority**! On them, it is always open season! Their critics accuse them of **trying to turn back the clock** on the gains they have made. If they are talking about turning back Satan's gains in control of our nation and turning back to the faith that once exalted this nation, I would love to **turn back that clock**!

Many very intelligent and sincere folk ask, "If there is a God, why doesn't He stop all this evil?" The stark, simple answer is, "Because He loves us!" He could stop it all this very moment! He knows very well, the day He **steps in with judgment**, the doom of **everyone not redeemed** has also been **sealed**! If God is permitting all this carnage to continue just to keep Heaven's doors open a little longer for sinners yet to repent: what should the spiritually alive Christian be doing? If we are truly walking with Him: we will be working for that closest to His own heart. It was for this cause Christ also died: the redemption of lost mankind and their reconciliation with the Father. How can you love someone very much, spend a lot of time around them, and not be concerned about what burdens them? Jesus said, "He that is not with Me is against Me, he that gathereth not with Me scattereth abroad." *Matthew 12:30* Are we of the Faith winning arguments, feeding our own egos, or winning souls?

God is absolutely sovereign. He always was and always will be. He does not, however, always exercise that sovereignty. He deliberately limited His sovereignty to make room for man's free will. What a marvelous, gracious thing for Him to do! Mankind has registered a terrible history of misuse and abuse of that trust. One day, God will say, "That's enough!" He will step in and reassert His absolute sovereignty! On that day our freedom of independent action will be ended. Choices already made will determine our destiny, and it will be sealed for eternity!

Few matters demand as much attention as the disease of AIDS. Vast sums of money, much research and efforts in education are being invested in seeking a cure. This is a horrible physical disease: almost one hundred percent fatal. How awful when children may inherit this disease from the blood of their own mothers! Yet, **there is a worse disease** we inherit from our parents! **Every descendent of Adam has been born SIN positive!** We are born afflicted with that one hundred percent terminal spiritual disease; that carries a sentence of death that is eternal!

    Could you or I announce we have an absolute cure for AIDS and prove it with facts, we would find ourselves among the wealthiest and most popular people on earth. We would be sought out from all over the world! Strangely enough, we do have wonderful news! **A cure has been found for the most infectious, deadly, universal disease in the history of mankind!** It has been perfected and paid for by a foundation established on that skull-shaped hill just outside the walls of Jerusalem, nearly two thousand years ago! The greatest of Physicians, who administers this cure, stands just outside the heart's door, asking, "Please let Me help you!" Wouldn't you think every one of us would rush to that door and open it inviting Him to step in? **You either have done so, or you have not!** Be wise, open that door!

    All Heaven is watching to see what we will do with God's cure for **SIN Positive**. When word of Sodom and Gomorrah's sins reached Heaven; God took up the matter, sending a delegation to check it all out. It was worse than reported! In spite of the horrible evidence, He would have spared the city had there been enough righteous still in it. Right now, The United States of America is being checked out by just such a delegation. We are being weighed in the balance as was Belteshazzer of old. There is every evidence we are being found terribly wanting as a nation. Just where do you stand? Waiting or wanting? Open that door; He will step in saying, "Peace be unto you!" If you fail to do so, He will step in with judgment! One way or the other, **He will come!** ❖

13 Mysteries of Godliness

The Bible has provided all necessary answers pertaining to truth and Godliness. We would like to believe we understand all of them, yet so many are seen as "through a glass darkly". We who minister the Gospel, do not like to dwell on what we do not know: especially when in debate with those of another persuasion. The most brilliant of minds have not been able to figure out these mysteries of Godliness. Most of those facts of truth and Godliness, essential to our concepts of God and living in a right relationship with God, are so clear; as the Word has said, "The wayfaring man, though a fool, need not err therein."

Some speak of contradictions in the Bible text. There are differing versions of the same incidents as seen by various writers. This does not undermine the veracity of the text. The varying points of view, yet presenting clearly the essential facts, only strengthens the witness. Were a judge to hear ten witnesses, from ten totally diverse educational, social, economic and ethnic backgrounds come up with verbatim testimonial agreement, he would know there had been collusion. It would have been a staged presentation. Peter said, "We have not followed cunningly devised fables, when we made known unto you the power and coming of our Lord Jesus Christ, but were eye witnesses of His majesty." *II Peter 1:16* The Bible has one Author, Who used many scribes. The content of each scribe's work reflects his background and personality without altering the main content of his transcription. Every basic statement of fact in the Bible is true! Everything we need to know is there. It is **all true**; yet does not present **all of** the truth there is to know. John, in his version of the Gospel said, of the teachings of Jesus alone, "And there are also many other things which Jesus did, the which, if they could be written every one, I suppose that even the world itself could not contain the books that should be written." *John 21:25*

What may seem to be contradictions in the Bible are simply gaps in our knowledge due to our failure to understand. I have come to understand more clearly as I read the Bible every year, the same passages take on new depths of meaning because of a broadened understanding due to new experiences in life and study. Each lesson taught by the Spirit sheds new light on yet other facets of truth. When something seems contradictory to me and I sense a gap in my understanding: I pray for an understanding heart. Sometimes new light answers the question. At other times I simply commit it all to Him, for I know He has it all figured out; and I am satisfied. However, I remain curious and the question lingers pending new light.

Too often we settle for consensus among those of our own doctrinal persuasion. We fear contention and desire acceptance. In this manner we become more **bound to a system** of men and **lose cohesion with devout men of all faiths**. God grant us the wisdom and love to live in peace and harmony, in spite of differing doctrines and definitions. We should be at peace with every other person on earth who loves the Lord! We need to be alert lest some theory of **theological correctness** obscure what the Holy Spirit would teach us. We need to take our problems up with the Author of the Book for we must adjust to the Mind of God above the minds of men. Jesus prayed that every one of His followers be bound as one with the Unity of the Trinity. *John 17* This is being led by the Spirit of God as advised in Romans eight. Please understand: this is not incitation to **rebellion**, but a call for **freedom** in the Spirit! We do well to remember, the Bible is the "Owner's Manual". We should learn to take the advice of our "Manufacturer"! He will tell us how to get the most out of life, how to avoid problems, what constitutes preventative maintenance and what to do when problems do develop.

One such question bothered me for many years. The answer, that cleared it up to my satisfaction: could well raise the hackles on the back of some seasoned theologian's neck. Jesus never talked hypothetically, dealt with approximations or "almosts". His words were yea and amen! When He said, "A certain rich man," there was a certain rich man! Exactness as to detail, is one of the basic tests for the authenticity of prophecy! I could not understand that portion in Matthew, twelve, twenty, where Jesus said, "For as Jonas was three days and three nights in the whale's belly; so shall the son of man be three days and three nights in the heart of the earth." Jesus made this statement in response to those requesting a sign. He said it was the wicked who needed signs to believe; then added, one precise sign would be given: the sign of Jonas the prophet. For years, I thought He was referring to time spent in the tomb. But He was not in the tomb three days and three nights. He was in the grave but a part of three days and only two nights. Through the years I heard the theories of: special Sabbaths, a Thursday crucifixion and other explanations. None seemed to be very convincing.

One day while meditating on the crucifixion and Easter: the question arose, "Just what did Jesus mean by three days and three nights in the heart of the earth, or bowels of the earth?" Was He speaking of the entombment of His crucified body, or His separation from the Father as He was cloaked in the sins of the world? Was He speaking of His **physical death** – separated from life or **spiritual death** – when separated from the Father while bearing our trespasses and sin?

Jesus frequently used the term "Mine hour is not yet come". But there in the garden He said, **"Now is mine hour come!"** *John 17:1* I have come to believe those three days and three nights in the bowels of the earth marked the **time of separation from the Father** as our Lord suffered isolation from the Father because of the sins of the world. Adam, God's created son, walked with God until he sinned and his sin separated him from his Creator. Fellowship was broken! There in Gethsemane, God's only begotten Son, Who had walked in fellowship with His Father from eternity's morning, **assumed the guilt of Adam** and the human race, **became separated** from fellowship with the Father. "For He hath made Him to be sin for us, who knew no sin; that we might be made the righteousness of God in Him." *II Corinthians 5:21* He was identified as a sinner separated from His father and isolated in the world of sin. He was born to die! "For this cause came I into the world." *John 12:27* Our Lord was **not recoiling from the prospect of separation of body and soul in physical death**. That was not the **bitter cup** He wished to avoid drinking. **It was His separation from the Father, and suffering spiritual death** from which He cringed. Jesus was isolated from the Father in the heart of the world He helped create! I find assurance in believing **that night in Gethsemane was the first of three nights of His separation from the Father**! I am certain the Heavenly Father, and all Heaven were in mourning that night of Christ's agony, but in the heart of the earth, Jesus suffered, bled and died, **alone**!

The garden of Gethsemane was an olive garden. Here at the **place of the wine press**, God permitted His Own Son to be crushed under the weight of the sins of the world until He sweat drops of blood. *Luke 22:44* The holy, sin-less, immaculate Son of God, was not only separated from His Father, but **He became sin**! All the guilt of all men, for all time, became His to bear. It was the assumption of all the spiritual filth of all men from Adam, to us, and all mankind to the end of time; and its burden of guilt that Jesus wished to avoid, if at all possible. Yet, He knew the suffering of that guilt was the very reason He became flesh. There in the garden, the **first drops of atoning blood were shed**!

More atoning blood was shed as our Lord was beaten and His blood flowed from His lacerated back. "He was **bruised for our iniquity**, the chastisement for our peace was upon Him, and **by His stripes we are healed**." *Isaiah 53:5* On the cross of Calvary, Jesus shed all His remaining blood, paid the full price for our redemption, and could cry, "It is finished!" Just three days and three nights from the time He accepted the burden for our sin, and was separated from the Father, Jesus walked out of the tomb triumphant! He had paid for the redemption of all mankind forever. Satan would be forever, a conquered foe!

May God help us to understand the awful price required for our deliverance from sin. If we could but understand the depth of Christ's suffering for us: nothing God could ask of us would ever seem too much!

The death, burial and resurrection of Jesus was observed from many points of view. The Jewish rulers, failing to understand the two visions of Messiah, considered Jesus an imposter and blasphemer worthy of death. Before we are too hard on them, let us remember they were God's custodians of the Law. In Deuteronomy, the Jews were commanded to put false prophets to death. *Deuteronomy 13:5* They could not understand how the same prophet saw Jesus as a sacrificial lamb and a lion: as a suffering servant and a coming king. Failing to recognize two distinct times of coming, they opted for the conquering Messiah who would set them free from Rome. Jesus was an imposter and blasphemer to them. Of course we know their own self-interest and sinful natures betrayed many of them. Don't forget, we too may be blinded and led astray by our own sinful and selfish natures. We come equipped with a natural prejudice all of our own.

The Roman point of view was a classical case of **political correctness**! They just couldn't have someone around who challenged the authority of Caesar.

For Mary, the mother of Jesus, it was the agony of a beloved son's murder and the fulfillment of the prophecy of Simeon, at His circumcision, "A sword shall pierce your heart also."

It was the end of everything for the disciples. Their hopes and dreams were destroyed; and they feared for their own lives.

Have you ever wondered how those awful scenes must have looked from Heaven? Can you imagine the Father, the hosts of Heaven, those legions of restrained angels watching from the battlements of Heaven? As Jesus came to earth **to become the Light of the world**, there was **a measure of darkness in Heaven**. The Son of God, Co-Creator of Heaven and earth, had absented Himself for approximately thirty-three years. He truly was the Lord "Who had gone into a far country to hew Himself out a kingdom!" How they must have been at attention that morning when a delegation of angels attended His physical birth in Bethlehem – as He became a Son of Man. How they must have recoiled with horror as God the Son, walking as the son of man, was abused and suffered such vile treatment! Jesus told Pilate, "I could call ten thousand angels to release me if I chose to do so." Can you imagine those eager angels, restrained only by the will of God, standing at attention in Heaven just awaiting His call to destroy our Lord's abusers and set Him free?

What terrible gloom must have prevailed as the Father and His heavenly hosts watched that **blackout** descend on Gethsemane, as sin separated our Lord from the fellowship of those He had known for eternities. The Scripture says angels did come to aid Him in the garden. What intense gloom must have prevailed as Jesus was crucified. What about that blackness of midnight that prevailed in the final hours of crucifixion: could Heaven have drawn a veil to shut out the scene?

On the morning of that third day; the earth turned in the path of light from the sun, and the light of dawn was spread across the Arabian desert toward the Judean hills. Two of those restrained angels, now released, were eagerly racing the dawn to a garden tomb not far from that skull-shaped hill. They arrived with a triumphant shout and rolled the stone away: not to let Jesus out, but to show the world the tomb was empty!

We know there is joy in Heaven over every sinner redeemed because of that shed blood. What must it have been like when He who shed that blood walked out of the tomb? We sing with joy, "Up from the grave He arose, with a mighty triumph over foes." What singing and shouting must have erupted in Heaven! What a cantata! Surely that was the original *Hallelujah Chorus*! He had risen; and was on His way home! I look forward to the day when the angels can tell me all about that resurrection morning! Sure hope you will be there, too!

I love to think of Mary of Magdela, lingering there by an empty tomb. Overwhelmed by her love for the Lord and brokenhearted because she could not minister to His broken body, she could not see clearly because of her tears. Approaching one thought to be a gardener, she pleaded, "Please, tell me where they have laid Him and I will take care of Him!" Could there be a more beautiful moment than when our Lord revealed His resurrection to Mary? He simply spoke her name in love – "Mary!" I identify most with Mary. For I, too, have had Him speak to me in love! I have the confidence that Jesus paid it all that repentant sinners might hear Him speak their name in love as they bow humbly at His feet! ✥

14 Our Inheritance

We are all children of destiny! We are not drifting flotsam on a sea of time, just nobodies going nowhere. We were created for a purpose having a destiny that is eternal. Our Creator God, housed our eternal spirits in bodies made from the dusts of the earth, just temporary housing for the journey through time. Our temporal existence is a period of probation, preparation and spiritual development: fitting us to be at home with Him; when He finally walks us home, as He did Enoch. In military terms, it is a staging area, a place for basic training. When we are ready and our earthly sojourn is over, our bodies go back to dust: but our eternal spirits go back to the God who created us in His own image. We are immortal, in spirit and will never cease to be. There is no annihilation of the soul. We were created to be a part of God's eternal family. He has prepared Heaven for His created children. He prepared Hell for Satan and the fallen angels. However, if we refuse to follow Him home, we will end up in Hell with Satan because we chose to follow him instead of our Heavenly Father! So many have followed Satan: God's Word reports, "Hell hath enlarged itself!" Just imagine that! So many on the broad road to destruction they were creating housing shortages in Hell! How awful!

Heaven is God's final home – a place prepared for a prepared people. So many persons would not feel at home in Heaven, even if they should get there. They have no interest in what Heaven represents. Their only interest in Heaven is occasioned by their fear of Hell. They know they do not wish to be there, if the place does actually exist! A man once told me he did not believe there was a Hell that existed as a place. I felt prompted to reply, "You mean, you hope there is no Hell: for if there is such a place, that is where you are headed as indicated by your lifestyle!" Surprisingly, that man replied, "I guess you are right!"

If your affections are centered in the materialistic and the sensual, you have no longing for what Heaven presents. We are told **not** to love the things of the world: for if we do, the love of the Father is not in us. If you do love self, the world, the flesh and the Devil you are locked into the pull of Hell upon your total being.

Probably a majority of the peoples of earth love sin. They only hate what it does to them. It is the consequences of sin they fear. No one is driven to spiritual redemption by fear alone. Our soul is reconciled with God through our response to the Savior's love! You cannot, in keeping with a whimsical statement, "scare Hell out of anyone!" There have been many case studies where someone, facing great danger or death, moved by fright, have confessed sin and made promises to God. However, when the present danger had passed, they reverted to their old patterns of behavior.

How to Walk with God

There had been no Godly sorrow for sin, no true repentance: hence, no true forgiveness and no spiritual rebirth! No real, lasting change had taken place. Anyone with common sense should be afraid of going to Hell. Fear may move you to face up to your spiritual condition, but you are truly redeemed by the drawing power of the love of God, and your response to that love! This is the pull that brings you safely home!

  We may be driven to repentance by fear, but we are drawn into fellowship with God, by His love. When God reaches down in love and we receive the light of his truth; we may respond in total surrender to His will, becoming new creations in Christ, **spiritually-reborn**. His love flowing through us provides the spiritual energy, the thrust necessary to break Satan's hold upon us and bring us under the drawing power of His love. This is well illustrated in Isaiah's experience at the temple during his hours of crisis. When he saw God in His holiness: he saw his own contrasting filth and cried out for cleansing. God did purge him of his sins and gave him a love for God, greater than all other affections or desires. This is the way we lose our love for the world and learn to love God with all our heart, mind and strength. We sing of this experience, "Things are different now, I am changed, can't you see: since I gave my heart to Jesus! Things I loved before have passed away: things I love far more have come to stay, since I gave my heart to Him!" In true spiritual conversion we change directions, value systems, motivations and Masters. These are evidence of a genuine experience of reconciliation with God. One of the prime evidences of life is the hunger drive. The newborn child does not have to be taught to seek nourishment from his mother. He starts trying to feed from the time he is born. Unless a professedly new-born Christian hungers and thirsts for righteousness, one may question his spiritual birth. Unless you hunger and thirst for righteousness, you will never pay the price to receive the fullness of God's love, nor make it all the way home! Too many professed Christians try to stay as close to worldly things as possible and still make it to Heaven. Professing to love God, they carry on a flirtation with the Devil. The pull of Hell has not yet been truly broken! They are not as yet set free! Not yet truly redeemed from sin's bondage!

  As beautiful as life can be now, it is but the preliminary to the main event. In God's training program, some seem to graduate ahead of their class. Many graduate with honors. When in my student pastorate in Providence, I frequently visited a lovely old lady, Mrs. Nicholson: who seemed to radiate the love of God. Always cheerful, always thoughtful of others, and constantly praising the Lord, even though she was old, ill, and did not have much of this world's treasure. She was always so appreciative of my calls; yet I felt I was the one being ministered to. New challenge and inspiration seemed to flow from her presence. The call announcing her passing reached me at Eastern Nazarene College. While driving home, the Lord gave me my first funeral message. Standing to speak at the funeral, I announced, "You may have come to hear a funeral message; I am here to deliver a commencement address!" There was confidence she could say with Paul, "I have finished the course and kept the faith," and I proceeded to **graduate** her, summa cum laude.

There was an extraordinary series of such home-goings in Toronto, Ontario. They occurred near the end of that pastorate. There had been a sense of having completed my work, but I did not have clear, new orders. A two-week vacation was taken hunting in New Brunswick, almost as much to take time to pray for guidance, as to hunt. Just short days after my return, a district superintendent called, inviting me to accept a church in New York. Thinking surely this is God's guidance, I scheduled a meeting with the church and was to fly down to meet them. Before leaving, it seemed wise to visit the old, sick shut-ins who depended upon my ministry. It seems now there were five of them. **Every single one of them**, said something such as, "Pastor, I don't what we would ever do if you left us. Old Brother Powell, a war veteran, was in a military convalescent home. His wife was in another nursing home; and I was their messenger boy, keeping them in touch with each other. During my visit, Brother Powell said, "You will never know what you have meant to Nance and me! You won't leave us will you?" I asked, "Why would you think I might be leaving?" He responded, "Oh, it's about the time ministers change pastorates." That really was not such a time. With that precious old man's plea still ringing in my ears, and tugging at my heart, too: I went to visit a lady in the Queen Elizabeth Hospital, a hospital for the terminally ill. Mrs. Markle was not in her room, but I found her in the solarium. Mrs. Markle was standing, looking out the window as I entered. She wheeled about and startled me by saying, "I just had the most awful feeling you were not coming! You will not leave me here alone will you?" I had met Mrs. Markle while visiting a parishioner in another hospital. It has always been customary to pray for all in the rooms I visit and to greet them all in Jesus' Name. Mrs. Markle was too ill to come to church, and I visited her in her home where she accepted my Lord as her Savior, too. On the way to my home from that last visit of the day, I felt like a man out courting who was already married! Immediately upon returning home, a phone call was placed to the superintendent in New York, apologizing for not being able to come, as I was not free to leave. He really did not understand why, although I tried to explain to him. But I knew! **I could not leave.**

That was in November. By the next May thirtieth, **all of those folk were in Heaven, except one**! Nance Powell had been transferred to a small private nursing home run by devout Christians! Brother Powell wanted so much to come to church for Easter services. Transportation was provided and that precious old man was so happy! I served him communion that morning. He took the cup and was drinking from it: when he took a heart attack and went home – the communion wine still on his lips. That truly was a last communion. Brother Powell could not have planned a more beautiful departure for home! He was there in the house of God he loved, among the people he loved and who loved him. How wonderful it will be to see him again! We sure will talk that one over in the by and by! How different that expected meeting would be if I had abandoned him!

Six months after God told me I could not leave, I came to the realization, **I could not stay**. My work was done! Think what an awful burden of guilt I should have had to bear had I left those old folk to die alone. No new pastor could have picked up on their care in the short time left to them. That is a vivid reminder of how important it is that we actually, honestly, truly be led by the Spirit of God. Only He could have known all that! God prevented me from "playing the fool" in my human limitations: and helped me "to keep the faith"!

We have so much to look forward to when we get home, but I must confess I am enjoying the journey tremendously! My frequently stated summation: "Heaven is a beautiful place, but I am in no hurry to get there. However, when God decides it is time to come home, He will not have to drag me kicking and complaining over the threshold." There is so much awaiting us there! "The Spirit Itself beareth witness with our spirit, that we are the children of God: and if children, then heirs of God, and joint-heirs with Jesus; if so be that we suffer with Him, that we may also be glorified together!" *Romans 8:16-17* My biggest concern is that I accomplish His full will for me while I am here. Henry W. Longfellow's poem, *The Psalm of Life* has thrilled and inspired me since childhood:

> "Tell me not in mournful numbers life is but an empty dream;
> And the soul is dead that slumbers and things are not what they seem!
> Life is real, life is earnest and the grave is not its goal.
> Dust thou art and to dust returneth, was not spoken of the soul!
>
> "Lives of great men (and women!) all remind us, we can make our lives sublime;
> And in passing leave behind us, footprints in the sands of time.
> Let us then be up and doing with a heart for any fate, still achieving, still pursuing.

Learn to labor and to wait!"

There came a time of special crisis in my ministry. We had completed four pastorates and four building programs. I was feeling terribly frustrated: for my surrender had been to serve God and to bring lost souls into reconciliation with Him. So much time, energy, prayer and emotion had gone into monuments of mortar and stone! Wonderful things had happened, but there had been but few Spirit-anointed revivals, and the people did not seem to have a vision for our commission to win the lost. We were just promoting programs, wrapt up in running a church. One day, sitting and meditating in my office, I prayed, "Lord, is this all there is to it? Is this what you died to accomplish? Don't let me miss out on what you really want to do through my life. Lord, take control and help me to achieve your purpose. When I look back from Heaven's shore, don't let me see sheaves that I have missed. Help me to accomplish everything possible, using the best I have, plus the grace you will give, as I trust and obey: **whatever the cost**." God did, I believe, lead to new fields and new depths; but for a while, I fussed at the cost. I failed to realize the difficulties He led me through were the answers to my own prayers!

Memory Cassettes

Millenniums before man invented audio and video cassette recorders and players: God created memory cassettes and told man how to program them! What a wonderful gift of God – **our memory**! "Precious memories, how they linger! How they ever flood my soul!" Almost all the writings in this book are memories being shared. Some of this material has been recorded on paper at earlier times, most of it is a transcript of playbacks from memory cassettes. Every conscious, active, creative thought we have ever had is programmed into memory. Almost all of our outlook on life, and our basic character is determined by what we program into memory! The mind will program what we put into it, and we are programming every conscious, waking moment. "As a man thinketh in his heart, so is he!" *Proverbs 23:7* We are urged, "Keep thy heart with all diligence, for out of it are the issues of life!" *Proverbs 4:23* It is said, "We are what we eat." There are elements of truth in that statement. It is absolutely true, however, "**We are what we think**!" You cannot have a dirty mind and a clean heart at the same time! James tells us chapter three, "Doth a fountain send forth at the same place sweet water and bitter. So no fountain yields both saltwater and fresh. But if ye have bitter envy and strife in your hearts, glory not, and lie not against the truth!" *James 3:11-12* God's Word assures us that when His Holy Spirit indwells us: a river of living water will flow from our inmost being. A professed Christian who seeks to read both pornographic material and the Bible is **mock-**

ing the Creator who designed his mind! Very little of the Bible will emerge from that man's mind, mouth or life!

Our youth today are urged to experiment with evil. There is a subtle temptation, appealing to both our human ego and sensuous nature, involved in the question, "How can you criticize it if you have never experienced it?" Some have said, "I'll try anything once!" Others think, "I'll go ahead and do it and ask God to forgive me later!" God will forgive if we are genuinely repentant and fully confess. He will forget that forgiven sin, but we cannot! It has been recorded on a memory cassette! The terribly rapid rise in teen suicides is largely due to what they programmed into their memory cassettes! Disillusioned, degraded, defeated, ashamed, they see nothing of hope or beauty in their present condition, and no hope in the future! They seek oblivion to escape! **There is no escape!** In Hell, the merciless rich man **remembered**!

Throughout the years, I've challenged youth to let God's Holy Spirit help them **reprogram their minds**; and then seek His guidance in programming memories, precious to remember! Early in life my mother challenged me to refuse to let Satan, or any member of his crew, dump his garbage in my mind! I do not have to resort to his garbage to understand God's contrasting holiness!

Have I said this before? If so please let me repeat, **I have no desire to appear to be deifying my mother**. Please do not think of me as doing so. References to my mother were not born of euphoria in the mind of an idealistic son seeking to canonize his mother as a super saint. My references to her reflect memories of a mother's beautiful, unselfish love: her spirit of God-given wisdom, and my own introduction to the reality of God's love. However, a deity did indwell my mother. I became fully aware of His presence, in and through her life. Only God knows how many times, when preaching or writing, I have heard the echo of her voice in my mind as she had once shared with me the truth that I was writing or preaching! What she had said was not as significant as that which God said to me as I remembered! There were so many precious, beautiful insights that she helped me to program into memory cassettes.

All of us are programming such cassettes every day! Will those memories bless or burn? Will they bring joy and peace or sorrow and regret? May I challenge you to carefully design and develop your programming under the directorship of God's Holy Spirit?

Were I to go blind tomorrow, I could still see Katahdin, in the golden glow of a subzero morning. I could see the changing leaves of autumn, and the smiling upturned faces of my children glowing with love! Were I to lose my hearing, I could still hear the gurgling, bubbly flow of a wilderness stream, the splat of a beaver's tail, the song of the birds, beautiful hymns of the faith and the laughter of loved ones. **All because of that glorious gift of memory!**

Treasure it, guard it, program into it only that which you wish to remember with delight, and will cause you to look, with anticipation, into eternities yet to come!

Have You Confirmed Your Reservation?

Jesus told His disciples, "I go to prepare a place for you. And if I go to prepare a place for you, I will come again, and receive you unto Myself, that where I am, there ye may be also." *John 14:* It was not God's will that anyone should spend eternity in Hell! Remember, if we go to Hell it will because we let Satan walk us through life to his designated place of abode! One day we will die, or the Lord will come, and our eternal existence will be sealed. This is no option! Just where we will spend eternity is a choice we **must** make! No one else can decide this for us. It is the set of our own will that determines our eternal destiny!

You may question whether or not there is life after death. Some think we die and cease to exist just like any other animal. I believe, to the point of conviction, we will spend eternity in a conscious state of existence in just one of two places; Heaven or Hell; because God said so! Since learning to walk with God and to talk with Him, He has told me many things that only He could know! These confidings have been confirmed as they have checked out in detail. That is why I expect to awake in His presence some day to spend eternity with Him. I believe that in Christ I have confirmed my reservation to that place He said He would prepare for me! Now if I am mistaken: nothing has been gained or lost! What about those who don't believe and have made no reservation? What happens to them because they were mistaken? Moments after death these consequences will no longer be just mere speculation or belief.

The concept of endless eternities is almost beyond our comprehension. It is difficult for the human mind to grasp such enormities. Never ending suffering in agony or never ending peace, joy and love! Time could very well be viewed as a measured period between eternities, past and future. There are many who view the time period, since the creation of the universe in terms of millions, or even billions of years. But a billion years would constitute just an introduction to eternity!

Many people of great courage, fortitude and strength suffer patiently for years, sustained by hope that suffering would end someday. Imagine suffering pain for one hundred, one thousand, one million, one billion years without hope. Can you imagine unending suffering lasting as long as the history of this present universe? suffering while age after age unfolded and fossilization took place? That would be horrible enough, but in eternity there is no hope, no end to suffering. It will then be eternally now!

Some have said, "If I go to Hell I'll have a lot of company!" I had a woman tell me one day, "I know my husband is in Hell and I want to be with him!" According to the only authority on the subject that I know of: there are no reunions in Hell! It is a place of horrible separation and loneliness. Loneliness is one of the most acute forms of mental and emotional suffering known to mankind. Many persons have committed suicide because they perceived they could no longer endure their loneliness: only to discover they had sealed that suffering as an eternal destiny!

When, for us, time passes away and eternity dawns, **everyone will know for sure**. The hope of the redeemed and the faithful will be fulfilled beyond all possible expectations, according to God's word. What will go through the minds of those who sold out there eternal birthright for some mess of earthly pottage? Can you imagine the realization they were suffering eternal agonies, with no hope of relief, as the price they must pay for sensual pleasures and a few years of self-indulgence? Endless hope or hopeless end: which are you programming for?

There used to be an old saying, "What goes up must come down!" That was before men knew something could be thrust beyond the pull of earth's gravity. One of the terrible fears of the early space program was that of being unable to bring a manned space capsule back to earth, and men would be forever lost in space. The specter of men orbiting earth or some distant planet or just drifting helplessly, hopelessly, endlessly in space as their life support systems ran out, was almost too terrible to think about.

One lunar spacecraft did have an explosion in one of its power units as it entered the pull of the moon's gravity. The attention of the entire world was riveted to radio, television and newspaper accounts as this real-life drama gripped the hearts and minds of almost everyone, throughout the entire world. Would these men actually be the first to be lost in space? People were praying for their safe return, all over the world! I vividly recall my own fascination with that rescue effort. The craft had left the sphere of earth's gravitation, and the only hope was to whip it about the moon, break with the moon's gravity and have enough thrust to come back under the pull of earth's gravity. I was watching that televised drama, and remember the anxiety as that capsule passed around the backside of the moon, and we lost all contact with those helpless men. I can still see the grim faces of those men at space control as they tensely waited out that period of communication blackout! Suddenly, that voice from that crippled spacecraft, "We have ignition!" Those astronauts, in full cooperation with mission control, had made the decisions and taken the action necessary to break from the moon's gravity with enough thrust to bring them back under the controlling gravity of earth. They were on the way home! Those astronauts took advantage of every provision for their safety, and in full cooperation with those directing the mission were brought safely to earth.

Those three men commanded the attention and concern of multiple millions of people, lest they be lost in space. However, according to God's Word, He is unable to rescue untold millions of people, under the pull of Satan, **orbiting Hell** because those lost persons will not cooperate! They will not make the decisions nor take the action that will enable them to break the pull of Hell upon their souls! Those who do not break free will not be orbiting about Hell throughout eternity, they will be spiritually conscious **within** it. They will fall into it at their death or the end of time. Strangely enough, few people seem to care. Even many in the church are prayerless and indifferent! Peoples of earth, refusing to do the will of God; and demanding their own freedoms: will one day find themselves helplessly and hopelessly trapped throughout endless eternities. While earth's mountains and the fossils buried in them crumble to dust, every human being will be in a conscious state of existence, somewhere!

The signal that was the key to release from my orbit of Hell was that beattitude, "Blessed are they which hunger and thirst after righteousness; for they shall be filled!" *Matthew 5:6* This verse came both as a signal from God at His Mission Control, that He was communicating with me, doing everything within His power to bring me home, and the catalyst that gave me the faith to break the pull of Satan, holding me in His orbit. Satan had told me before, "You can't make it!" He was lying! I could and did break free when I followed God's instructions. There is a very real consciousness of the gravitation of Heaven, drawing me home. I am very conscious of my "call to the heights". Have you been set free? Do you want to be? He is reaching down to all of us. May we reach up and touch Him by faith!

Perhaps you do not believe this? Want to make sure? Ask the One who really knows! He will give you the correct answer! Please ask Him while you can still influence the outcome! He will tell you exactly how to break the gravitational pull of Hell on your soul, and give you enough thrust to bring you back under His control.

Best Yet to Come

What a rich store of memories God has given. He has presented so many beautiful things to remember. More wonderful still: **the best is yet up ahead**! Our best days are not back there in the yesterdays, but up ahead in our tomorrows. "The path of the just is as a shining light, that shineth more and more unto the perfect day." *Proverbs 4:18* Our focus must not be on earth's sunsets, but on eternity's sunrise. This is not to speak of the fantasy world of the sentimentalist. We must speak of God's world of eternal realities. Those things now verified by our physical senses, are temporal and passing.

He has proven His presence real, His word true and His promises kept. He has said, in effect, **You haven't seen anything yet**! Just wait until you see what I have "reserved for those who walk uprightly." "For the Lord God is a sun and a shield: the Lord will give grace and glory: no good thing will He withhold from them that walk uprightly!" *Psalms 84:11* **I rejoice in the past, but I do not live in it!** I have shared the past with Him as we have walked together. I walk with Him now in joyous fulfillment and in excited anticipation concerning our walk through the tomorrows! God has provided a glorious future. Let us not disappoint Him and shortchange ourselves. So many live in spiritual poverty, even though they are children of the King of Glory! We are shocked when people of wealth live in squalor and die of malnutrition. Yet, so many people, professedly Christian, are doing even worse!

The Journey Home

Just what is your inheritance in Christ Jesus? Ask Him! "The eyes of your understanding being enlightened; **that ye may know** what is the hope of His calling, and what the riches of the glory of His inheritance in the saints." *Ephesians 1:18*

Do you wish to receive your legacy provided in your Heavenly Father's will? Do everything possible to get your hands upon a Bible. Read the Gospel of John, the First Epistle of John and Romans, chapter 8, and pray with your Bible open. Ask God to talk to you through His word. Pray that the Holy Spirit, Author of the Book, will teach you what you need to know. I assure you, He will speak! Pray that you may understand. Pray, "Lord if this is Your Book and you care about me, help me to understand what you want me to know!" He will communicate with you, personally! Where, when, how? I do not know; **but He will**! He will step into your life, too, saying, "Peace be unto you!" You will suddenly discover: **You are walking with God!**

Via Con Dios!

Rev. Carlton P. Gleason, Sr.

P.S.

If I do not have the opportunity to meet you on this side of the horizons of earth and time, please identify yourself on the other side of life, in eternity. Have a wonderful journey! I'll see you in the morning!
c.p.g.

CREATED TO WALK WITH GOD

Biographical Data

Born to former missionaries to Israel, Ralph Emerson and Christine Marple Gleason

Ordained to the Gospel Ministry in 1950

Pastored for twenty-five years: led churches in four building programs including three complete churches

Served as vice chairman on the Board of Directors for "Transport for Christ" at its founding, as a chaplaincy to the transport industry (then based in Toronto, Ontario with Rev. Jim Keyes as president)

Served several years as an administrator – approximately six years with Dr. Jerry Falwell in the building of Liberty University